EUROPE IN FIGURES

Fifth edition **2000**

London:

The Stationery Office

This publication was designed by Eurostat, the Statistical Office of the European Communities, for educational purposes. It does not necessarily reflect the official opinions of the institutions of the European Communities.

It would not have been possible to produce this publication without the assistance of:
● Eurostat authors' services,
● Mr Fons Theis, Mr David Bond (Unit C1) for coordination
● Mr John Wright
● and Mrs Valerie Port for production and proof reading.

The Secretariat-General of the Commission and the following Directorates-General also contributed:

DG I (External Relations), DG II (Economic and Financial Affairs), DG III (Industry), DG V (Employment, Industrial Relations and Social Affairs), DG VI (Agriculture), DG VII (Transport), DG VIII (Development), DG X (Information, Communication, Culture and Audiovisual Media), DG XI (Environment, Nuclear Safety and Civil Protection), DG XII (Science, Research and Development), DG XIII (Information Society: Telecommunications, Markets, Technologies - Innovation and Exploitation of Research), DG XIV (Fisheries), DG XVI (Regional Policy and Cohesion), DG XVII (Energy), DG XXIII (Enterprise Policy, Distributive Trades, Tourism and Social Economy), as well as the EIB, the Council, the Committee of the Regions, the Economic and Social Committee, the Court of Auditors, the Court of Justice, the European Parliament and the Office for Official Publications of the European Communities.

Luxembourg: Office for Official Publications of the European
              Communities, 2000

UK ISBN 0 11 702658 1
EC ISBN 92-828-7781-7

Catalogue No : CA-24-99-036EN-C

Printed in Great Britain

Preface

Europe is a Community that has been built gradually: the Treaty of Rome, the Single Act, the Treaty on European Union and the Treaty of Amsterdam have been important steps in this process of building Europe. Major successes have already been obtained with the development of the single market in 1993 and, more recently, with the introduction of the euro, an operation that will be completed when the notes and coins of the new currency enter circulation at the start of 2002. Other steps in building Europe lie ahead for the European Union.

The European Community was conceived from the outset as an open structure. Austria, Finland and Sweden opted to join in 1995, and other countries have shown their interest in becoming full members.

At the core of this process lies Eurostat. By compiling, harmonising and disseminating information covering every area of economic and social life it is fulfilling its vocation: to provide the European Union with a high quality statistical information service.

The purpose of this publication, which has been prepared especially with schools in mind, is to provide particularly accurate, impartial and objective information for everyone who is interested in the European Union and its members, and also in the world's major economic powers.

This fifth edition reiterates one of the statistical profession's primary ambitions: to explain things to ensure better understanding.

Yves Franchet

Contents

vi Contents

Abbreviations

Member States of the European Union

B	Belgium
DK	Denmark
D	Germany
EL	Greece
E	Spain
F	France
IRL	Ireland
I	Italy
L	Luxembourg
NL	Netherlands
A	Austria
P	Portugal
F	Finland
S	Sweden
UK	United Kingdom
EU-6	Belgium, Federal Republic of Germany, France, Italy, Luxembourg, Netherlands
EU-9	EU-6 plus Denmark, Ireland and United Kingdom
EU-10	EU-9 plus Greece
EU-12	EU-10 plus Spain and Portugal
EU-15	EU-12 plus Austria, Finland and Sweden
EUR-11	Belgium, Germany, Spain, France, Ireland, Italy, Luxembourg, the Netherlands, Austria, Portugal and Finland

Note: Throughout this publication EU Member States are listed in alphabetical order of their names in the national language

Other European countries

AD	Andorra
CH	Switzerland
CY	Cyprus
IS	Iceland
LI	Liechtenstein
MT	Malta
NO	Norway
TR	Turkey

CECs

AL	Albania
BG	Bulgaria
BA	Bosnia-Herzegovina
CZ	Czech Republic
EE	Estonia
HR	Croatia
HU	Hungary
LT	Lithuania
LV	Latvia
MK	Macedonia, the Former Yugoslav Republic
PL	Poland
RO	Romania
SK	Slovakia
SI	Slovenia

Currencies

ECU or ecu	EMS unit
EUR	euro
BFR	Belgian franc
DKR	Danish krone
DM	German mark
DR	Greek drachma
ESC	Portuguese escudo
FF	French franc
FMK	Finnish markka
HFL	Dutch guilder
IRL	Irish pound
LFR	Luxembourg franc
LIT	Italian lira
OS	Austrian schilling
PTA	Spanish peseta

SKR   Swedish krona
UKL   pound sterling
CAD   Canadian dollar
USD   United States dollar
YEN   Japanese yen

Other abbreviations

bn   billion (= thousand million)
grt   gross register tonnage
GWh   Gigawatt hour (106 kWh)
ha   hectare
hl   hectolitre
kg   Kilogram
Kgoe   Kilogramm of oil equivalent
kWh   kilowatt hour
m3   Cubic metre
Pkm   passenger-km
sq km   Square kilometre
t   tonne (metric ton)
TJ   terajoule = 1012 j
tkm   Tonne-km
toe   tonne of oil equivalent
TWh   terawatt hour = 109 kWh

ABU   adult bovine unit
ACE   Action by the Community relating to the environment
ACP   African, Caribbean and Pacific countries (signatories of the Lomé Convention)
ALA   Countries of Asia and Latin America
ASEAN   Association of South-East Asian Nations
AWU   annual work unit
Benelux   Economic Union of Belgium, the Netherlands and Luxembourg
BIS   Bank for International Settlements
BLEU   Belgo-Luxembourg Economic Union (B/L)
CAE   Community actions for the environment
CAP   common agricultural policy
CEC   Central and Eastern European country/country of Central and Eastern Europe
CFC   chlorofluorocarbons
CFP   common fisheries policy
CIET   Centre for Information on Education Techniques
cif   cost, insurance and freight
CMEA/COMECON
   Council for Mutual Economic Assistance
Coreper   Committee of Permanent Representatives
CSCE   Conference on Security and Cooperation in Europe
DC   developing country
EAGGF   European Agricultural Guidance and Guarantee Fund
ECB   European Central Bank
EBA   Ecu Banking Association
EBRD   European Bank for Reconstruction and Development
EC   European Community
ECNR   European Council for Nuclear Research

ECSC   European Coal and Steel Community
EDC   European Defence Community
EDF   European Development Fund
EEA   European Economic Area
EEAgency
       European Environment Agency
EEC   European Economic Community
EFTA   European Free Trade Association
EIB   European Investment Bank
EIONET
       European Environmental Information and Observation Network
EMCF   European Monetary Cooperation Fund
EMF   European Monetary Fund
EMI   European Monetary Institute
EMS   European Monetary System
EMU   Economic and Monetary Union
EOEC   European Organization for Economic Cooperation
EONR   European Organization for Nuclear Research
EPO   European Patent Organization
ERDF   European Regional Development Fund
ERM   Exchange Rate Mechanism
ESA   European Space Agency
ESA   European System of Integrated Economic Accounts (Eurostat)
ESCB   European System of Central Banks
ESF   European Science Foundation
ESF   European Social Fund
ESPRIT   European strategic programme for research and development in
       information technology
EU   European Union
Eureka   Community programme for research in technology
FIFG   financial instrument for fisheries guidance
FOD   French overseas department(s)
fob   free on board
GATS   General Agreement on Trade in Services
GATT   General Agreement on Tariffs and Trade
GDP   gross domestic product
GFCF   gross fixed capital formation
GNP   gross national product
GSP   generalized system of preferences
GVA   gross value added
IBRD   International Bank for Reconstruction and Development (World
       Bank)
ILO   International Labour Organization
IMF   International Monetary Fund
JHA   cooperation in the fields of justice and home affairs
LDC   least developed country/countries
LU   livestock unit
MFN   most favoured nation
MMI   Maghreb, Mashreq and Israel
NACE   General industrial classification of economic activities within the
       European Communities
NAFTA   North American Free Trade Agreement
NATO   North Atlantic Treaty Organization

NCI	New Community Instrument
NIC	newly industrialized countries
NIS	Commonwealth of Independent States
NUTS	Nomenclature of Territorial Units for Statistics
OCTs	overseas countries and territories
OECD	Organization for Economic Cooperation and Development
OEEC	Organization for European Economic Cooperation
OPEC	Organization of Petroleum Exporting Countries
OSCE	Organization on Security and Cooperation in Europe
PHARE	Poland-Hungary assistance in the restructuring of economies
PPS	purchasing power standard
PTOM	overseas countries and territories
R&D	research and development
SDR	Special Drawing Rights
SGM	standard gross margin(s)
SITC	Standard International Trade Classification
SME	small and medium-sized enterprise(s)
S&T	science and technology
Stabex	system for the stabilization of export earnings (of the ACP and PTOM)
Sysmin	system of aid for mining products – special financing facility for mining products of the ACP and PTOM
TAC	total allowable catches
TACIS	technical assistance to the Commonwealth of Independent States
UAA	utilized agricultural area
UNCTAD	
	United Nations Conference on Trade and Development
UNO	United Nations Organization
VAT	value added tax
WEU	Western European Union
WTO	World Trade Organization
EU-12	refers to the twelve Member States before the accession of Austria, Finland and Sweden on 1 January 1995
EU-15	includes the fifteen Member States, even for data relating to periods before the accession of Austria, Finland and Sweden
EUR-11	Countries participating in EMU (EUR-11): Belgium, Germany, Spain, France, Ireland, Italy, Luxembourg, the Netherlands, Austria, Portugal and Finland

Germany: Germany is usually taken to be as constituted after unification on 3 October 1990. However, certain data concern only the territory of the Federal Republic before unification (referred to as the 'old Länder').

General explanation of symbols used:

*	*estimated*
.	*not applicable*
:	*not available*
0	*less than half the unit used*
–	*zero*

1 The development of the EU

1.1 Key dates

1947
Marshall Plan for economic revival of a Europe devastated by war
17 MARCH 1948
Benelux Treaty enters into force
1948
Creation of Organisation for European Economic Co-operation (OEEC) to administer Marshall Plan
1949
Creation of Council of Europe based in Strasbourg
9 MAY 1950
Schuman Declaration
18 APRIL 1951
Signing of Treaty of Paris establishing European Coal and Steel Community (ECSC)
MAY 1953
Common market in coal and steel comes into effect
1952–1954
Development and failure of plan for European Defence Community (EDC)
25 MARCH 1957
Signing of Treaties of Rome establishing European Economic Community (EEC) and European Atomic Energy Community (Euratom)
1 JANUARY 1958
EEC and Euratom established
1962
Introduction of Common Agricultural Policy (CAP)
1967
Executive institutions of the three Communities (ECSC, EEC and Euratom) merged
1 JULY 1968
Customs union completed
22 JANUARY 1972
Signing of Treaties of Accession of Denmark, Ireland, Norway (where accession is later rejected by referendum) and UK
1 JANUARY 1973
Denmark, Ireland and UK join European Community (EU-9)
1979
European Monetary System established
28 MAY 1979
Signing of Treaty of Accession of Greece
JUNE 1979
First election of European Parliament by direct universal suffrage
1 JANUARY 1981
Greece joins European Community (EU-10)
12 JUNE 1985
Signing of Treaties of Accession of Portugal and Spain
1 JANUARY 1986
Portugal and Spain join European Community (EU-12)
FEBRUARY 1986–1 JULY 1987
Signing of treaty and entry into force of the Single European Act

3 OCTOBER 1990
Unification of Germany
7 FEBRUARY 1992
Signing of Maastricht Treaty setting up the EU
2 MAY 1992
Signing in Oporto of treaty setting up European Economic Area
1 JANUARY 1993
Completion of European Single Market
1 NOVEMBER 1993
Establishment of EU with entry into force of Maastricht Treaty
1 JANUARY 1994
Establishment of European Economic Area
24 JUNE 1994
Signing of Treaties of Accession of Austria, Finland, Norway (where
accession is later again rejected by referendum) and Sweden
1 JANUARY 1995
Austria, Finland and Sweden join EU (EU-15)
2 OCTOBER 1997
Signature of Amsterdam Treaty
2 MAY 1998
Decision of the European Council on Member States participating in
phase III of Economic and Monetary Union (EMU)
1 JANUARY 1999
Entry into force of phase III of EMU

The countries of Europe, 1998

		Accession dates		Accession dates			
							Ireland
							Italy
							Luxembourg
The European Union	*Belgium*	*1951*	*Greece*	*1981*			
	Germany	*1951*	*Portugal*	*1986*	*Schengen Agreement*		*Luxembourg*
	France	*1951*	*Spain*	*1986*			*Belgium*
	Italy	*1951*	*Austria*	*1995*			*Netherlands*
	Luxembourg	*1951*	*Finland*	*1995*			*Germany*
	Netherlands	*1951*	*Sweden*	*1995*			*France*
	Denmark	*1973*					*Spain*
	United Kingdom	*1973*					*Portugal*
	Ireland	*1973*					*Italy*
EEA	*Belgium*	*Netherlands*			*EFTA*		*Switzerland*
	Denmark	*Austria*					*Norway*
	Germany	*Portugal*					*Iceland*
	Greece	*Finland*					*Liechtenstein*
	Spain	*Sweden*			*CEECs*		*Albania*
	France	*United Kingdom*					*Bulgaria*

The countries of Europe, 1998

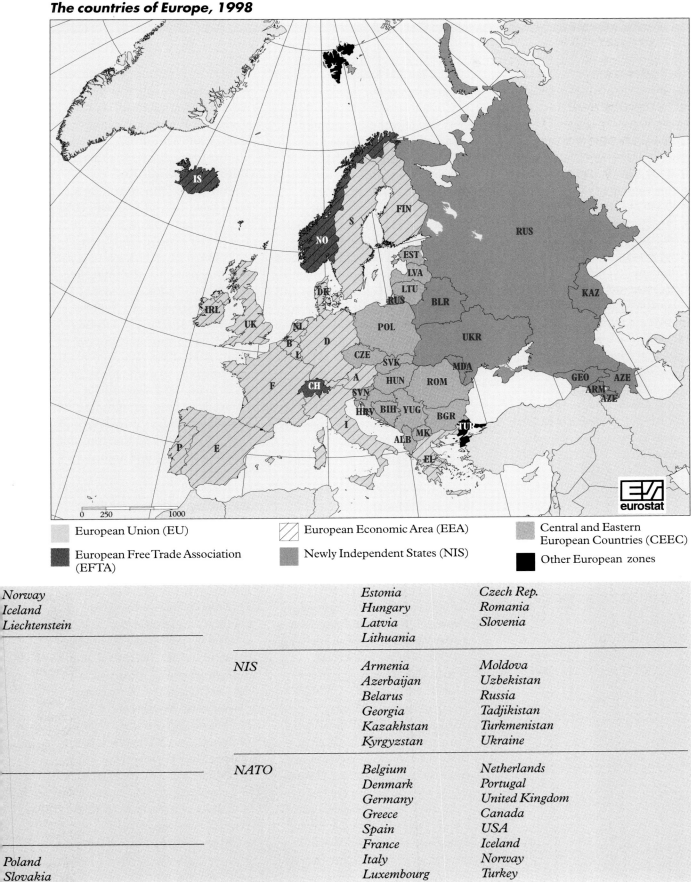

Norway		Estonia	Czech Rep.
Iceland		Hungary	Romania
Liechtenstein		Latvia	Slovenia
		Lithuania	
	NIS	Armenia	Moldova
		Azerbaijan	Uzbekistan
		Belarus	Russia
		Georgia	Tadjikistan
		Kazakhstan	Turkmenistan
		Kyrgyzstan	Ukraine
	NATO	Belgium	Netherlands
		Denmark	Portugal
		Germany	United Kingdom
		Greece	Canada
		Spain	USA
		France	Iceland
Poland		Italy	Norway
Slovakia		Luxembourg	Turkey

1.2 From the ashes of war . . .

The European Community rose from the ashes of a divided Europe at the end of World War Two. While various organisations for economic, financial and cultural cooperation were formed initially, the first major step was the creation of the European Coal and Steel Community (ECSC) in 1952. This was followed by the establishment of the European Economic Community (EEC) and the European Atomic Energy Community (Euratom) in 1958.

From six original members, the Community grew to nine in 1973, ten in 1981, and twelve in 1986. In 1995, by which time it had become the European Union, it expanded to fifteen. In parallel with its geographic expansion, it also acquired greater 'depth' thanks to the introduction of common policies and actions in the economic, monetary and social spheres.

How the EU began

Western European countries were first brought together to develop close and effective co-operation within the **Organisation for European Economic Co-operation (OEEC)**, set up in 1948 to administer US aid under the Marshall Plan. By gradually liberalising trade and payments, the OEEC also boosted commerce between its members. In 1960 it was transformed into the **Organisation for Economic Co-operation and Development (OECD)**, which was gradually joined by all major western industrialised nations.

In 1949 the idea of a united Europe was given further substance with the establishment of the **Council of Europe**. But its achievements have been largely confined to protecting human rights and to the cultural and social fields. Neither the OEEC nor the Council of Europe was a supra-national body because Members refused to yield sovereignty. The actual process of building Europe was launched on 9 May 1950 when French Foreign Minister Robert Schuman proposed that all European countries set up a coal and steel community to be administered by a supra-national 'high authority'. This led to the signing in 1951, by France, Italy, Germany and the three Benelux countries, of the Treaty of Paris establishing the **European Coal and Steel Community (ECSC)**. In May 1953, the common market in coal and steel came into effect. However, plans for a **European Defence Community**, merging the armed forces of the six ECSC Member States into a European army, fell through in 1954 when the French Parliament rejected them.

The building of Europe continued in the economic sphere with 1957 witnessing the signing of the two Treaties of Rome establishing the **European Economic Community (EEC)** and the **European Atomic Energy Community (Euratom)**. Both came into being on 1 January 1958. While the union of the people of Europe remained the long-term objective, the first task was to create a common market permitting free movement of persons, goods, services and capital. In 1962 the **Common Agricultural Policy (CAP)** came into force. In 1967 **Value Added Tax (VAT)** on goods and services was introduced EEC-wide. In the same year a single Council of Ministers and a single Commission began presiding over the ECSC, EEC and Euratom. On 1 July 1968, **customs union** was achieved.

Growing bigger and deeper

In the 1970s and 1980s, the European Community (EC) expanded from six to twelve members. In the 1990s this grew to 15. Enlargement seems set to continue, with the former communist countries of central and eastern Europe – Bulgaria, Estonia, Hungary, Latvia, Lithuania, Poland, the Czech Republic, Romania, Slovenia and Slovakia and three Mediterranean countries: Cyprus, Malta and Turkey – pressing for membership. However, this will necessitate bringing their political and economic circumstances in line with those of existing EU members. Hand in hand with Union enlargement has gone its deepening. This started with a common trade policy, competition policy, the CAP and a common transport policy. Such common policies were extended, as the EC was enlarged, to cover fisheries, regional development, energy, research and development and social affairs. The EC has also organised development aid to and cooperation with Member States' former colonies and dependent territories, currently extending to 71 countries in Africa, the Caribbean and Pacific. The deepening of the Community was also marked by the setting-up in 1974 of the **European Council** (meeting of Heads of State or Government), the first election of the **European Parliament** by universal suffrage in 1979 and the establishment, in 1979, of the **European Monetary System (EMS)**. The latter was designed to create stable exchange rates between Member State currencies and lead to **economic and monetary union (EMU)**.

1.3 From Community to Union

The Single European Act, the Treaty on European Union and the Treaty of Amsterdam have been the main vehicles for strengthening the European Community and for transforming it into European Union (EU).

The Single European Act – signed in 1986 and coming into force on 1 July 1987 – amended and supplemented the Treaties of Rome. Its main aim was to add new momentum to European integration by establishing a single internal market in 1993 and strengthening economic and social cohesion. But it was only a step on the road to European union. The Treaty on European Union – signed in Maastricht on 7 February 1992 and coming into force on 1 November 1993 – established a European Union founded on the European Community. Its main aim was the establishment of economic and monetary union. But it also embraced two additional forms of cooperation that had grown up alongside the Communities:

political cooperation; and cooperation in legal and home affairs. These three areas were designated as the three 'pillars' of European Union (see box). On 29 March 1997, following the Turin European Council, a new Inter-governmental Conference was opened to review the Treaty. Based on the genuine political will of everyone to strengthen the EU, the Conference focused on four key objectives: to bring Europe closer to its citizens; to abolish the final barriers to free movement; to make Europe's presence felt in the world; and to adopt an institutional system which would work in an enlarged Union. In June 1997 the Treaty of Amsterdam gave the EU a new framework.

Main indicators for the Member States of the European Union

(1997, except where specified)

	EU-15	EUR-11	Belgium	Denmark	Germany	Greece	Spain	France
Total population (m, 1998)	374.6e	290.8e	10.2	5.3	82.1e	10.5	39.3	58.7
Activity rate (%) (1)	55.4	54.0	50.5	65.4	57.7	48.9	49.1	55.4
Unemployment rate (%)	10.7	11.6	9.2	5.5	10.0	9.6	20.8	12.4
% of total employment in:								
agriculture	5.0	5.3	2.7	3.8	2.9	19.8	8.3	4.6
industry	29.4	30.5	27.5	26.2	34.7	22.5	29.9	26.6
services	65.6	64.2	69.8	70.0	62.4	57.7	61.8	68.8
Total taxes and social contributions as % GDP	42.6	43.2	46.6	53.1	41.6	na	36.2	46.3
Gross value added at market prices (PPS bn, 1996) (2)	6,276	4,951	192	92	1,516	119	520	1,022
of which:								
% agriculture	2.4	2.5	1.2	4.0	1.0	14.3	3.7	2.4
% industry	31.2	32.1	28.5	27.8	32.5	23.8	33.2	27.2
% services	66.5	65.3	70.3	68.2	66.5	62.0	63.1	70.4
GDP at current prices, PPS per person (2)	18,079	18,654	20,416	20,596	20,030	12,216	13,936	18,916
Export/import ratio, goods(3)	107.4	113.4	108.3	110.0	117.3	42.8	87.5	106.0

(1) Labour force expressed as a % of the population of working age.
(2) ECU, using purchasing parity standard exchange rates. These adjust for differences in the cost of living between countries and thus give a better indicatio
(3) Exports to and imports from countries outside EU-15 and EUR-11 respectively.
e   estimate

The three pillars of the EU

European Community

- Treaty of Rome revised by the Single European Act and the Treaty of Maastricht
- Democratisation of the institutions
- Rules on crossing Member States' external borders
- Immigration policies – cooperation between customs, police and judicial authorities
- New fields of competence
- Increased powers

Common foreign and security policy

- Common foreign policy: systematic cooperation; common positions and action; general foreign policy approach; possible common strategies
- Common defence policy based on the Western European Union (WEU)

Justice and home affairs

- Increased cooperation: asylum policy; combating drug abuse; combating international fraud

A single currency – economic and monetary union

On 2 May 1998 the European Council decided that the following Member States would join the third phase of economic and monetary union (EMU): Austria, Belgium, Finland, France, Germany, Ireland, Italy, Luxembourg, the Netherlands, Portugal and Spain. Bilateral conversion rates between participating currencies were pre-announced.

Some weeks later, the European Monetary Institute (EMI), which had overseen the European Monetary System, was dissolved and replaced by the European Central Bank (ECB).

The main task of the independent ECB is to ensure price stability through a single monetary policy. The third phase of EMU, culminating in the issue of bank notes and coins in 2002, began on 1 January 1999.

The UK reserved the right not to enter the third stage of EMU and to enter the final stage at a later date after approval by its Parliament. Denmark negotiated a derogation not to participate in the third stage, unless this was approved by a new referendum. Sweden, which had decided not to participate initially, and Greece did not meet the necessary conditions.

reland	Italy	Luxem-bourg	Nether-lands	Austria	Portugal	Finland	Sweden	UK	
3.7	57.6	0.4	15.7	8.1	10.0	5.1	8.8	59.1e	Total population (m, 1998)
55.4	47.7	51.2	60.9	58.4	57.7	60.1	60.8	61.8	Activity rate (%) (1)
10.1	12.1	2.6	5.2	4.4	6.8	13.1	9.9	7.0	Unemployment rate (%)
									% of total employment in:
10.9	6.5	2.4	3.7	6.9	13.3	7.8	3.2	1.9	agriculture
28.6	31.7	23.3	22.9	29.6	31.0	27.4	25.6	26.9	industry
60.6	61.8	74.3	73.4	63.5	55.7	64.8	71.2	71.2	services
34.1	44.5	45.6	45.9	44.9	37.9	47.5	54.1	35.9	Total taxes and social contributions as % GDP
61	1,018	11	270	150	114	77	148	966	Gross value added at market prices (PPS bn, 1996) (2)
									of which:
6.0	2.9	0.9	3.1	1.5	14.8	4.0	2.4	1.5	% agriculture
38.3	31.5	21.9	28.2	31.6	85.2	34.0	39.0	31.6	% industry
55.7	65.6	77.2	68.7	66.9	–	62.0	58.6	66.9	% services
6,782	18,474	29,440	18,996	20,400	12,543	17,311	18,123	17,786	GDP at current prices, PPS per person (2)
43.7	114.5	108.3	109.0	90.6	69.0	131.2	126.3	91.5	Export/import ratio (3)

living standards and similar data.

Treaty of Amsterdam – some key points

The aim of the Treaty of Amsterdam is to lay the foundations for the Europe of the 21st century. A key challenge is preparing as effectively as possible for the next EU enlargement.

The new Treaty puts employment and citizens' rights at the very heart of the Union. A high level of employment, now defined as a matter of common interest, is now specifically included among key EU objectives.

The Treaty strengthens the Union's social action. Member States formally confirmed their allegiance to social rights and stressed the need to combat discrimination at work and the importance of equal opportunities.

European citizens may now go to the Court of Justice on matters they consider to be contrary to fundamental rights. If the European Council determines the existence of a 'serious and persistent breach' of these principles, a Member State may have certain EU rights suspended, including voting. And the EU may also take appropriate action to combat 'discrimination based on sex, racial or ethnic origin, religion or belief, disability, age or sexual orientation'.

Consumer rights are also strengthened.

The Treaty stresses the European citizen's right to information.

The remaining barriers to the free movement of persons are removed and the safety of individuals is strengthened. In the five years following the entry into force of the Treaty, the Council was to adopt measures aimed at ensuring the free movement of people and the absence of any controls – either on EU citizens or those of non-member countries – when crossing borders between Member States.

Finally, in future nominations for the President of the Commission will have to be approved (or rejected) by the European Parliament.

Rotation of the EU Presidency

Member states take it in turn to preside over the EU, each holding the presidency for a six-month period.

	1st half year	2nd half year
1997	Netherlands	Luxembourg
1998	United Kingdom	Austria
1999	Germany	Finland
2000	Portugal	France
2001	Sweden	Belgium
2002	Spain	Denmark
2003	Greece	

1.4 The EU and the rest of Europe

EU Member States, and in some cases the EU itself, belong to various international bodies of which other European and Western nations are members. These include the Council of Europe, OECD and NATO. Together with most members of the European Free Trade Association (EFTA), the European Community forms the European Economic Area. Following the collapse of communism, the EU entered into relations with central and eastern European countries (CECs), including those of the former Soviet Union, which now make up, with the exception of the three Baltic countries, the Commonwealth of Independent States (NIS). These took the form of the Conference on Security and Cooperation in Europe (CSCE), assistance programmes and cooperation agreements.

The Council of Europe

The Council of Europe, set up on 5 May 1949, is an inter-governmental organisation with a membership (in 1997) of 40 countries, including the EU-15. Its aim "is to achieve a greater unity between its members for the purpose of safeguarding and realising the ideals and principles which are their common heritage and facilitating their economic and social progress".

In promoting cooperation between its members, its activities may, in principle, extend to all areas. apart from defence. In practice, it operates in three main areas: defending and fortifying pluralist democracy and human rights; attempting to find solutions to social problems; and furthering the growth of a genuine European cultural identity.

Organisation for Economic Co-operation and Development (OECD)

All EU Member States are also members of the OECD, created in 1960 out of the former OEEC, and now with 29 members, including USA, Canada and Japan. The OECD aims to coordinate the economic and social policies of its members with the aim of promoting economic well-being and contributing to the harmonious operation of the world economy.

North Atlantic Treaty Organisation (NATO)

NATO was set up in 1949 under the North Atlantic Treaty to guarantee the security of its member countries through a policy of collective defence. It has 19 members, including 11 EU Member States. France, although a member, ceased

The forty members of the Council of Europe

Belgium	Hungary
Denmark	Iceland
Germany	Liechtenstein
Greece	Lithuania
Spain	Malta
France	Norway
Ireland	Poland
Italy	Romania
Luxembourg	San Marino
Netherlands	Slovakia
Austria	Slovenia
Portugal	Switzerland
Finland	Turkey
Sweden	Bulgaria
United Kingdom	Albania
Andorra	Moldova
Cyprus	Russia
Latvia	Former
Croatia	Yugoslavian
Ukraine	Republic of
Czech Republic	Macedonia
Estonia	

The twenty-nine members of the OECD

Belgium	South Korea
Denmark	Poland
Germany	Canada
Greece	Iceland
Spain	Japan
France	Mexico
Ireland	New Zealand
Italy	Norway
Luxembourg	Switzerland
Netherlands	Turkey
Austria	USA
Portugal	Australia
Finland	Hungary
Sweden	Czech Republic
United Kingdom	

to take part in the integrated defence system in 1966; in 1996 it became a member of the Military Committee again. The North Atlantic Council, composed of representatives of the 19 governments, defines policy. In 1994 it offered former Warsaw Pact countries a 'partnership for peace' which is leading to cooperation and the strengthening of relationships with central and eastern European countries; the Czech Republic, Hungary and Poland joined the alliance in March 1999.

Western European Union (WEU)

Some EU Member States also belong to the WEU, set up in 1954 following the collapse of the European Defence Community. It is the only purely European organisation involved in defence. Following the Treaty of Amsterdam, the WEU is destined to become an essential component of the defence of the EU and grow in stature as a means of strengthening the European pillar of NATO.

European Free Trade Association (EFTA)

The European Free Trade Association (EFTA) was set up at the UK's instigation in 1960 following the failure of a British proposal for a large free trade area incorporating the European Community. Its composition changed following the EU accession of some members. In 1997 it had four members: Iceland, Liechtenstein, Norway and Switzerland. EFTA has succeeded in eliminating customs duties and other barriers to trade between member countries and the EU. EU-EFTA trade has always been considerable and accounts for almost a quarter of all EU imports and exports.

The nineteen members of NATO

Belgium	Denmark
Germany	Greece
Spain	France
Italy	Luxembourg
The Netherlands	Portugal
United Kingdom	Canada
Iceland	Norway
Turkey	USA
Czech Republic	Hungary
Poland	

The ten members of the Western European Union

Belgium	Italy
Germany	Luxembourg
Greece	Netherlands
Spain	Portugal
France	United Kingdom

Associate members

Iceland	Turkey
Norway	

Observers

Austria	Ireland
Denmark	Sweden
Finland	

Partner-observers

Bulgaria	Lithuania
Czech Republic	Poland
Estonia	Romania
Hungary	Slovakia
Latvia	

The members of EFTA

1959	Iceland
Austria	Liechtenstein
Denmark	Norway
Norway	Sweden
Portugal	Switzerland
Sweden	
Switzerland	1995
United Kingdom	Iceland
	Liechtenstein
1991	Norway
Austria	Switzerland
Finland	

European Economic Area (EEA)

The development of the single European market made it desirable for EFTA countries to reorganise their relationship with the EU. They were therefore associated with preparations for the single market and some EFTA countries applied for EU membership. Negotiations for the creation of a European Economic Area (EEA) got under way in 1989. This led to a treaty establishing the EEA on 1 January 1994 with the EU-15 plus Iceland and Norway. Liechtenstein has since joined.

European Economic Area (EEA)

Belgium	Netherlands
Denmark	Austria
Germany	Portugal
Greece	Finland
Spain	Sweden
France	United Kingdom
Ireland	Iceland
Italy	Liechtenstein
Luxembourg	Norway

Organisation for Security and Cooperation in Europe (OSCE)

The EU has participated in the Conference on Security and Cooperation in Europe (CSCE) – later, from 1994, the Organisation for Security and Cooperation in Europe (OSCE) – since its inception. The CSCE met for the first time in Helsinki in 1975. This led to the Helsinki Final Act covering security in Europe, economic, scientific, technical and environmental cooperation and human rights. Acknowledging the changes in central and eastern Europe in 1989 and 1990 – the unification of Germany, the collapse of communist regimes and the growth of democracy – the Paris summit of 1990 confirmed the role

Main indicators for non-EU countries in Western Europe

(1997 except where specified)

	Iceland	Norway	European Economic Area (including Liechtenstein)	Switzerland
Total area (000 sq kms)	103.0	323.9	3,618.2	41.3
Total population ('000, 1998)	272.4	4,417.6	380e	7,093.5
Population density (inhabitants per sq km)	2.6	13.5	104.4	171.3
Life expectancy (male)	76.2	75.4	74.1e	75.9
Life expectancy (female)	80.6	81.0	80.5e	82.0
No. in lower education	30.0	333.0	:	561.0
No. in upper education	50.0	1,155.0	:	2,208.0
No. in higher education	39.0	602.0	:	823.0
Persons in employment (m)	0.1	2.2	:	3.8
of which:				
% in agriculture	8.6	4.5	:	4.6
% in industry	25.5	23.3	:	25.4
% in services	65.9	72.0	:	70.0
Unemployment rate (%)	3.7	3.5	:	4.2
Imports from EU15 (ECU m) (1)	1,035	21,719	:	51,604
Total imports (ECU m) (1)	1,782	31,246	:	6,988
Exports to EU15 (ECUm) (1)	988	32,064	:	40,172
Total Exports (ECU m) (1)	1,630	42,083	:	67,225
GDP at market prices (ECUbn)	5.7	124.2	6,902.0	232.0
GDP at current prices, PPS per person (1996) (2)	21,491.6	22,776.5	18,135.6	22,859.2
Gross value added at market prices (PPSbn, 1996)	:	88.9	:	154.4
of which:				
% agriculture	11.0	2.3	2.4	2.5
% industry	26.8	35.9	31.2	31.2
% services	62.2	61.8	66.5	66.3
% construction	5.3e	:	:	6.9e

(1) Data for Switzerland include Liechtenstein.
(2) ECU using purchasing parity standard exchange rates. These adjust for differences in the cost of living between countries and thus give a better indication of relative living standards and similar data.
e   estimate

of the CSCE as a political framework for peace and harmony in Europe. At the summit, the CSCE was institutionalised through the establishment of new structures and institutions. OSCE now plays a key role in the prevention of conflicts and management of crises, particularly through its special powers in the field of preventive diplomacy. In 1997, following the admission of central and eastern European countries, including Russia, OSCE had 54 members t he EU is represented in OSCE in its own right.

The members of the OSCE

Belgium	United Kingdom	Czech Republic	San Marino
Denmark	Iceland	Estonia	Slovakia
Germany	Liechtenstein	Georgia	Slovenia
Greece	Norway	Hungary	Tajikistan
Spain	Switzerland	Kazakhstan	Turkey
France	Albania	Kyrgyzstan	Turkmenistan
Ireland	Armenia	Latvia	Ukraine
Italy	Azerbaijan	Lithuania	United States
Luxembourg	Belarus	Malta	Uzbekistan
Netherlands	Bosnia Herzegovina	Moldova	Vatican
Austria	Bulgaria	Monaco	Yugoslavia (suspended)
Portugal	Canada	Poland	
Finland	Croatia	Romania	
Sweden	Cyprus	Russia	

The Former Yugoslav Republic of Macedonia (FYROM) is an observer. Japan takes part in the work of the OSCE as a 'non-participant state'.

1.5 The EU spreading east

In 1989 the Berlin wall came down, ending the division of Germany. Communism collapsed and the liberalisation of political systems began – first in all the USSR satellites, then in the USSR itself. EU relations with the central and eastern European countries (CECs), and those of the ex-Soviet Union, take place within the framework of the Organisation on Security and Cooperation in Europe (OSCE), assistance programmes and cooperation agreements.

The EU and the CECs: aid and cooperation

The CECs now view EU membership as offering increased assurance against a return of the old order, a guarantee of economic development and a means of avoiding the potential disruption of ethnic disorder. As early as 1989, the EU decided to help CECs in their transition to a market economy, their economic development and the consolidation of democracy. The assistance programme – called the Phare Programme – now covers 11 countries. The European Union does not just want to help CECs but to turn them into genuine partners. This lies behind the objective of the agreements of association, or Europe Agreements, signed with Poland, Hungary, the Czech Republic, Slovakia, Romania and Bulgaria. These include not only the establishment of free trade but also provisions introducing economic and technical cooperation, financial aid and a political dialogue mechanism. In return CECs must implement rules similar to those in the Treaty of Rome prohibiting restrictive business practices, abuse of dominant positions and public aid that distorts competition.

EU and NIS

Another programme – the Tacis Programme – covers EU technical assistance to Russia and the other NIS republics of the ex-Soviet Union – Armenia, Azerbaijan, Belarus, Georgia, Kazakhstan, Kyrgyzstan, Moldova, Russia, Tajikistan, Turkmenistan, Ukraine and Uzbekistan.
More details on CECs, NIS and the Phare and Tacis programmes may be found in chapter 18.

2 How the EU is run

EU Institutions are unlike any other. The EU is much more than an intergovernmental organisation; it has a legal 'personality' of its own and far-reaching powers. It is not a federation where national governments and parliaments are subordinate to central federal institutions. What makes it unique is the principle by which tasks are shared between the Commission – responsible for tabling proposals in the general interest – and the Council, which takes decisions. The European Parliament – the direct representative of the people – participates in decision-making through its budgetary and legislative powers and its political control. This system of political institutions ensures that account is taken of the interests and problems of all Member States – whatever their size and economic strength.

The European Court of Justice – as the supreme judicial authority – ensures community law is applied uniformly. The Court of Auditors – the EU's financial conscience – monitors EU finances and points out areas where management needs improving. The Economic and Social Committee and the Committee of Regions advise the Community's decision-making institutions on economic, social and regional concerns. By providing loans for capital investment projects, the European Investment Bank contributes to balanced economic development.

How EU decisions are made

Acts adopted by Community Institutions under the Treaties are genuine 'European legislation' directly applicable to all Member

EU at a glance

European Parliament
- *Monitors the Commission, whose appointment is subject to its approval.*
- *Takes part in the legislative process via the 'co-decision' procedure.*
- *Participates in adopting the budget and monitors Community spending.*

European Council
- *Gives impetus for development plus general political guidelines.*

Council of the EU
- *Represents Member States' interests and is the EU's legislature. Assisted by Coreper (Committee of Permanent Representatives of the Member States to the Communities).*

Commission
- *Has the exclusive right to table legislation. Endeavours to ensure compliance with provisions of Treaties and other Community legislation. Responsible for implementation of Community policies.*

Court of Justice
- *Monitors lawfulness of Community acts and organs and Member States' compliance with Community law.*

Court of Auditors
- *Provides Council and Parliament with a statement of reliability and exactitude of the accounts and lawfulness of underlying transactions. Submits report on financial year just ended. Assists Council and Parliament in monitoring and implementing the budget.*

Economic and Social Committee
- *Has a consultative role. Can deliver an opinion on its own initiative.*

Committee of the Regions
- *Has a consultative role. Can deliver an opinion on its own initiative.*

States. Initially restricted by the Treaties of Rome to Commission and Council working closely together, Community decision-making, by virtue of the Single European Act (1986), the Treaty on European Union (1993) and the Treaty of Amsterdam (1997), now involves the European Parliament in the legislative process. The Commission proposes, the Council decides. In an increasing number of cases Parliament has equal power, exercised jointly with the Council, to adopt regulations and directives.

A Parliament for Europe

The European Parliament frames EU law, controls budgets and generally supervises the Community – but with powers more limited than national parliaments. Since 1979 the 626 European Parliament Members, or MEPs, have been elected by direct universal suffrage in line with national voting systems. The number of seats allocated to each Member State depends mainly on its population. Elections are held every five years.

MEPs are organised into political groups of which there are currently (Autumn 1999) eight. A President and 14 Vice-Presidents are elected by the MEPs. The Parliament is based in Strasbourg, France and meets there each month. Extra meetings and Commission meetings are held in Brussels. The administrative staff are based in Luxembourg.

Since the adoption of the Single European Act and the Maastricht Treaty, the Parliament now has real legislative powers. These include co-decisions with the Council on such things as the internal market, workers' rights, the environment, consumer affairs, EU-wide transport links, culture, education and public health. It has the power of assent in various areas including,

among other things, funding and institutional matters and all key international agreements. A system called a cooperation procedure, which involves the Commission, applies to decisions adopted by a qualified majority of the Council in areas such as the internal market, social policy, research, economic and social cohesion and the environment. The Parliament supervises the Commission's activities, and can censure it. It is involved in appointing the Commission President and in approving the Commission before it

is appointed by joint agreement of the governments.

The Parliament can amend certain items of the budget and it is the President of the Parliament who formally announces the final adoption of the budget. Among a wide range of budgetary powers, it can reject the EU budget drawn up by the Commission and adopted by the Council of Ministers.

A key Parliamentary role is giving political impetus to the EU. It can request that policies are extended or amended, that new ones are initiated, and it can ask the

---

European Parliament Presidents since the introduction of direct elections by universal suffrage (term: two-and-a-half years)

1979: Simone VEIL (France)
1982: Piet DANKERT (Netherlands)
1984: Pierre PFLIMLIN (France)
1987: Sir Henry PLUMB (UK)
1989: Enrique BARÓN CRESPO (Spain)
1992: Egon KLEPSCH (Germany)
1994: Klaus HÄNSCH (Germany)
1997: José Maria GIL-ROBLES GIL-DELGADO (Spain)
1999: Nicole FONTAINE (France)

Turnout in European elections

	1979	1984	1989	1994(1)	1999
EU-15(2)	63.0	61.0	58.5	56.9	49.9
B	91.6	92.2	90.7	90.7	91.0
DK	47.1	52.3	46.1	52.9	50.4
D	65.7	56.8	62.4	60.0	45.2
EL	78.6	77.2	79.9	80.4	75.3
E	:	68.9	54.8	59.1	64.4
F	60.7	56.7	48.7	52.7	46.8
IRL	63.6	47.6	68.3	44.0	50.7
I	85.5	83.9	81.5	74.8	70.8
L	88.9	87.0	87.4	88.5	85.8
NL	57.8	50.5	47.2	35.6	29.9
A	:	:	:	67.7	49.0
P	:	72.2	51.1	35.5	40.4
FIN				57.6	30.1
S	:	:	:	41.6	38.8
UK	31.6	32.6	36.2	36.4	24.0

(1) Figures for Austria, Finland, Sweden are for 1995 and 1996 when their first European elections took place.
(2) In 1979, 1984, 1989, 1994, the data are for EU-12.

Commission to submit proposals in certain fields. The Maastricht Treaty confirmed Parliament's right to receive petitions from any EU citizen or organisation. Its Ombudsman examines complaints from any citizen about EU maladministration. The Amsterdam Treaty simplifies different procedures.

Number of seats in the European Parliament (626) in 1998

B	25
DK	16
D	99
EL	25
E	64
F	87
IRL	15
I	87
L	6
NL	31
A	21
P	25
FIN	16
S	22
UK	87
Total	626

A Council for decisions

The **Council of the EU** exercises legislative and decision-making powers. It is also where representatives of Member State governments can assert their interests and try to reach compromises. It ensures general coordination of Community activities. Key objectives include the establishment of a single market without internal frontiers and guaranteeing freedom for goods, persons, services and capital – and a single currency. The Council is also responsible for intergovernmental cooperation in: common foreign and security policy; justice and home affairs (including, for example, immigration and asylum);

combating terrorism and drugs; and judicial cooperation.

The Council has one representative at ministerial level of each Member State, with the power to commit his or her Government. Therefore its members are politically accountable to national parliaments and public opinion. The Council usually meets at its Brussels headquarters although it meets in Luxembourg in April, June and October. Where the Council acts as legislator, the initiative lies with the European Commission, which submits a proposal to it. The Council examines the proposal and may amend it before adoption.

The European Parliament takes an active part in the legislative process. In a wide range of issues, Community legislation is adopted jointly by Parliament and Council – on the basis of the 'co-decision' procedure. The Treaties lay down the cases in which the Council acts by simple majority, qualified majority or where unanimity is required. The Council always tries to obtain as broad a consensus as possible before acting. The Council is presided over for six months by each Member State in rotation. Each Member State has a Permanent Representation to the EU in Brussels. They meet each week in the Permanent Representatives Committee (Coreper). This prepares the Council's work. The Council is assisted by a General Secretariat in Brussels which carries out the administration for the Council's work and ensures it runs smoothly and provides continuity.

The European Council

EU heads of state or government, assisted by their ministers for foreign affairs and the President of the European Commission, gather at least twice a year at meetings of the **European Council.**

The European Council plays a key role in providing impetus for the development of the Union and policy guidance in every area of its activity. It is presided over by the Head of State or Government of the Member State that holds the Presidency of the Council.

Shares of Council votes

Germany, France, Italy, United Kingdom	10 votes
Spain	8 votes
Belgium, Greece, Netherlands, Portugal	5 votes
Austria, Sweden	4 votes
Denmark, Finland, Ireland	3 votes
Luxembourg	2 votes

The European Commission – the driving force

The European Commission is responsible for proposing and implementing Community policy and is the many ways the EU's driving force. It manages common policies, implements the budget and directs the administration. The Commission has 20 Members, appointed after a vote of approval by the European Parliament and by common agreement of Member States, usually for a renewable five-year term. Under the Maastricht Treaty, the European Parliament is consulted before governments nominate the Commission's future President; under the Amsterdam Treaty, a formal approval by Parliament is necessary.

As a guardian of the Treaties, the Commission ensures that legal provisions adopted by the Community institutions are implemented. It has the exclusive right to draw up proposals for Community legislation. In its function as the executive body it adopts implementing regulations, applies the rules of the Treaties to individual cases – especially within the frame work of competition policy, administers the different

Community funds and negotiates trade agreements. Commissioners agree to be completely independent of governments and the Council, which cannot dismiss them. Only a censure motion of Parliament can lead to the collective resignation of the Commission, which is then replaced.

There are two Commissioners each for France, Germany, Italy, Spain and UK and one each for other Member States. Each is responsible for a 'portfolio'. The Commission meets in Brussels every week. Its staff of about 17,000 are split between Brussels, Luxembourg and a number of other places.

Judging the EU

The **Court of Justice** is the EU's supreme judicial authority – an independent body ensuring Community law is applied uniformly. It consists of 15 judges and nine advocates-general appointed by common agreement of Member State governments. They hold office for a renewable term of six years. The judges' independence is guaranteed by statute. They are irremovable and their deliberations are secret. They elect one of their members as President for three years.

The Court's task is to ensure that the law is observed in the interpretation and application of the Treaties. Various actions may be taken against Member States that transgress. National courts cooperate with the Court. They seek preliminary rulings on interpretation of the content or scope of Treaties and Community Acts etc. The Court of Justice is the only court competent to deliver final interpretation of Community law or to find the act of an EU Institution void.

A **Court of First Instance,** attached to the Court of Justice, was set up in 1989. It is composed of 15

Commission Presidents	
1958–67	*Walter HALLSTEIN (Germany)*
1967–70	*Jean REY (Belgium)*
1970–72	*Franco Maria MALFATTI (Italy)*
1972–73	*Sicco MANSHOLT (Netherlands)*
1973–77	*François-Xavier ORTOLI (France)*
1977–81	*Roy JENKINS (UK)*
1981–85	*Gaston THORN (Luxembourg)*
1985–95	*Jacques DELORS (France)*
1995–99	*Jacques SANTER (Luxembourg)*
1999–	*Romano PRODI (Italy)*

judges appointed on the same basis as the latter. The Court of First Instance has jurisdiction to hear all actions brought by individuals and organisations against acts of EU Institutions.

Through its judgments and interpretations, the Court of Justice is helping to build up a body of European case law applicable to all: Community Institutions, Member States, national courts, firms and private individuals. The Maastricht Treaty has strengthened the Court's authority by granting it power to impose a fine or penalty on a Member State not complying with its judgments. The Treaty of Amsterdam gives the Court direct responsibility regarding the observance of human rights and its jurisdiction is extended to the fields of immigration, visas and the crossing of borders and, where appropriate, police and judicial cooperation in criminal matters. Both Courts are in Luxembourg.

The EU's 'financial conscience'

The **Court of Auditors** was established in 1977 as an independent body. Its key task is to monitor EU finances. The Court checks whether financial management has been sound by ascertaining whether, to what extent and at what price financial management objectives have been achieved. Since the Maastricht

Treaty the Court provides the European Parliament and the Council of the European Union with a Statement of Assurance as to the reliability of the accounts and the legality and regularity of the underlying operations. The Court is a collegial body of 15 members, one from each Member State, appointed unanimously for a renewable six-year term by the Council after consultation with the Parliament. It carries out its control and consultative functions independently and autonomously. It is free to organise its own work and adopts its decisions by a majority of members. The Court of Auditors can be described as the EU's 'financial conscience'.

Advising the decision-making institutions

The **Economic and Social Committee (ESC)** and the **Committee of the Regions** advise the Community's decision-making bodies on Europeans' social, occupational and regional concerns, various aspects of EU policy and proposed legislation. The ESC is a consultative body that brings together different economic and social interest groups with the united aim of promoting European union. It tries to ensure that the Commission, the Council and Parliament are aware of the views of these groups on current Community priorities. It must be consulted by the Commission and the Council before certain decisions can be taken. It may also, either on request or on its own initiative, issue opinions on all aspects of Community legislation.

Set up by the Maastricht Treaty, the Committee of the Regions enables local and regional authorities to have a direct say in EU work. Its 222 members represent local and regional authorities and are appointed for terms of four years. It is based in Brussels. It must be consulted before decisions affecting especially regional interests are taken. The Amsterdam treaty expands the area of obligatory consultation.

Banking on the EU

The European Investment Bank's task is to contribute to balanced development, integration, and economic and social cohesion by providing long-term loans for capital investment projects furthering EU policy objectives. Luxembourg-based, it is administered by a board of governors, usually Member State finance ministers, a board of directors and a management committee appointed by the governors. The EIB's capital, subscribed by Member States, totalled ECU 62 billion until 31 December 1998. From 1 January 1999 it was increased to ECU 100 billion. It enables the Bank to grant loans and issue guarantees up to a ceiling of ECU 250 billion, representing 250% of subscribed capital.

Throughout the EU, the EIB aims to finances investments whose purpose is to:

- foster economic advancement of less prosperous regions
- improve transport and telecommunications infrastructure
- protect the environment and improve quality of life
- enhance international competitiveness of industry and integration at the EU level
- support the activities of small and medium-sized enterprises
- improve security of energy supplies.

The Bank is structured to adjust its activities to match the changing priorities of EU policies and world economic trends. Through borrowing on capital markets it is actively developing a future market for the single currency. Outside the EU, the EIB helps implement EU cooperation and development aid policy in over 120 countries, including those in Central and Eastern Europe aspiring to EU membership. The Bank raises nearly all it needs to finance its lending by borrowing on capital markets, mainly through public bond issues. Its 'triple A' credit rating enables it to obtain the most favourable conditions available. Working on a non-profit basis, it passes on the benefits to recipients of its loans. In 1997 the EIB raised over ECU 23 billion on the world's capital markets. This, together with its lending of ECU 26.2 billion, makes it one of the world's most important borrowers and lenders.

3 How the EU pays its way – and the policies it pursues

3.1 EU finances

From the outset, the EU has tried to implement common policies aimed at promoting economic and social progress and improving living conditions by removing the barriers dividing Europe, strengthening economic unity and closing gaps between regions.

The main financial instrument is the Community budget. This has been financed since 1970 from the EU's own resources, and supervised since 1977 by the Court of Auditors. In 1997 the total EU budget came to ECU 82 billion. This was 1.2% of Member States' GDP – or ECU 220 for each EU citizen. Some specific activities are financed by extra-budgetary resources. In the coal and steel sector the European Coal and Steel Community (ECSC) has resources from borrowings and a levy on production. The main channel for Third World aid is the European Development Fund (EDF), to which Member States contribute directly.

Another major source of funds is loans granted by the European Investment Bank (EIB) to support economic development in the regions and the Third World. Such loans are mostly financed through borrowing. In 1978 the EU set up the New Community Instrument (NCI) which allows it to grant loans financed by funds borrowed directly by the Commission and channelled through the EIB.

Budget reflects policy

The budget reflects EU policy. Apart from spending on the Common Agricultural Policy (CAP) and external action – which together account for over half the total – the Community budget is mainly directed at investment to enhance the EU's economic potential. The Commission, the Council of Ministers and the European Parliament are all involved in drawing up the budget. Each year the Commission draws up a preliminary draft budget, which is sent to the Council. The Council then either adopts it or amends it by qualified majority to produce a draft budget that goes to Parliament. Parliament discusses it at first reading and can either approve and adopt it or propose modifications. The budget is then re-examined by the Council. It can either accept the modifications and amendments by qualified majority and adopt the budget – or make further changes. In the latter case the budget returns for its second reading in Parliament, which then has the final say. At this point it can reintroduce the amendments and finally adopt the budget. If it rejects the draft, the Council is obliged to produce another.

Most EU spending – totalling ECU 84 billion if the EDF and ECSC are counted – consists of the operating costs of the various programmes. At ECU 4 billion, administration costs are only 5% of the budget; the EU operates with around 30,000 officials. Almost 90% of spending is on economic, social, cultural and regional programmes in Member States or the Third World.

Structure for spending

In 1988 the three structural funds – the European Regional Development Fund (ERDF) set up in 1975, the European Social Fund

General EU budget in 1997		
Revenue	%	Amount (ECU million)
Agricultural duties	2.4	2,015.5
Customs duties	14.8	12,203.2
VAT	42.0	34,587.7
Fourth resource	40.0	32,947.2
Miscellaneous	0.7	612.0
Total revenue	100.0	82,365.6

Expenditure		
General budget	%	Amount (ECU million)
EAGGF Guarantee Section	49.2	41,305.0
Structural Funds	31.7	26,634.9
EAGGF Guidance Section	4.3	3,580.0
ERDF	13.2	11,122.6
ESF	7.3	6,143.4
Cohesion Fund	2.8	2,326.0
FIFG	0.4	367.9
Research	3.8	3,160.4
External action	5.7	4,826.5
Administration	5.1	4,283.6
Repayments and other	2.6	2,155.2
General budget – Total	98.1	82,365.6
EDF	1.6	1,325.0
ECSC	0.3	265.5
Grand total	100	83,956.1

Note: FIFG – Financial Instrument for Fisheries Guidance. See text for other abbreviations.

Number of EU staff shown in the 1997 budget

European Parliament	4,109
Council	2,529
Commission	21,190
administrative	16,789
R&D	3,712
publications Office	525
other	164
Court of Justice	953
Court of Auditors	503
Economic and Social Committee and Committee of the Regions	739
Total	30,023

Trends in EU spending 1986 to 1997

Year	Expenditure (ECU million)	Expenditure per citizen (ECU)	% of Community GDP	% of Member States public' expenditure
1986	35,820.2	111.3	1.01	2.1
1987	36,234.8	112.3	0.96	2.0
1988	42,495.2	131.3	1.04	2.2
1989	42,284.1	130.1	0.95	2.0
1990	45,608.0	139.5	0.95	2.0
1991	55,016.2	159.6	1.05	2.2
1992	60,844.1	175.7	1.11	2.2
1993	66,733.4	191.8	1.21	2.3
1994	61,478.7	176.1	1.06	2.1
1995	68,408.6	183.9	1.06	2.1
1996	78,840.5	211.3	1.17	2.3
1997(1)	83,956.1	224.3	1.18	2.4

(1) 1997 Budget

General Budget 1993-1999 financial perspectives - commitment appropriations

(million ECU)

	1993	1994	1995	1996	1997	1998	1999
Common agricultural policy	36,657	36,465	37,944	40,807	41,555	42,323	43,110
Structural measures	22,192	23,176	26,329	28,262	29,958	31,783	33,614
Internal policies	4,109	4,370	5,060	5,337	5,557	5,789	6,010
External measures	4,120	4,311	4,895	5,264	5,576	5,981	6,465
Administration	3,421	3,634	4,022	4,191	4,316	4,380	4,445
Reserves	1,522	1,530	1,146	1,152	1,152	1,152	1,152
Compensation	0	0	1,547	701	212	99	0
Total commitment appropriations	72,021	73,486	80,943	85,714	88,326	91,507	94,796

(ESF), established in 1958, and the European Agriculture Guidance and Guarantee Fund (EAGGF), Guidance Section, set up in 1964 – were reformed to make them more efficient. Substantial additional financial resources were made available for the period 1989–93. The aim was to permit more effective implementation of structural measures in the run-up to the internal market – and to strengthen the economic and social cohesion of the Community by closing gaps between more advanced regions and social groups and those less-developed. Further changes were introduced in 1993 with resources again increased for the period 1994–99. In addition, a Cohesion Fund was set up for the economically least-developed Member States – Greece, Spain, Ireland and Portugal. This was intended to help these countries to cope with transition to economic and monetary union through improvement of their transport systems and environmental protection.

Financial resources allocated to structural and cohesion funds have risen substantially over the past decade – from ECU 7 billion, or some 19% of the Community budget, in 1988 to around ECU 31 billion, or 35%, in 1997. The Cohesion Fund contributes to projects in the fields of the environment and trans-European transport infrastructures in poorer Member States. Up to the end of 1999 only Greece, Spain, Ireland and Portugal will be eligible for this aid. Maintaining economic and social cohesion is essential for future EU development. This will be even more so after enlargement, in view of the generally very low level of incomes per person in applicant countries. So further reform of the Structural Funds is a central element of the Commission's Agenda 2000 proposals on EU development in the early years of the 21st century.

Appropriations for the Structural Funds – 1994–99

(ECU million at 1994 prices) (1)

Objective	Appropriation
1. Underdeveloped regions	93,976
2. Regions experiencing industrial decline	15,366
3+4. Long-term unemployment	15,206
5a. Adaptation of agricultural structures	6,400
5b. Development of rural areas	6,877
6. Regions with low population density	712
Community initiatives	13,894
Transitional and innovative measures	1,539
Total	153,969

(1) 1995 prices for a total amount of 4,747 million ecus for Austria, Finland and Sweden.

Appropriations for the Structural Funds by Member State, 1994–99

(ECU million at 1994 prices) (1)

Objective	B	DK	D	EL	E	F	IRL	I
1: Underdeveloped regions	730	–	13,640	13,980	26,300	2,190	5,620	14,860
2: Regions experiencing industrial decline	341	120	1,566	–	2,415	3,773	–	1,462
3+4: Long-term unemployment	465	301	1,942	–	1,843	3,203	–	1,715
5a: Adaptation of agricultural structures	195	267	1,143	–	446	1,932	–	814
5b: Development of rural areas	77	54	1,227	–	664	2,238	–	901
6: Nordic regions	–	–	–	–	–	–	–	–
Community initiatives	288	102	2,212	1,154	2,781	1,605	444	1,898
Total	2,095	844	21,729	15,134	34,448	14,941	6,064	21,650

Objective	L	NL	A(2)	P	FIN(2)	S(2)	UK
1: Underdeveloped regions	–	150	166	13,980	–	–	2,360
2: Regions experiencing industrial decline	15	650	101	–	183	160	4,580
3+4: Long-term unemployment	23	1,079	395	–	343	520	3,376
5a: Adaptation of agricultural structures	40	165	388	–	354	208	450
5b: Development of rural areas	6	150	411	–	194	138	817
6: Nordic regions	–	–	–	–	460	252	–
Community initiatives	20	421	146	1,061	153	128	1,415
Total	104	2,615	1,607	15,041	1,687	1,406	12,998

(1) In addition to these amounts, a total of 64 million ecus has been set aside for the development of networks in the context of Community Initiatives and 1 539 million ecus for innovative actions.
(2) 1995 prices

3.2 A quick look at key EU policies

Agriculture

The creation of the Common Agricultural Policy (CAP) was motivated by the desire to ensure that food supply problems experienced by Member States – particularly severe during the war and just after – should not recur. It was also intended that farmers should be able to gain a fairer and more reliable income from the land. In turn this would help arrest the rapid depopulation of the countryside. The effects of the CAP go well beyond the management of agricultural markets. The measures adopted complement policies in other fields including those for development of regions, promotion of employment, environmental protection and consumer health.

The CAP has evolved considerably over the past decade to adapt to new requirements arising from economic change, the development of the internal market and the shifting demands and priorities of people and their representatives, but its fundamental principles have remained intact. By the early 1980s, the CAP had largely achieved its original aims set in 1957. In global terms, the EU has risen to be the biggest importer and second biggest exporter of agricultural products.

But success has brought with it a number of less desirable side-effects. Above all, growth of the notorious 'butter mountains' and 'wine lakes' questioned the acceptability of a policy that in certain sectors induced farmers to produce food that was not needed. Several measures were introduced throughout the 1970s and 1980s in attempts to reduce costs and eliminate surpluses. Finally, the Council of Ministers decided in 1992 to have a root and branch review of the CAP, leading to the most radical reform since its creation 30 years earlier.

The reformed CAP maintained the objectives and fundamental principles established in 1957. But, in a radical departure, it turned an exclusively price supporting policy into one that also sought to offer direct income support. Key elements were a cut in prices for key commodities and withdrawal of land from production – the by now well-known 'set aside'. The 1992 reform has been judged a broad success, but further changes are now planned to meet the challenges of the next century. The common fisheries policy (CFP), drawn up in 1983, was reformed in 1992. It aims to protect stocks from over-fishing, guarantee fishermen their livelihoods and ensure consumers and the processing industry regular supplies of fish at reasonable prices.

Turning green

Since 1972 the EU has been laying the foundations for a common policy on the environment. The first two action programmes consisted mainly of measures to restore the environment on a European scale. In 1983 the third programme highlighted the fundamental principle that is the current basis of policy – prevention is better than cure. It was the Single European Act that laid down the explicit legal and political bases of a meaningful policy on the environment. The Maastricht and Amsterdam Treaties strengthened the introduction of the concept of sustainable develop-ment, reinforcing the obligation to integrate environmental protection requirements into the definition and

4 The environment

4.1 A sensitive balance

Our environment is the world we live in. It consists of the air we breathe, the water we drink and use, the land we inhabit and on which we grow our food, and the animals and plants surrounding us, as well as the infrastructure built by human beings.

The environment is the result of complex interactions between the physical environment, nature and people. Normally, the overall system is in equilibrium but it is a sensitive balance.

Once the balance is disturbed – mainly by human activities – various environmental changes become apparent. This results in today's environmental problems: climate change due to the greenhouse effect; stratospheric ozone depletion; acidification of soils and water; algae blooms in lakes and seas; loss of biodiversity etc.

The rising human population is taking ever more space from nature and exploiting natural resources ever more intensively, putting the environment under more and more strain.

Public awareness of environmental problems is growing – at both local and international level and national and international environment policies are playing an ever-increasing role.

The EU plays a key part in implementing decisions taken by the UN World Conference on the Environment – known as Rio '92 – and the programme it adopted, Agenda 21. The EU is also a signatory to a number of conventions aimed at safeguarding land and sea – the Oslo and Paris Conventions (marine protection), the Basle Convention on Wastes etc. Believing that only European – or even world-wide – regulation can help overcome threats to the environment, the Community has been running a series of projects since 1972. Work on these has been stepped up since the Single European Act and the Treaty on European Union came into force.

The Union has drawn up environmental action programmes. The fifth, now under way, was launched in 1992 and has been updated with new goals.

In 1990 the EU created the European Environment Agency (EEAgency). The area it covers is larger than the EU's 15 Member States. The EEAgency embraces the EFTA area and has agreements with Central and Eastern European countries to assist in developing harmonized monitoring systems.

A first result of the EEAgency's work has been the production in 1995 of 'Europe's Environment, the Dobris Assessment', which describes the European environment as a whole. This can be seen as a of 'state-of-the-art' inventory of problems to be remedied. An update was published in June 1998 and a state of the environment report for the EU has been published by the EEAgency.

4.2 The problem of pollution

The air we breathe

Atmospheric pollution is the presence in the ambient air of pollutants – gas, solids or liquids – in amounts harmful to human beings, nature or property. Atmospheric pollution is the major contributor to climate change, stratospheric ozone depletion, acidification and photo-chemical smog (photo-oxidation). It is also a big partial contributor to eutrophication and the dispersion of toxins.

An objective of the 5th Environmental Action Programme is to cut atmospheric pollution from human activities such as energy production and consumption, manufacturing, transport and agriculture.

Most emissions of atmospheric pollutants are related to the energy used in human activities – mainly in manufacturing, energy supply, transport, agriculture and households. Energy consumption depends on climatic conditions, industrial structure and transport needs. In the north, long winters boost the need for heating; in the south hot summers demand special air-conditioning. National energy consumption per person can be very high when there is large-scale production of basic chemicals, metals or pulp and paper. Specialised production of goods leads to the exchange and transport of products and a rise in heavy goods vehicle traffic, leading to further emissions. Daily commuting between and inside towns and seasonal tourism greatly influence emissions of carbon dioxide, nitrogen oxides, volatile organic hydrocarbons and heavy metals.

Pollution by CO_2

Although carbon dioxide (CO_2) occurs naturally and is harmless in

Inland emissions of CO_2

	total, m tonnes			tonne per capita		
	1985	1990	1995	1985	1990	1995
EU-12	2,841.4	2,930.5	2,880.7	8.4	8.5	8.2
EU-15	2,997.3	3,087.7	3,047.6	8.4	8.5	8.2
B	99.1	104.8	111.3	10.1	10.5	11.0
DK	60.9	52.8	59.9	11.9	10.3	11.5
D	990.7	952.3	848.9	12.9	12.0	10.4
EL	66.7	71.1	78.2	5.7	7.0	7.5
E	177.9	203.8	238.1	4.6	5.3	6.1
F	359.8	354.1	347.5	6.5	6.2	6.0
IRL	26.0	30.4	31.9	7.3	8.7	8.9
I	339.1	390.8	405.1	6.0	6.9	7.1
L	10.0	10.6	8.7	27.3	27.8	21.4
NL	141.2	153.0	170.9	9.7	10.2	11.1
A	51.0	55.0	56.7	6.8	7.1	7.1
P	25.1	39.1	47.9	2.5	4.0	4.8
FIN	46.8	51.6	56.4	9.6	10.4	11.1
S	58.0	50.6	53.6	7.0	5.9	6.1
UK	544.9	567.7	532.3	9.6	9.9	9.1

itself, its growing atmospheric concentration adds to the greenhouse effect and leads to global warming. The scale of CO_2 emissions makes it the key pollutant accelerating climate change or global warming.

The main sources of CO_2 emissions are combustion of fossil fuels, either in power stations or in transport. Changes in land use, such as drainage of moors, can also cause high releases of CO_2.

There is no efficient way of eliminating CO_2 except by using alternative energy sources such as wind, geothermal heating or nuclear power, or through massive energy saving. The energy sector is crucial to reducing CO_2 emissions. Compliance with EU commitments, within the UN Framework Convention of Climate Change, on freezing CO_2 emissions at the 1990 level by the year 2000 touches all economic activities.

In addition to freezing CO_2 emissions by the year 2000, EU countries have decided to cut their emissions by 15% from the 1990 level by the year 2010. Some 30–40% of cuts will be met by joint EU instruments such as norms, rules and energy taxation. Member States are responsible for ensuring that the remaining reduction occurs and for determining feasible ways to use alternative energy sources.

SO$_2$ and NO$_2$

Sulphur dioxides (SO_2) and nitrogen dioxide (NO_2), together with ammonia, are the main contributors to acidification. The acidifying potential of SO_2 is almost 1.4 times more than nitrogen oxides, but around half that of ammonia. Therefore, although the total amount of SO_2 emissions are similar to those of NO_2, SO_2 seems to dominate the acidifying threat to the environment. As most fossil fuels contain varying quantities of sulphur, electricity production by conventional power stations, transport and refineries and basic metal industries have been the main sources of EU SO_2 emissions. Due to intensive abatement measures, drastic falls in SO_2 emissions occurred from 1980–1995. Sulphur recovery systems in refineries have contributed to a very big cut in SO_2. Another key contribution has come from filtering and lime scrubbing of exhaust gases in industry and power stations, which has also cut emissions of particles and heavy metal aerosols. Such reductions are very much in line with EU goals of ensuring that long-term sulphur deposits do not exceed critical loads. The current EU target is to cut SO_2 emissions by 35% of 1985 figures by the year 2000.

NO_X emissions affect the EU environment in several ways. Acidification is the main impact but atmospheric fallout also adds to the eutrophication of water and terrestrial ecosystems. NO_X (a mixture of nitrogen oxides, mainly NO_2), and volatile organic hydrocarbon concentrations in cities in hot weather, can lead to the formation of free radicals, such as ozone and peroxides, that are toxic to plants and human health. Like SO_X (a mixture of sulphur

Emissions of CO$_2$ from selected activities as share of total emissions, 1995

	Total emissions m tonnes	Electricity and heat production	Industry	% share of Transport	Households, commerce, etc	Agriculture
EU-12	2,880.7	31.4	0.9	26.1	19.1	1.7
EU-15	3,047.6	31.1	0.8	26.4	19.0	1.7
B	111.3	20.6	0.7	22.4	24.4	3.1
DK	59.9	49.9	0.2	22.9	10.9	3.8
D	848.9	38.2	0.6	21.4	21.4	0.7
EL	78.2	49.7	2.0	24.3	6.9	3.3
E	238.1	33.0	1.1	32.3	7.9	2.2
F	347.5	8.0	1.0	37.1	24.9	2.4
IRL	31.9	39.2	3.1	21.3	25.4	2.5
I	405.1	31.1	1.2	26.9	16.9	2.1
L	8.7	4.6	..	44.8	16.1	..
NL	170.9	28.7	0.4	21.1	19.0	5.1
A	56.7	23.1	0.5	31.2	22.6	..
P	47.9	40.1	1.3	30.1	5.8	2.7
FIN	56.4	38.8	0.4	21.3	11.0	2.8
S	53.6	14.4	0.6	40.7	16.2	2.1
UK	532.3	32.7	0.8	25.7	20.9	0.5

oxides mainly sulphur dioxide) and CO_2 emissions, the combustion of fossil fuels in power stations and vehicles greatly contributes to total NO_2 emissions. The EU target is to cut NO_2 emissions by 30 % of 1990 levels by the year 2000.

Water – vital to life

Water is essential to life. There should be sufficient water of a high enough quality to maintain the various biological processes. Both surface and ground water are used in human activities. There has been a large rise in surface water used by human beings since its introduction as a coolant in electricity production and for irrigation in agriculture.

Water pollution poses another threat to the environment. For many uses, water needs to be of good quality but this is often unavailable due to human pollution. This in turn increases the pressure on available, unpolluted resources. The water we use is part of the hydrological cycle. The annual water quantity remaining after natural evapo-transpiration is called the 'renewable water resource'. In principle, this can be used for human purposes. We abstract water from this for our use.

Human activity has a big impact on water availability. Formerly, most water that fell as rain was absorbed by the soil, resulting in ecological-rich wetlands and replenishing or refreshing aquifers before the surplus entered rivers. But now water tables are no longer replenished as before. This, combined with high abstraction, can lead to a fall in ground-water levels, and cause certain areas to dry up. Such an effect is increasingly present throughout the EU. Another negative effect is that in areas where much of the land is built up, rainfall quickly swells the rivers, which may lead to catastrophic flooding – for example, the Rhine and the Meuse in 1993 and 1995 and the Oder and Danube in 1997.

A major source of freshwater abstraction in nearly all Member States is cooling in electricity generation – from 8 to 74% of all use. In Mediterranean countries large amounts are used for irrigation, whereas abstraction for public supply generally is 10 to 20% of the total.

Water availability plays a key role in consumption. Where there is an abundant and cheap supply, we use more. Consumption varies substantially from one Member State to the next – from 50 litres per person a day in Portugal to 500 litres in Sweden.

Waste water treatment

Treatment plants have been built in all EU countries but the type and percentage of population covered still vary greatly from one to the next.

A precondition is a good sewerage system that collects the waste water and takes it to a central point. If no treatment is available, waste water will have to be discharged directly into surface water. The degree of sewerage varies from about 50% of the population in Greece to over 95% in several northern and central European countries.

Major industries often have their own treatment plants. In some countries, industrial waste water treatment can be almost 50% of overall public waste water treatment.

Biological treatment, as it removes more of the impurities from waste water, is preferable to simple mechanical treatment, but as can be seen from the table on population served by waste water treatment works, biological treatment is still not standard in one or two EU countries. Even with biological treatment, efficiency varies greatly depending on techniques used and the composition of waste water; efficiency ranges from 65% to over

Man-made SO$_X$ and NO$_X$ emissions

	Kg SO_2 per person			Kg NO_X per person		
	1985	1990	1994	1985	1990	1994
B	:	:	:	:	:	:
DK	:	:	:	67.5	62.5	:
D	:	67.1	36.8	:	33.3	27.1
EL	50.3	:	:	31.0	33.3	:
E	57.0	58.3	:	22.1	30.3	:
F	26.7	22.9	17.4	28.6	27.9	25.8
IRL	39.8	63.2	:	25.8	36.6	:
I	30.6	29.6	:	28.1	46.7	:
L	45.1	26.2	:	59.7	:	:
NL	17.9	13.9	9.5	38.9	37.0	34.9
A	25.1	13.9	7.3	30.7	26.9	21.7
P	19.8	28.6	26.1	9.6	21.9	25.9
FIN	77.9	52.1	22.0	66.1	58.2	65.4
S	31.9	15.9	11.0	:	48.0	44.6
UK	66.4	65.3	46.5	43.3	50.3	41.5
IS	31.5	32.2	30.1	66.4	82.4	86.5
NO	23.4	12.5	7.8	55.1	53.5	51.2
CH	11.7	6.3	4.4	27.7	24.7	19.1

Water resources and water abstraction In EU and EFTA Member States

(M m3 except where specified)

	Potential renewable resources	Abstractions (1990)					
		Total	% ground Water	public use	irrigation supply	manufacturing industry	production of electricity
B	16,500	:	:	:	:	:	:
DK	6,115	1,200	100.0	625	365	225	3,500
D	178,000	58,852	13.1	6,769	1,841	8,410	33,786
EL	60,500	:	:	:	7,700	...	135
E	116,290	33,289	16.5	4,296	24,116	1,900	3,000
F	191,000	38,287	:	6,080	:	4,233	23,045
IRL	52,198	:	:	:	:	:	:
I	175,000	:	:	:	:	:	:
L	1,644	261	:	47	:	160	22
NL	91,000	7,900	13.4	1,277	:	1,379	5,140
A	84,000	4,078	65.8	626	200	1,509	1,642
P	72,885	7,288	42.1	578	3,836	238	2,684
FIN	110,200	2,347	10.2	424	:	1,619	249
S	173,975	2,968	20.5	977	94	1,721	26
UK	147,329	:	:	7,782	:	:	:
IS	170,000	:	91.5	82	0	10	0
NO	393,000	:	:	750	:	:	:
CH	53,250	2,665	35.3	1,162	:	:	1,503

95% of the 'biochemical oxygen demand' or BOD.

There is, however, a growing share of advanced treatment that, in addition to BOD elimination, also eliminates nitrogen and phosphorus compounds from waste water. This cuts the nutrient load on surface water and helps reduce the risk of its eutrophication, which is the enrichment of water by nutrients, especially compounds of nitrogen and/or phosphorus, causing an accelerated growth of algae and higher forms of plant life to produce an undesirable disturbance to the balance of organisms present in the water and to the quality of the water concerned.

The vital role of soil

Fertilisers, both natural and artificial, help increase crop yields, provided they are used under the right conditions and at the right time. If not, some nutrients are leached by rainwater and carried into the ground-water. This increases its nitrate content – sometimes to very high levels, as can be seen in certain EU regions. The spreading of manure slurry can lead to vastly-increased levels of chemicals in ground-water if more is applied to the soil than can be absorbed by plants.

The use of herbicides and pesticides destroys organisms such as earthworms and reduces soil aeration. If pesticides are not correctly used, the harmful substances will be leached through the soil into the ground water.

The EU has set a target of cutting the quantity of pesticides applied per unit of arable land by the year 2000 and promoting control of crop parasites – both animal and plant – using biological methods rather than chemical pesticides and insecticides. Fewer pesticides mean less threat to the environment. The European Commission has regulated the marketing of plant protection products via Directives. This will play a key role in the authorisation and use of new products.

Refuse tips pose another threat to soil quality. The leaching of waste by rainwater carries soluble chemical elements into the ground-water and water bodies.

Waste is now managed more carefully – with an eye on environmental protection. Some tips are being set up on an impermeable layer with a drainage system that collects the percolated water and prevents pollutants leaching into the soil. Regulations also ban dumping dangerous products into the sea; special tips have to be provided.

Population served by waste water treatment in EU and EFTA Member States: Total public sewage treatment

	% of resident population				of which at least biological treatment % of resident population			
	1970	1980	1990	1995	1970	1980	1990	1995
B	3.8	22.9	:	:	3.8	22.9	:	:
DK	54.3	:	98.0	:	22.4	:	90.0	:
D	:	:	85.5	:	79.7	:	:	:
EL	:	0.5	:	34.0	:	:	:	:
E	:	17.9	48.0	48.3	:	:	41.9	37.7
F	19.0	43.6	69.0	77.0	:	58.5	:	:
IRL	:	11.2	:	45.0	:	:	:	:
I	14.0	30.0	:	:	:	:	:	:
L	28.0	81.0	90.4	87.5	:	:	71.1	68.4
NL	44.0	72.0	93.0	96.0	29.0	65.0	92.0	96.0
A	17.0	38.0	72.0	75.7	:	28.0	67.0	73.3
P	...	2.3	20.9	:	:	:	11.5	:
FIN	26.0	65.0	76.0	77.0	37.0	65.0	76.0	77.0
S	63.0	82.0	94.0	:	44.0	81.0	94.0	:
UK	:	82.0	87.0	:	:	76.0	79.0	:
IS	:	:	2.0	4.0	20.0	27.0	44.0	52.0
NO	21.0	34.0	57.0	67.0	:	73.0	94.0	94.0
CH	35.0	73.0	94.0	94.0	:	73.0	94.0	94.0

Use of fertilisers on agricultural land (arable land+ permanent crops+grassland)

(Kg/ha)

	Nitrogen (N)		Phosphate (P_2O_5)		Potash (K_2O)		Total commercial	
	1985	1995	1985	1995	1985	1995	1985	1995
EU-15	76.7	69.6	36.0	25.9	38.9	30.5	161.6	126.0
EU-12	77.5	70.3	33.7	24.6	36.3	29.0	142.4	119.5
B	127.4	108.3	61.0	33.9	91.0	64.8	279.5	207.0
DK	134.8	103.1	37.3	16.9	51.5	34.3	223.6	154.3
D	190.8	102.1	88.1	23.1	123.7	37.5	402.6	162.7
EL	78.3	66.0	31.3	29.1	9.6	10.8	119.3	105.9
E	31.3	30.1	15.0	16.9	10.1	13.8	56.5	60.8
F	77.2	80.2	47.0	34.6	58.4	50.0	182.6	164.7
IRL	54.9	96.4	23.3	32.5	30.4	39.7	108.6	168.6
I	60.5	55.2	39.7	32.8	20.4	25.1	120.6	113.1
L	134.8	142.2	45.4	31.2	61.8	48.4	242.1	221.8
NL	247.0	185.9	40.2	29.5	59.2	43.9	346.4	253.1
A	47.0	36.6	25.8	16.9	37.9	20.1	110.6	69.7
P	30.3	34.2	15.4	18.3	7.5	12.7	53.1	65.1
FIN	83.0	84.7	63.6	34.6	61.6	39.3	208.2	158.6
S	70.3	69.5	24.4	16.7	25.2	17.3	119.9	103.5
UK	84.2	88.0	23.6	24.2	27.8	30.7	135.5	143.0

Waste

EU environmental legislation defines waste as 'any substance or object which the holder discards or intends or is required to discard'. In general, household waste consists of left-over food, packaging, used care products, rags etc. Industrial waste might include all sorts of residues from manufacturing processes – packaging, cleaning products, used oil and grease and products past their expiry date.

EU policy tries to ensure waste is managed so it no longer poses a health risk or threat to the environment – or results in distortion of the internal market. The Commission has outlined six areas for action:

- waste prevention
- recycling and reuse
- optimum final disposal
- improved management of disposal sites, and
- rehabilitation of polluted sites
- regulation of transport

The Commission has looked into improving the comparability of data on waste in Member States. It developed the European Waste Catalogue (EWC), with detailed descriptions of different types of waste, in particular the hazardous ones.

Since the Second World War, the growth in industrial production has led to a big rise in waste. Cheap energy has led to a relative fall in the cost of consumer goods, and a boost in products with short life spans. General prosperity has transformed lifestyles. People buy new clothes, furniture etc much more often. To increase turnover, traders are distributing mass publicity material supplied by a printing industry taking advantage of cheap paper. This all ends up as waste.

An OECD study shows a correlation between the trend in GDP, final consumption of

Quantities of waste produced by selected activities, and types of waste

(1 000t)

		Sectors						Types		
	Year	Municipal	Agriculture	Mining and quarring	Manu-facturing industry	Energy production	other	Demolition waste	Dredging sludges	Waste water treatment sludges
B	1988	3,410	:	:	27,000	1,069	2,830	680	4,805	687
DK	1985	2,430	:	:	2,304	1,532	:	1,747	:	1,263
D	1990	27,958	:	19,296	81,906	29,598	:	:	:	:
EL	1990	3,000	90	3,900	4,304	7,680	:	:	:	:
E	1990	12,546	112,102	70,000	13,800	:		22,000	:	10,000
F	1990	20,320	400,000	100,000	50,000	9,800		:	:	600
IRL	1984	1,100	22,000	1,930	1,580	130	860	240	:	570
I	1991	20,033	:	:	34,710	:	:	34,374	:	3,428
L	1990	170	:	:	1,300	:	:	5,240	:	15
NL	1990	7,430	19,210	391	7,665	1,553	:	12,390	17,500	320
A	1990	4,783	880	21	31,801	1,150	:	18,309	111	365
P	1990	2,538	:	202	662	165	15	:	:	:
FIN	1990	3,100	23,000	21,650	10,160	950	150	7,000	3,000	1,000
S	1990	3,200	21,000	28,000	13,000	625	3,850	1,200	:	220
UK	1990	20,000	80,000	107,000	56,000	13,000	15,400	32,000	21,000	1,000
IS	1990	80	:	:	135	:	:	:	:	:
NO	1990	2,000	18,000	9,000	2,000	:	:	2,000	:	100
CH	1990	3,000	:	:	1,000	:	:	2,000	:	260

households and the production of municipal waste.

Industrialised and heavily urbanised countries produce more waste than rural economies, where organic kitchen waste is recycled, either as feed for domestic animals or garden fertiliser, and agricultural waste is recycled directly on to arable land to improve the structure of the soil and fertility. So definitions of waste can vary from country to country.

According to the OECD, municipal waste includes household and similar waste from commerce, offices, small businesses and institutions (schools, hospitals etc). It also embraces bulky and garden waste as well as similar waste from rural areas.

The introduction of cheap, disposable packaging has vastly increased the quantity of waste. Traditionally, such waste has been collected by municipal refuse

Municipal waste production

(kg par habitant)

	1980	1985	1990	1992	1994
B	313	:	351	476	:
DK	399	475	569	566	520
D	:	:	318	:	:
EL	259	302	295	310	:
E	270	276	323	354	365
F	575	548	538	540	:
IRL	188	311	315	:	:
I	248	265	353	352	:
L	352	357	445	484	:
NL	498	478	497	501	596
A	:	:	626	604	:
P	203	235	303	332	:
FIN	:	510	622	:	413
S	302	317	374	:	362
UK	:	:	608	:	:
IS	:	:	314	307	560
NO	416	458	472	519	543
CH	362	403	437	410	380

collection services. Today, waste management is also in the hands of private companies, mostly on behalf of municipalities.

More and more waste treatment is in large plants. This means waste can be sorted prior to final treatment – combustion, composting or recycling – or tipping. In a small number of plants, checks can be made for hazardous products. A disadvantage of central waste treatment could be the long distance waste is transported before processing.

Municipal waste is dealt with in various ways: the oldest and commonest is tipping. Modern tips are managed so that – after pre-treatment to eliminate harmful substances – the waste forms methane for recovery as tip gas. There is an increasing move to incineration, particularly in industrialised and densely-populated countries. Here, generally, the waste's energy is reused. Another way of reducing municipal waste is composting into products that can be used as fertiliser and for soil improvement in farming and gardening.

Many waste materials are recycled or reused to extract secondary raw materials, particularly if collected separately. They can then be used in a variety of ways – for example, scrap metal as raw material in foundries, waste oil or timber as fuel.

As packaging is a large part of landfill waste and is a key source of secondary raw materials, most countries now collect waste glass and paper separately for recycling. Some packaging waste, such as disposable bottles, could be avoided by reintroducing reusable packaging – not always an easy option – or, for certain non-food products, dispensing with packaging entirely.

Hazardous waste presents a special problem for industry. Certain activities produce harmful substances that pose a major threat to the environment and the public. According to the Council Directive on hazardous waste – in which 14 hazardous properties are defined – waste must have one or more of these broadly defined properties to be described as hazardous. Further implementation of this European legislation has led the Commission to draw up a Hazardous Waste List to support the definition of waste based on its toxicological characteristics and concentrations. But the official EU list of hazardous waste is not yet in line with existing national definitions. And national definitions also show big differences.

The Directive on hazardous waste requires Member States to follow certain rules in processing, transportation and final disposal, and introduce a system of notification for all such waste.

Percentage of paper and glass recycled

	Paper and cardboard (%)			Glass (%)		
	1985	1990	1993	1985	1990	1993
B	14	:	11	42	:	55
DK	31	35	:	19	:	62
D	40	40	46	44	54	70
EL	25	28	30	15	15	20
E	57	51	78	13	27	29
F	34	37	42	26	29	46
IRL	10	:	:	7	23	29
I	38	:	:	25	48	52
L	:	:	:	:	:	:
NL	50	50	:	49	67	76
A	37	78	:	38	:	68
P	37	45	:	10	27	29
FIN	39	43	:	21	36	46
S	43	43	50	20	:	59
UK	28	32	32	12	21	29
NO	23	26	32	:	:	67
CH	39	49	54	46	65	78

Production, treatment and disposal methods of hazardous waste

(1 000t)

		Total amounts generated	Total amounts to be managed	Transfrontier movements – Imports	Transfrontier movements – Exports	Physico/ chemical treatment	Thermal treatment, incineration	Recovery operations	Landfill
B	1995	776	:	:	:	:	:	:	:
DK	1994	194	:	24	34	:	108	24	62
D	1990	8,949	:	:	:	:	:	:	:
EL	1992	450	:	:	:	:	:	88	:
E	1990	:	:	:	:	:	:	:	:
F	1994	7,000	2,634	429	71	340	1,558	:	728
IRL	1990	:	:	:	:	:	:	:	
I	1991	3,387	:	:	:	3,090	:	:	284
L	1995	180	:	:	:	:	:	:	:
NL	1993	1,688	1,757	237	163	255	160	130	510
A	1995	1,000	1,000	:	:	122	190	345	410
P	1994	1,365	1,368	3	1	16	37	3	145
FIN	1992	558	:	:	:	450	44	202	23
S	1985	500	:	34	64	:	:	:	45
UK	1993	2,020	:	66	0	668	224	195	936
IS	1994	6	5	:	1	:	5	2	:
NO	1994	500	471	4	323	10	19	83	:
CH	1993	837	711	8	126	231	254	55	171

4.3 Protecting and conserving nature

Each EU country has its system of protecting wild flora and fauna as well as natural eco-systems and landscapes. But nature recognises no national borders. Landscape, habitats and living organisms – like pollution and the weather – cross national borders freely. Measures in one country – and the degree to which they are effective and enforced – have consequences for distant as well as neighbouring lands. Therefore, EU countries work closely on the conservation of nature and cooperate with countries outside the EU as well as with non-governmental organisations.

Policies for protection

Long ago, several Member States adopted nature conservation policies to try to maintain the wide variety of semi-natural habitats still remaining and protect plants and animals under particular threat. The EU has developed – and is still developing – legislation to improve the protection of endangered species and habitats. Two key measures are the Birds Directive – which requires Member States to protect some 175 species of birds – and the Habitats Directive. These measures cover both the maintenance of suitable habitats and a ban on hunting or shooting the species in question. The Habitats Directive aims to create a European network of protected areas, called Natura 2000. So far, Member States have concentrated on identifying and mapping sites for this network.

Assisted by numerous non-governmental nature conservation organisations, Member States have designated a number of exemplary habitats as nature reserves. These vary widely in size and the level of protection. In the 5th Environmental Action Programme – the EU policy and action on the environment and sustainable development – the creation of this network and the maintenance or restoration of natural habitats and protection of wild fauna and flora are key targets for the year 2000.

Concern over diminishing populations of wild birds due to various environmental pressures – such as pesticide use, pollution, habitat loss and hunting and collecting – has led to the need for conservation. Since a large number of species of EU wild birds are migratory, measures in one country would be rendered ineffective by lack of coordination with others. Therefore EU action requires Member States to maintain wild bird populations and protect their eggs, nests and habitats. A particularly important part of this legislation is the conservation of habitats of certain threatened species through designation of Special Protection Areas (SPA). The list of such species is continuously updated in line with scientific research.

Intensive farming methods have added to the problem, in particular the use of pesticides. This has cut the populations of insects and their host plants that are the basis of the food chain. It has long been recognised that to conserve and protect wild animals you must protect the plants and habitats they need to survive. The first recorded protected area was the New Forest in England, designated a hunting reserve in 1079.

This century the concept of protected areas has been broadened to cover areas of outstanding natural beauty and habitats with a particularly rich or unique range of species.

It is increasingly recognised that some EU policies – particularly in agriculture and regional development – have a direct, and sometimes detrimental, impact on habitats and species. Nature conservation is a part of Community economic development projects. For example, there are systematic checks to ensure that projects financed under Community structural funds do not damage habitats listed as important by the EU Birds Directive.

Measures in the Birds Directive have been extended to protect other threatened animals, plants and habitats of EU importance. The aim is to establish an EU-wide network of protected areas to maintain the distribution and populations of threatened species and habitats, on land and in seas.

The network of Special Areas of Conservation (SAC), established under the Natura 2000 project will include the SPAs of the Birds Directive. EU Member States are incorporating planning and development policies in their land use to encourage and manage landscape important for wild fauna and flora. Features such as rivers, hedgerows, lakes and ponds are essential for migration, dispersal and genetic exchange of wild species.

Protected areas included in Natura 2000 network at 17 March 1997

	Birds Directive (SPAs)			Habitats Directive (SACs)		
	Number	Total area (km2)	Share of national territory (%)	Number	Total area (km2)	Share of national territory (%)
B	36	4,313	14.1	102	903	3
DK	111	9,601	22.3	175	±11,000	±25.5
D	502	8,598	2.4	9	128	0
EL	29	1,930	1.5	164	18,969	14.4
E	150	25,208	5	122	3,078	0.6
F	105	7,360	1.4	–	–	–
IRL	106	2,054	2.9	–	–	–
I	101	4,530	1.5	±2,800	±33,250	±11.0
L	6	14	0.5	–	–	–
NL	26	3,411	8.2	27	2,820	6.8
A	44	2,482	3	97	±3,620	±4.3
P	36	3,323	3.6	*30	414	:
FIN	15	967	0.3	415	25,599	7.6
S	225	22,177	4.9	1,047	43,736	9.7
UK	140	5046	2.1	255	13,322	5.5
Total EU-15	1,632	101,014	3.1	±5,243	±156,839	±4.8

*Portugal: SACs in Madeira and Azores only

4.4 Spending on environmental protection

The public has become increasingly aware of the need to protect the environment against pollution. Protective measures are designed to prevent damage, or repair that already done. Environmental protection is now a priority concern of economic policy. The general aim is sustainable development. All measures in this area cost money. But investing in anti-pollution measures means spending less on subsequent cleaning-up and helps prevent irreparable damage. It also creates markets for environmental goods and services, with benefits for exports and employment.

To encourage firms to protect the environment governments can use regulatory measures or levy taxes directly linked to pollution. The 'polluter pays' principle is one weapon in the fight against pollution. It is easier to quantify spending on environmental protection than to estimate the benefits. An effort is being made to produce comparable expenditure data at European level. Since data are not yet completely harmonised, the following tables have to be interpreted with caution.

Spending on the environment is generally divided into public and private expenditure. The former includes all government spending; the latter covers investment and current outlays by businesses in capturing emissions and/or rendering them less harmful.

The second table shows the size of investment and current outlays of the public sector in various EU and OECD countries. The importance of the public sector differs among countries, due in part to the way environmental protection is organised. For example, some countries have privatised waste water collection and treatment. The way environmental problems are perceived varies from country to country. Problems are linked directly to the industrial structure in different countries. A country where service industries predominate might have to spend less in all fields than a country with an important basic industry.

EU environmental spending was an estimated 90 billion ECU in 1994 or 1.4% of EU GDP. Waste water treatment accounts for the largest share, followed by waste and air.

Expenditure on pollution control financed by the public sector

(% of GDP)

	1985	1987	1988	1989	1990	1991	1992
B	:	:	:	:	:	:	:
DK	0.7	0.8	0.9	0.5	0.5	0.6	:
D	0.7	0.8	0.8	0.8	0.8	0.9	0.9
EL	0.7	0.5	0.5	0.5	0.6	0.5	:
E	:	0.5	0.5	0.6	0.6	0.6	:
F	0.6	0.6	0.8	0.9	0.8	0.9	0.9
IRL	:	:	:	:	:	:	:
I	:	:	0.2	0.5	:	:	:
L	:	:	:	:	:	:	:
NL	1.0	0.9	:	0.9	0.9	1.1	1.2
A	1.0	1.0	1.0	:	1.0	1.0	:
P	:	:	0.4	0.4	0.8	0.7	0.8
FIN	:	:	:	:	:	:	:
S	:	0.6	:	:	:	0.8	:
UK	0.7	:	:	:	0.4	:	:
IS	0.3	0.3	0.3	0.3	0.3	0.4	0.4
NO	:	:	:	:	:	:	:
CH	0.7	:	0.7	0.8	:	:	1.0

Investment and current expenditure in the business sector and public sector

(US$ per capita)

		Business sector				Public sector		
	Year	Water	Waste	Air	Year	Water	Waste	Air
B	:	:	:	:	:	:	:	:
B	:	:	:	:	:	:	:	:
DK	:	:	:	:	1991	56.6	37.8	1.9
D	1991	36.9	18.4	52.4	1991	86.3	47.6	0.4
EL	:	:	:	:	:	:	:	:
E	:	:	:	:	1991	45.8	24.1	1.0
F	1992	23.7	22.0	19.8	1992	86.1	62.8	:
IRL	:	:	:	:	:	:	:	:
I	1989	12.8	19.2	19.2	1989	29.5	43.6	:
L	:	:	:	:	:	:	:	:
NL	1992	48.0	17.7	45.1	1992	91.8	77.4	3.2
A	1991	78.1	17.2	81.2	1991	142.1	60.2	5.9
P	1991	:	:	:	1991	28.6	17.1	0.1
FIN	1992	36.2	14.0	44.5	:	:	:	:
S	1988	:	:	:	1991	63.2	40.9	:
UK	1990	80.8	37.6	30.1	1990	11.1	33.3	13.4
IS	:	:	:	:	1992	:	78.0	:
NO	:	:	:	:	:	:	:	:
CH	1993	30.4	30.3	45.3	1992	103.2	101.3	5.5
USA	1992	50.5	87.7	68.8	1992	96.8	51.3	4.0
CAN	1989	19.7	9.5	20.8	1990	55.3	33.5	:
JPN	1990	:	:	:	:	:	:	:

Source: Eurostat and OECD, joint questionnaire.

5 Population

5.1 6.4% of the world's population

The EU's population on 1 January 1997 was 374 million – 6.4% of the world total. The 6.4% share compares with 10.4% in 1960 and Eurostat's projection of just over 4% in 2020. Population can increase both naturally (births minus deaths) and because of a net inflow of migrants. The EU's natural increase per thousand fell from 7.7 in 1960 to 0.8 in 1996, one of the world's lowest. It ranged from Ireland's 5.2 to –1.1 in Germany. Italy also had a negative rate (–0.3). Such low growth, typical of developed countries, results mainly from fewer babies being born and from people living longer. The EU has had an ageing population for the past 60 years.

Migration to the EU has been positive for the last 40 years – in 1996 it increased the population by 2 per thousand. On 1 January 1996, 17.5 million non-nationals lived in EU countries – 4.7% of the total population. Two-thirds were from non-EU countries.

Becoming older

In 1996, 23.7% of the EU population was aged under 20 and 20.8% over 60. 3.9% were over 80, double the 1960 figure.

Ireland has 33.5% of its population under 20, Italy only 21%. Ireland also has the lowest percentage over 60 (15.2%); Italy the highest at 22.6%. The populations of all Member States are ageing. Italy, Sweden and Greece are the most seriously affected but the trend is spreading to Spain, Portugal and even Ireland.

This is a global problem – which will affect even the Third World sooner or later – and is perhaps the most important social phenomenon of the late 20th century. A fall in the number of people at work will, among other things, make it difficult to pay for pensions and put a strain on social protection.

Population projections

Eurostat's population projections for the countries of the European Union, analysed by sex and age, for the period 1995–2050, are based on two major sets of hypotheses:
The 'low' scenario is based on the following assumptions:
- *continuation of the downtrend in the average number of children per woman to a level of approximately 1.4 for the generations of women born recently;*
- *a slight rise in life expectancy at birth;*
- *a return to more moderate levels of net immigration, giving an annual increase, from 2000, of almost 400,000 persons for the 15 Member States.*

The 'high' scenario is based on the following assumptions
- *a rising fertility rate per generation, to a level of 1.95 children per woman;*
- *continuation of the strong upward trend in longevity over the next five decades;*
- *net immigration of 800,000 persons per annum, as from 2000, into the countries of the European Union.*

The ageing of the population

The expression 'ageing of the population' means an increase in the proportion of the elderly in a given population.
The population can age either because of a fall in the birth rate, which reduces the number of young people and narrows the base of the age pyramid, or because people live longer, which causes the top of the age pyramid to become wider.

EU actual and projected population

(millions)

— Observed
— High scenario
— Low scenario

450
425
400
375
350
325
300

1960 1965 1970 1975 1980 1985 1990 1995 2000 2005 2010 2015 2020

EU population as a percentage of world population

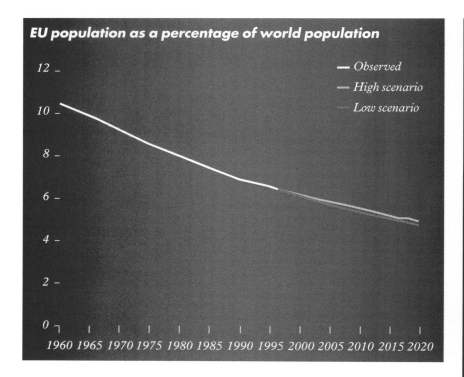

EU population by age group, 1960–2050

(%)

	0–19	20–59	60+
1960	31.7	52.8	15.5
1960	31.7	52.8	15.5
1965	32.3	51.3	16.5
1970	32.1	50.3	17.6
1975	31.5	50.2	18.3
1980	30.0	52.1	17.8
1985	27.8	53.3	18.9
1990	25.5	54.7	19.8
1995	23.9	55.5	20.6
2000	23.1	55.4	21.5
2005	22.5	55.2	22.3
2010	21.8	54.4	23.7
2015	21.2	53.6	25.2
2020	20.7	52.4	26.9
2025	20.1	50.7	29.2
2030	19.8	48.8	31.4
2035	19.6	47.5	32.9
2040	19.5	47.1	33.4
2045	19.4	46.9	33.7
2050	19.4	47.0	33.6

Eurostat baseline population scenario.

Population by age group, 1 January 1996

(%)

	0–19	20–39	40–59	60+	of which: 80+
EU-15	23.7	30.4	25.1	20.8	3.9
Belgium	24.0	29.7	24.9	21.4	3.8
Denmark	23.5	29.8	27.0	19.7	3.9
Germany	21.5	30.7	26.7	21.0	4.0
Greece	23.9	29.5	24.7	21.9	3.5
Spain	24.3	31.9	22.9	20.9	3.4
France	26.0	29.4	24.4	20.1	4.1
Ireland	33.5	29.1	22.2	15.2	2.6
Italy	21.0	30.8	25.6	22.6	4.1
Luxembourg	23.9	31.4	25.6	19.1	3.4
Netherlands	24.3	31.9	26.0	17.8	3.1
Austria	23.2	32.2	24.8	19.7	3.8
Portugal	25.4	30.5	24.0	20.1	2.8
Finland	25.4	27.7	27.9	19.0	3.2
Sweden	24.6	27.4	26.1	22.0	4.7
UK	25.3	29.8	24.4	20.5	4.0

5.2 People live longer

In 1996 the EU recorded 3.7 million deaths – a gross mortality rate of 10 per thousand.

The **infant mortality** rate (the number of deaths during the first year of life) is a key indicator of a country's economic and social health. The EU has one of the world's lowest. It fell from 34.5 per thousand in 1960 to 5.6 in 1995. The drop in Portugal was 90%; in Spain and Italy over 85%.

Life expectancy at birth in the EU is also among the world's best: in 1996 it was 74.0 years for men and 80.5 for women. In the USA it was 72.7 (men) and 79.4 (women); in Japan 77.0 and 83.3. In France, a baby girl is likely to live to 81.9 years, almost eight years longer than a boy. However the gap in the UK is only five years.

Life expectancy at birth

	Men					Women				
	1960	1970	1980	1990	1996(1)	1960	1970	1980	1990	1996(1)
EU-15	67.5 e	68.6 e	70.5 e	72.8	74.0	72.7 e	74.6 e	77.1 e	79.4	80.5
Belgium	67.7	67.8	70.0	72.7	73.5	73.5	74.2	76.8	79.4	80.2
Denmark	70.4	70.7	71.2	72.0	72.8	74.4	75.9	77.3	77.7	78.0
Germany	:	:	:	72.0	73.3	:	:	:	78.4	79.8
Greece	67.3	70.1	72.2	74.6	75.0	72.4	73.8	76.8	79.5	80.3
Spain	67.4	69.2	72.5	73.3	74.4	72.2	74.8	78.6	80.4	81.6
France	66.9	68.4	70.2	72.7	74.0	73.6	75.9	78.4	80.9	81.9
Ireland	68.1	68.8	70.1	72.1	73.2	71.9	73.5	75.6	77.6	78.5
Italy	67.2	69.0	70.6	73.6	74.9	72.3	74.9	77.4	80.1	81.3
Luxembourg	66.5	67.1	69.1	72.3	73.0	72.2	73.4	75.9	78.5	80.0
Netherlands	71.5	70.7	72.7	73.8	74.7	75.3	76.5	79.3	80.9	80.3
Austria	66.2	66.5	69.0	72.4	73.9	72.7	73.4	76.1	78.9	80.2
Portugal	61.2	64.2	67.7	70.4	71.0	66.8	70.8	75.2	77.4	78.5
Finland	65.5	66.5	69.2	70.9	73.0	72.5	75.0	77.6	78.9	80.5
Sweden	71.2	72.2	72.8	74.8	76.5	74.9	77.1	78.8	80.4	81.5
UK	67.9	68.7	70.2	72.9	74.4	73.7	75.0	76.2	78.5	79.3

(1) Provisional or estimated data
e   estimate
Source : Eurostat

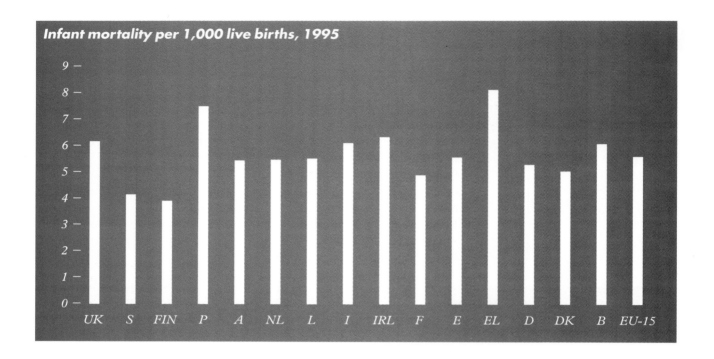

Infant mortality per 1,000 live births, 1995

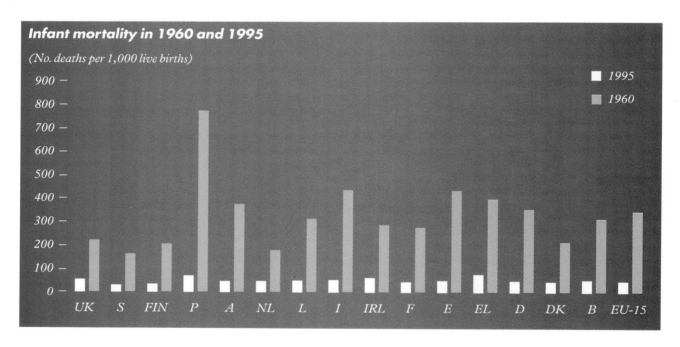

Infant mortality in 1960 and 1995

(No. deaths per 1,000 live births)

■ 1995
■ 1960

5.3 Fewer babies, more divorces

In 1996, 4 million live births were recorded in the EU compared with 5.8 million in 1960. There has been a big fall in larger families.

Between the mid-1960s and 1975, EU fertility was in rapid and constant decline. Thereafter, it has fallen at a slower pace, with occasional interruptions. The latest data suggest a halt in the long-term fall. Ireland is the only EU country where, despite a big drop in the last 10 years, fertility is still nearly at generation replacement level. In others, the fertility rate is below the replacement rate (just over 2 children per woman); if the fertility rate does not rise, the population will eventually decline.

More births outside marriage

Another change in recent decades has been the steady rise of births outside marriage. From 1970 to 1995 these rose from 5.6% of all births to 23.4%. In 1995, Sweden (50.0%), Denmark (46.5%), France (37.2%), UK (33.6%) and Finland (33.1%) had the highest proportions. In Italy (8.1%) and Greece (3.0%) they were much lower.

Marrying less, divorcing more

In 1996, 1.9 million people got

Fertility indicators

The completed fertility indicator shows the number of children born to women of the same generation, i.e. to those born in the same year, by the end of their childbearing years or by the standard cut off age of 50. This figure is an indication of the fertility of a generation, since it represents the average number of children born to each woman in the specific generation (longitudinal analysis).

The total fertility indicator is the sum of the fertility rates by age group for all women between 15 and 49 in the same calendar year (cross-sectional analysis). It indicates the fertility recorded during the calendar year under review. It is thus affected by the differing behavioural patterns of women whose situations vary greatly during their childbearing years. The two indicators reflect two different sets of circumstances, since a woman's childbearing behaviour depends as much on her present situation as on the life she has lived and her attitude to the future. The completed fertility of generations provides a longitudinal view of fertility but it can be calculated only when the childbearing years are over. The total fertility indicator does not represent the figure for any actual generation but provides short-term fertility data every year.

Total EU fertility

— Total fertility rate
— Completed fertility

3.0							
2.5							
2.0							
1.5							
1.0							

| 60 | 65 | 70 | 75 | 80 | 85 | 90 | 95 |
| 33 | 38 | 43 | 48 | 53 | 58 | 63 | 68 |

Calendar year/Generation

married in the EU – a rate of 5.1 per thousand compared with 8.0 in 1960. First marriages fell from 91% of the EU-15 total in 1960 to 83% in 94. In 1995, Portugal and Denmark had the highest marriage rates (6.6 per thousand). But in Sweden and Ireland they were 3.8 and 4.3 respectively. Marriages between young single people are steadily falling and the average age of first marriage steadily rising. In 1994, men were on average 3.0 years older at first marriage than in 1975 and women 3.3 years. In Portugal, the average age of a woman at first marriage was 24.8 in 1995 compared with 29.0 in Denmark.

The age difference between partners at first marriage appears stable throughout the EU with men some 2.5 years older on average. In

Completed fertility (average lifetime births per woman) for female generations born 1930 to 1960 (1)

	1930	1935	1940	1945	1950	1955	1958	1959	1960
EU-15	2.40	2.37	2.24	2.05	1.96	1.90	1.85	1.83	1.81
Belgium	2.30	2.27	2.17	1.94	1.84	1.83	1.85	1.84	1.86
Denmark	2.36	2.38	2.24	2.06	1.90	1.84	1.86	1.87	1.88
Germany	2.17	2.16	1.98	1.79	1.72	1.67	1.65	1.65	1.63
Greece	2.21	2.02	2.01	2.00	2.07	2.03	1.90	1.93	1.93
Spain	2.59	2.67	2.59	2.43	2.19	1.90	1.81	1.78	1.72
France	2.64	2.58	2.41	2.22	2.11	2.13	2.12	2.10	2.08
Ireland	3.50	3.44	3.27	3.27	2.99	2.66	2.46	2.40	2.36
Italy	2.29	2.29	2.14	2.07	1.90	1.79	1.69	1.67	1.63
Luxembourg	1.97	2.00	1.92	1.82	1.72	1.68	1.66	1.70	1.72
Netherlands	2.65	2.50	2.21	1.99	1.90	1.87	1.86	1.84	1.84
Austria	2.32	2.45	2.17	1.95	1.89	1.70	1.69	1.69	1.66
Portugal	2.95	2.85	2.61	2.31	2.12	1.97	1.94	1.90	1.86
Finland	2.51	2.30	2.03	1.87	1.85	1.89	1.93	1.94	1.94
Sweden	2.11	2.14	2.05	1.96	2.00	2.03	2.05	2.04	2.05
UK	2.35	2.41	2.36	2.17	2.03	2.02	1.98	1.97	1.94

(1) Estimates for generations which have not yet completed their productive career are based on the assumption that future fertility rates by age will be the same as the most recent observations.

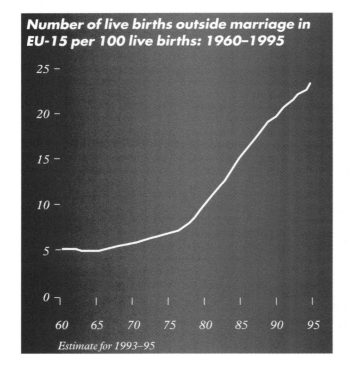

Number of live births outside marriage in EU-15 per 100 live births: 1960–1995

Estimate for 1993–95

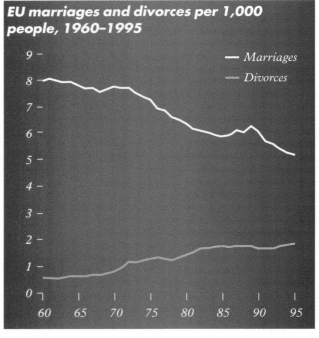

EU marriages and divorces per 1,000 people, 1960–1995

— Marriages
— Divorces

some EU countries, such as Italy and Greece, there seems to be a link between falling marriage rates and declining fertility as children in these countries tend to be born in wedlock. But marriage rates do

seem to have stabilised in most Member States from 1993 to 1995.

From 1960–1985 there was a more-or-less unbroken rise in the number of EU divorces. They soared from

170,000 per year to 625,000. After 1985 the number seemed more or less stable – but it started to rise again in 1992–1996, albeit with striking contrasts between some Member States. Divorce is still much more common in Scandinavia, for example, than in Mediterranean countries. It seems likely that nearly a third of EU couples married in 1995 will divorce before long.

Average age at first marriage in EU, 1975 to 1994

☐ *Men*
☐ *Women*

IRL: 1992; E, I, UK: 1994; EU-15: estimate for 1994

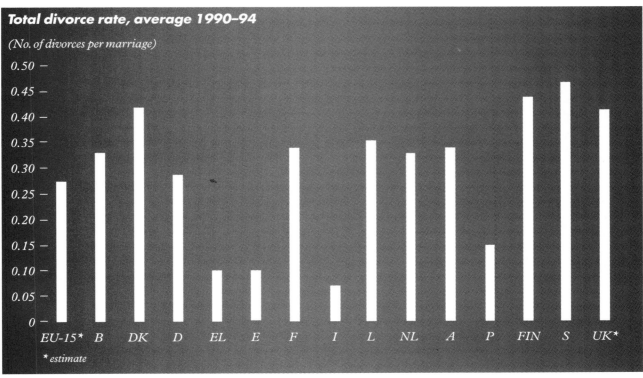

Total divorce rate, average 1990–94

(No. of divorces per marriage)

* estimate

5.4 EU immigration

On 1 January 1995, the EU's 372 million inhabitants included 14.1 million (3.8%) nationals of non-EU countries. There were also 5.6 million EU citizens living in a Member State other than their own.

In 1996, most non-nationals from non-EU countries (74.1%) lived in Germany (5.3 million), France (2.3 million) and the UK (1.2 million). They accounted for 6.5%, 4.0% and 2.1% respectively of these countries' populations. Luxembourg has the largest percentage of non-national residents – 32.6%, but these are mostly from other EU countries.

In the EU as a whole, half of the non-EU foreigners come from other European countries, especially Turkey and the former-Yugoslavia. The large number of non-nationals in the EU can be explained by

immigration in response to the need for labour – especially in jobs considered menial or badly paid – and by the appeal of the EU to those outside.

In 1995, Germany welcomed over half of EU immigrants, putting migration to other Member States in the shade. In that year, immigrants to EU countries included 47% who were citizens of another EU country, either coming home or moving within the EU. Another 31% were nationals of non-EU European countries and 22% were non-Europeans.

Breakdown of resident population 1996

('000)

	Total	Nationals	Non EU Nationals	Nationals of other EU countries
EU-15	370,662	352,964	12,014	5,684
Belgium	10,143	9,233	355	555
Denmark	5,251	5,028	176	47
Germany	81,817	74,644	5,362	1,812
Greece	10,465	10,310	111	44
Spain	39,742	39,243	263	236
France	56,652	53,055	2,275	1,322
Ireland	3,626	3,509	45	72
Italy	57,269	56,585	559	125
Luxembourg	407	274	13	120
Netherlands	15,494	14,768	534	191
Austria	8,040	7,319	611	110
Portugal	9,921	9,752	127	42
Finland	5,117	5,048	55	14
Sweden	8,837	8,306	353	179
UK	57,881	55,889	1,174	818

Immigration to EU by nationality 1996 (main groups)

German	274,289
British	136,265
Former Soviet Union	106,784
Turkish	86,723
Polish	82,705
Italian	54,950
Dutch	51,722
Former Yugoslavia	50,300
USA	45,084
Portuguese	38,580

5.5 The shrinking EU household

Private households in the EU now have fewer members on average – many with only one or two.

According to 1990/91 censuses, EU-12 had 131 million private households compared with 111 million in the 1981/82 censuses. This 18% rise was far higher than the 2.6% increase in total population.

Only in Greece did household size stay stable from 1981–91. And only in Spain, Portugal, Greece and Ireland was the average household size still above 3 in 1991. The fall elsewhere was due to fewer babies, more divorce and people living longer and on their own, especially widows. One-person households now account for over 30% of the total in Denmark, Germany and the Netherlands. Of the EU-15's 140 million households, the country with the smallest average size is Sweden (2.1 people). And in Sweden 40% of households consist of one person and half of all households have no children.

In EU-12 there are nearly 9 million single-parent households, 85% of them headed by the mother.

FURTHER READING

Eurostat publications

A social portrait of Europe
Demographic statistics yearbook 1997
Asylum-seekers and refugees: a statistical report
   Volume 1: EC Member States
   Volume 2: EFTA countries
Migration statistics 1996
Population, Households and Dwellings in Europe: Main results of the 1990/1991 Censuses, 1996
Beyond the predictable: Demographic changes in the EU up to 2050, Statistics in Focus 1997/7
Decline in births halted in 1996, Statistics in Focus 1997/10
About one marriage in four in the EU ends in divorce, Statistics in Focus 1997/14

Electronic products

Eurostat Yearbook CD-ROM
Eurostat's New Cronos database (Regio)

Other publications

Social Europe: periodical and supplements

Single-person EU households

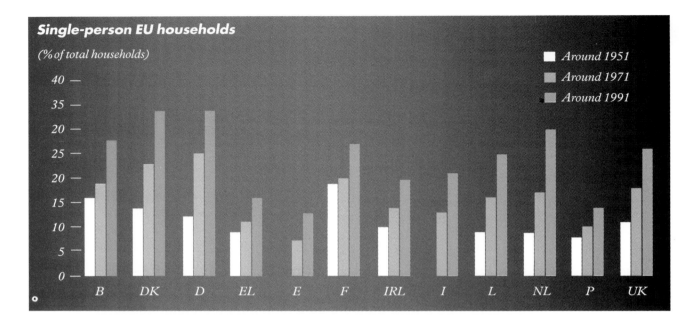

(% of total households)

Around 1951
Around 1971
Around 1991

Average number of persons per household

	1981/82	1990/91
EU-12	2.8	2.6
Belgium	2.7	2.5
Denmark	2.4	2.2
Germany	2.5	2.2
Greece	3.1	3.1
Spain	3.6	3.3
France	2.7	2.6
Ireland	3.6	3.3
Italy	3.0	2.8
Luxembourg	2.8	2.6
Netherlands	2.7	2.4
Portugal	3.3	3.1
UK	2.7	2.5

Source: Community programme of
population censuses, 1990/91.

Breakdown of EU-12 private households by size

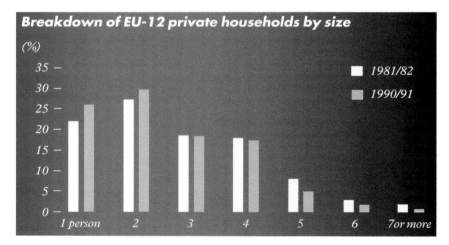

(%)

1981/82
1990/91

6 Education

Full-time schooling for at least eight years

The starting age for full-time compulsory schooling ranges from four in Luxembourg to seven in Scandinavian countries. The age at which it ends varies from 14 to 16. Luxembourg, the Netherlands and the UK have the longest duration of compulsory education at eleven

years while Spain and France have ten years. All other Member States stipulate nine years, except Italy (eight). Belgium, Germany and the Netherlands have an additional two to three years compulsory part-time schooling.

Increasing numbers of four-year-olds are in pre-primary education. In countries such as Belgium,

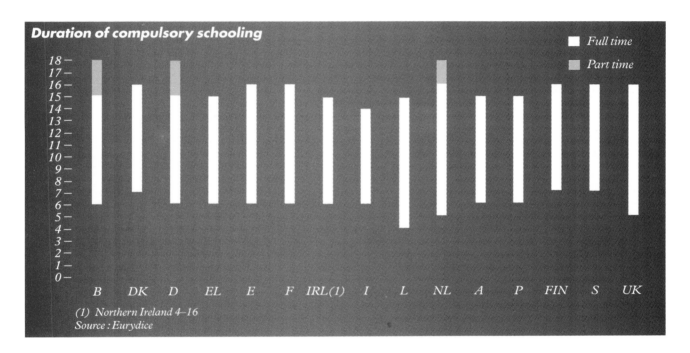

Duration of compulsory schooling

(1) Northern Ireland 4–16
Source : Eurydice

Percentage of four-year-olds in pre-primary education, 1980/81–1994/95

	B	DK	D	EL	E	F	IRL	I	L	NL	A	P	FIN	S	UK
1980/81	100	54	65	38	69	100	54	:	94	96	57	18	18	28	:
1990/91	99	74	71	51	95	100	55	:	94	98	66	46	26	48	:
1994/95	100	79	71	54	100	100	53	96	94	97	71	55	29	58	93

Source: Eurostat – Joint Unesco, OECD, Eurostat data collection (UOE)

Participation rates in education of those aged 16–18 and 19–21, 1994/95

(% of those of relevant age)

Age	EU-15	B(1)	DK	D	EL(1)	E	F	IRL	I	L	NL	A	P	FIN	S	UK
16–18	82	97	82	92	66	73	91	84	:	:	91	81	67	88	94	71
19–21	47	59	46	47	41	48	55	38	:	:	59	28	43	44	32	39

Source: Eurostat – Joint Unesco, OECD, Eurostat data collection (UOE)

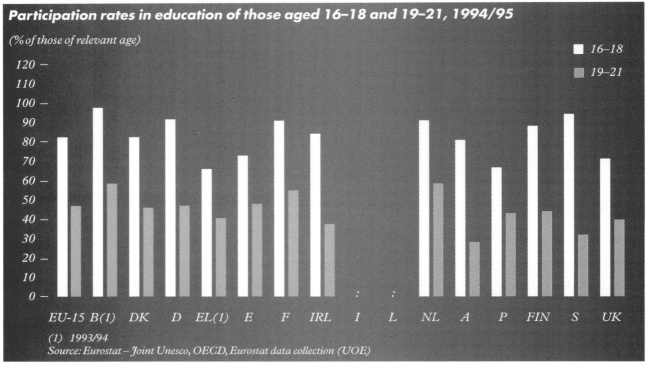

Participation rates in education of those aged 16–18 and 19–21, 1994/95

(% of those of relevant age)

Legend: ■ 16–18   ■ 19–21

(1) 1993/94
Source: Eurostat – Joint Unesco, OECD, Eurostat data collection (UOE)

Number of students in tertiary education, EU-15, 1980/81–1994/95

('000s)

	EU-15	B	DK	D	EL	E	F	IRL	I	L	NL	A	P	FIN	S	UK
1980/81	6,736*	217	115	1,525	121	698	1,176	55	1,126	:	364	137	90	113	:	828
1994/95	11,791	353	170	2,156	296	1,527	2,073	122	1,792	2	503	234	301	205	246	1,813
% rise from 1981 to 1995	75*	63	48	41	145	119	76	121	59	:	38	71	231	81	:	119

* estimate.
Note: For some countries, the figures for tertiary education in recent years may be slightly affected by the inclusion of programmes that were not
   included previously.
Source: Eurostat – Joint Unesco, OECD, Eurostat data collection (UOE)

France, Luxembourg and the
Netherlands this has been the norm
for at least 15 years.

By age 16, EU students will have
spent nearly three-quarters of their
lives in school. On average, 82% of
16 to 18-year-olds then remain in
education. The lowest staying-on
rates are in Greece, Spain, Portugal
and the UK. The EU average for
those aged 19 to 21 remaining in
education falls to 47%. Large falls –
over 50 percentage points – in the
participation rate as students pass
the age of 18 are seen in Sweden
and Austria, which have the lowest
participation rates for 19–21 year

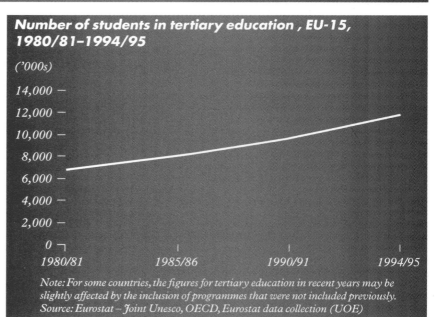

Number of students in tertiary education , EU-15, 1980/81–1994/95

('000s)

Note: For some countries, the figures for tertiary education in recent years may be
slightly affected by the inclusion of programmes that were not included previously.
Source: Eurostat – Joint Unesco, OECD, Eurostat data collection (UOE)

Women per 100 men in upper secondary and tertiary education, 1994/95

	EU-15	B	DK	D	EL	E	F	IRL	I	L	NL	A	P	FIN	S	UK
Upper Secondary	102	99	100	85	94	111	95	106	99	90	88	84	109	121	117	117
Tertiary Education	103	98	108	77	98	111	122	97	110	:	89	92	131	112	122	104

Source: Eurostat – Joint Unesco, OECD, Eurostat data collection (UOE)

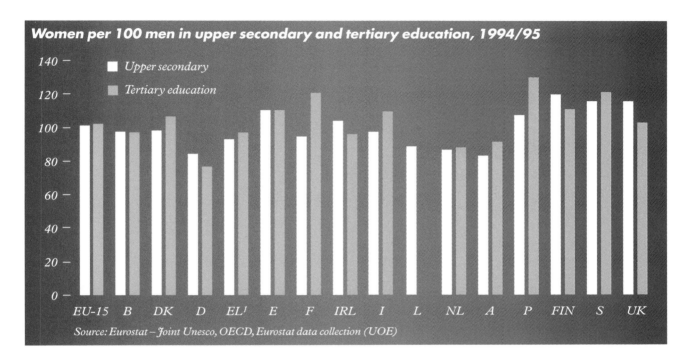

Women per 100 men in upper secondary and tertiary education, 1994/95

Source: Eurostat – Joint Unesco, OECD, Eurostat data collection (UOE)

olds. Many in this age group go on to other forms of training but, for some, 18 is the end of their education.

Sharp rise in students

There has been a big rise in the number of EU students in tertiary education in the last 15 years – up by 75% from 6.7 million to 11.8 million, even though the number of those in the 18–29 age-group rose by only 3%.

There are many reasons for this rise.

A major stimulus must be the realisation that tertiary education increases job potential. Another factor is the increasing number of women in post-compulsory education.

In 1980/81 there were 75 women to 100 men in tertiary education. They now outnumber men while female to male participation in upper secondary education rose from 88 per 100 in 1980/81 to 102 in 1994/95.

However, traditional differences remain between the sexes in the subjects studied. In the EU as a whole, about five times as many men as women graduated in 1994/95 with engineering qualifications and three times as many with degrees in mathematics and computer sciences. Women predominated in the arts and medical sciences, including nursing.

Graduates by field of study, EU-15, 1994/95

(% of total)

	Men	Women
Total	100	100
Humanities, Applied arts, Religion	8	14
Social sciences, Business studies	26	25
Law	6	6
Natural sciences	7	5
Mathematics, Computer sciences	6	2
Medical sciences	9	21
Engineering, Architecture	28	5
Others	10	21

Source: Eurostat – Joint Unesco, OECD, Eurostat data collection (UOE)

Another inequality is that chances of progressing beyond compulsory education are still linked to social background. It is clear there is a direct relationship between the head of household's education and that of his or her children.

Education for life

There is now a clear EU focus on lifelong learning and vocational training. These are seen as the key to enhancing job prospects and fighting social exclusion. Helping young people attain a certified vocational qualification is a Maastricht Treaty priority. In the EU as a whole around 29% of those aged 15–19 took part in initial vocational education and training programmes in 1993/94.

In 1993/94, 45 of every 100 people in such training were women. But in Ireland and Finland women were in a majority.

Continuing vocational training (CVT) is of growing importance. A

Proportion of young people aged 16–19 not in education by educational attainment level of head of household, 1996

| | Educational level of head of household % | | |
	Lower secondary or less	Upper secondary	Tertiary
EU-15	26*	9*	4*
B	10	5	2
DK	:	:	:
D	15	8	4
EL	32	12	6
E	29	10	4
F	12	6	1
IRL	27	11	5
I	34	11	6
L	18	9	3
NL	22	12	7
A	33	20	7
P	31	3	3
FIN	15	11	5
S	:	:	:
UK	:	:	:

Source : Eurostat – European Union Labour Force Survey (LFS) 1996

Participation rates in initial vocational education and training of those aged 15–19, 1993/94

(%) Age	EU-15	B	DK	D	EL(1)	E	F	IRL	I	L(2)	NL	A	P	FIN(3)	S	UK(3)
15–19	29*	45	21	40	21	22	28	17	:	28	30	55	12	24	37	30

(1) 1992/93
(2) The fact that students attend education/training in neighbouring countries may influence these rates
(3) Rates for 16-19 year olds and not 15–19
Source: Eurostat –Vocational Education and Training data collection (VET)

survey showed nearly 60% of enterprises with 10 or more employees in the then EU-12 carrying out some form of CVT in 1993. The bigger the firm, the greater the opportunities offered. In CVT courses, as in initial vocational training, sex equality seems the norm.

Internationalisation of education

European Commission initiatives to encourage the spirit of EU citizenship include the promotion of foreign language learning and the mobility of students and teachers across countries. Erasmus is an example of a Community scheme which encourages this. In 1995/96, 85,000 participated in this student exchange, which includes EFTA countries. The UK was the most popular destination, chosen by 26% of Erasmus students – a sign, perhaps, of the popularity of English as a foreign language.

In the EU as a whole, 90% of pupils in general secondary education were learning English, 33% French, 18% German and 9% Spanish in 1994/95. In many Member States, the proportion learning English was over 90%.

Participation rates in initial vocational education and training of those aged 15–19, 1993/94

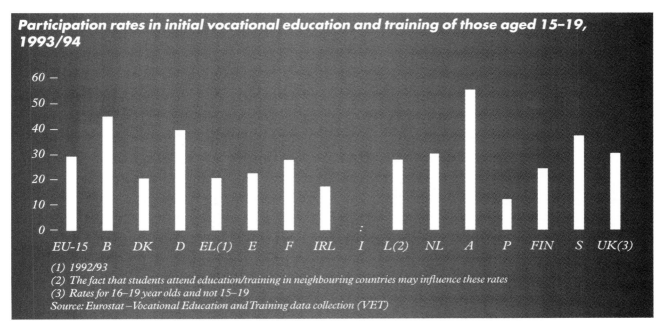

(1) 1992/93
(2) The fact that students attend education/training in neighbouring countries may influence these rates
(3) Rates for 16–19 year olds and not 15–19
Source: Eurostat – Vocational Education and Training data collection (VET)

Participants in vocational education and training by sex, 1993/94

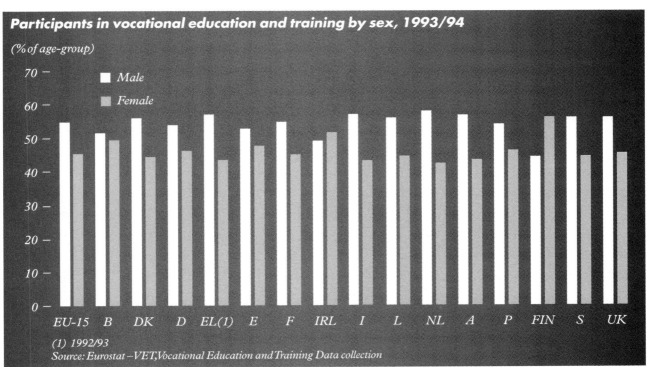

(1) 1992/93
Source: Eurostat – VET, Vocational Education and Training Data collection

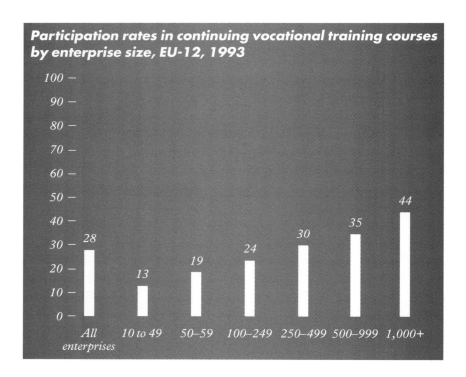

Participation rates in continuing vocational training courses by enterprise size, EU-12, 1993

Participation rates of employees on CVT courses by sex, 1993

	EU-12	B	DK	D	EL	E	F	IRL	I	L	NL	P	UK
Male	29	25	32	25	13	21	39	42	16	24	27	15	40
Female	27	28	34	22	13	18	33	44	11	26	24	11	37
All	28	25	33	24	13	20	37	43	15	25	26	13	39

Source: Eurostat – Continuing Vocational Training Survey (CVTS) 1994

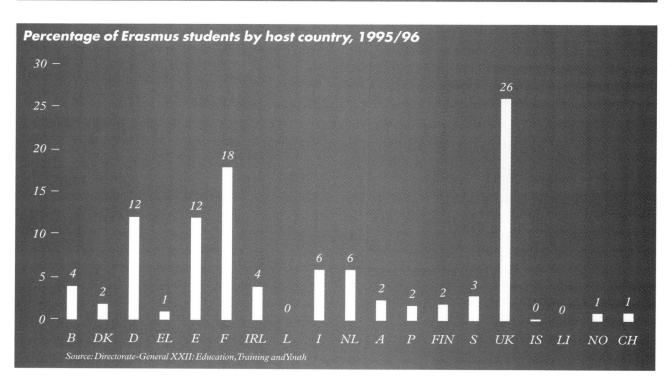

Percentage of Erasmus students by host country, 1995/96

Source: Directorate-General XXII: Education, Training and Youth

Percentage of pupils in secondary general education learning selected foreign languages, 1994/95

	EU-15	B(F)(1)	BVL	DK	D	EL(2)	E	F	IRL(3)	I	L	NL(3)	A	P	FIN	S(1)	UK
English	90*	60	70	94	93	69	95	95	.	73	76	99*	:	74	99	99	.
French	33*	.	97	16	24	51	8	.	70	34	98	65*	:	52	11	17	:
German	18*	5	22	68	.	4	0	28	26	4	98	78*	.	2	33	45	:
Spanish	9*	3	0	5	1	–	.	32	4	0	10	–	:	0	:	2	:

(1) 1993/94
(2) 1995/96
(3) Full-time only
Source: Eurostat – Joint Unesco, OECD, Eurostat data collection (UOE)

In order to facilitate comparison between countries, data on education in each Member State are allocated to the various category levels of the International Standard Classifieation of Education (ISCED)[1]. The levels are as follows:

Pre-primary education (ISCED 0)

Education preceding primary education. In the vast majority of cases it is not compulsory.

Primary education ISCED 1)

Begins between the ages of four and seven depending on the Member State, is compulsory in all cases and usually lasts for five or six years.

Lower secondary education (ISCED 2)

Compulsory schooling in all Member States. The end of this level often coincides with the end of compulsory full-time schooling.

Upper secondary education (ISCED 3)

Begins around the age of 14 or 15 and refers to either general, vocational or technical education. It can lead to the standard required for admission to tertiary education.

Higher education (ISCED 5,6,7)

ISCED 5 covers programmes which generally do not lead to the awarding of a university degree or equivalent but admission to this level requires the successful completion of a programme at the upper secondary level.
ISCED 6 covers programmes leading to a first university degree or equivalent.
ISCED 7 covers programmes leading to a post graduate degree.

1. This classification has recently been revised for future data collections.

DATA SOURCES:

The UOE data collection

The UOE (UNESCO/OECD/EUROSTAT) data collection is an instrument through which the three organisations jointly collect annually internationally comparable data on key aspects of the education system using administrative sources.

The European Union Labour Force Survey (LFS)

The European Union Labour Force Survey (LFS) is the leading source of data on employment and unemployment in the European Union (EU). It covers the whole EU population living in private households. The LFS has been held every year since 1983 and includes two sets of questions on education and training received and on current education and training. Data on the new Member States have been collected since 1995.

The Vocational Education and Training Data Collection (VET)

The Vocational Education and Training Data Collection (VET) is the first statistical exercise aimed at improving the information base in the area of initial vocational training at European level. The project was launched by Eurostat in co-operation with DGXXII, in

July 1994 and the data collection was made on a programme-by-programme basis. The data covers vocational education and training programmes defined as iany structured activity which aims to provide (especially young) people with the skills, the attitudes and broad and more specific knowledge necessary for an occupation or family of occupation and leads to a recognised qualification.

The Continuing Vocational Training Survey (CVTS)

The ContinuingVocational Training Survey (CVTS) was carried out in 1994 and asked about the training offered by enterprises in 1993. Data were collected in the then 12 Member States of the EU from a representative sample of enterprises with 10 or more employees. The samples were structured so as to provide results for 6 size groups of enterprises and for 20 sectors of the economy. The survey excluded the agriculture, forestry and fishing sector and also public administration and the health and education sectors.

7 Research and development

In the EU as a whole over ECU 128.9 billion was spent on research and development (R&D) in 1996. This was 4% higher than in 1995 but it remained around 2% of GDP. Some 2.1 million people were involved in R&D with noticeable differences between countries, regions and sectors.

In 1996 the four Member States with highest R&D spending were Germany (ECU 42 billion), France (ECU 28 billion), UK (ECU 18 billion) and Italy (ECU 10 billion). When spending is compared to the size of Member State economies, Sweden is in the lead with R&D spending equivalent to 3.5% of GDP. The EU average (1.9%), and the corresponding percentages for all Member States except Sweden, are below the USA (2.6%) and Japan (2.8%).

Most EU R&D is in the business enterprise sector (63%). The rest is split between government (16%) and higher education (20%).

People working in R&D

The 2.1 million people working in EU R&D (1995) formed 1.27 % in 1996 of the labour force. Sweden and Finland have the highest proportions with Denmark, Germany, France and the Netherlands also above the EU average. The proportion employed can also vary from one region to another.

R&D input by Member State, 1995

	R&D expenditure as % of GDP	R&D personnel as % of labour force
B	1.59	1.23
DK	1.96	1.81
D	2.28	1.50
EL(1)	0.48	0.75
E	0.84	0.94
F	2.35	1.46
IRL	1.41	1.17
I	1.01	0.81
NL	2.08	1.44
A[1]	1.49	1.16
P	0.59	0.53
FIN	2.35	1.97
S	3.58	2.18
UK(2)	2.02	1.28

(1) 1993.
(2) Personnel figure is for 1993.
For Austria, Finland and Sweden, based on ILO data.

Government support for R&D

Financial support of R&D by Member State governments and the European Commission is important. In 1996 the former allocated some ECU 55.3 billion. A further ECU 2.6 billion came from the Commission. Public sources provided on average some 45% of R&D funds – about 0.8% of EU GDP – a lower proportion than the USA but higher than Japan. Member States' spending on research ranges from ECU 710 (1995) per person a year in Sweden to ECU 36 in Greece (1993). Most EU R&D public funding goes to three main types of research. For some years, the most important has been university research. The second largest amount is spent on such things as space exploration, distribution and rational use of energy, industrial production and technology. The third key area is defence. Funding here is declining and varies considerably by country – from fairly high percentages in the UK and France to around zero in Ireland, Austria, Belgium and Denmark.

Measuring success

R&D success is difficult to measure. Well-known indicators such as the number of Nobel Prizes awarded,

R&D input by sector

	R&D expenditure as % of GDP, 1996	R&D personnel as % of labour force, 1995
Business enterprise	1.19	0.59
Higher education	0.39	0.46
Government	0.30	0.20
All sectors	1.91	1.27

Source: Eurostat estimates

Total personnel (head counts) as a percentage of the labour force, 1995

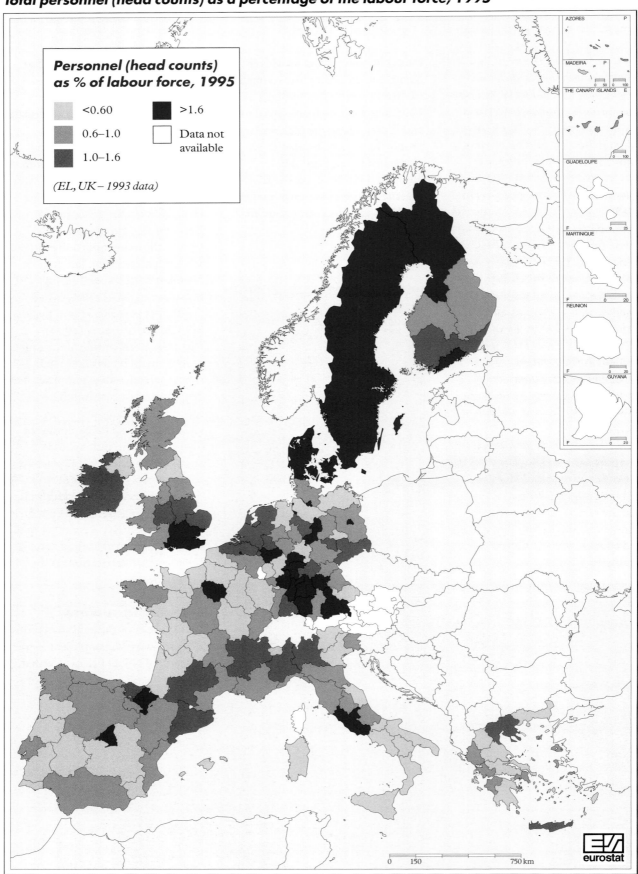

Personnel (head counts)
as % of labour force, 1995

<0.60	>1.6
0.6–1.0	Data not available
1.0–1.6	

(EL, UK – 1993 data)

scientific publications and patents do not give a full picture. But for some key sectors they do give some indication and show EU R&D output to be less than that of the USA or Japan.

The number of patents applied for is an important measure of R&D output. Germany, UK, France Sweden, Finland and Netherlands apply for the largest number.

The EU actively supports R&D

Although there was earlier R&D financing, mainly in the energy field, the EU first laid down its own policy in the mid-1980s. It started framework funding programmes together with specific programmes within them. Spending grew from ECU 284 million in 1980 to ECU 2 billion for 1993. An average ECU 3.1 billion a year is earmarked for the fourth framework programme (1995–1998). Of this 28% is devoted to information and communications technologies, 16% to industrial technologies, 9% to the environment, 13% to life sciences and technologies, 18% to energy and the rest to such areas as transport, socio-economic research and cooperation with Third World countries.

EU-funded research is aimed primarily at strengthening the scientific and technological base of EU industry so that it can be more internationally competitive. It also assists other Community policies, such as those covering energy, transport, the environment, fisheries and agriculture. The Community's own research is carried out by the Joint Research Centre (JRC). This consists of eight institutes in six countries, employs around 2,000 staff and had a total budget of ECU 273 million in 1996. It also hosts 200 visiting scientists.

The total budget of the third framework programme (covering the years 1990–1994) was equivalent to 3.8% of all government civilian research funding in Member States. Since the early 1990s the European Union has been cooperating with the countries of Eastern and Central Europe in supporting their scientific and technological systems. In addition to Community framework programmes for research and technological development and the Structural Funds, there are many other

Government R&D spending in the EU, USA and Japan, 1996

	EU	USA	JPN
Spending, m ECU at current exchange rates	*55,310*	*54,380*	*20,353*
As % of GDP	*0.82*	*0.94*	*0.56*

Sources: Eurostat, OCDE

Patent applications and scientific publications

	EU	USA	JPN
Total number of patent applications(1) at the European Patent Office, 1994	*28,635*	*20,308*	*7,941*
Total number of scientific publications(2) 1995	*207,973*	*203,164*	*52,599*

(1) By year initial application for patent first filed anywhere in the world (priority year).
    Source: European Patent Office
(2) Source: REIST2.

European Commission research budget

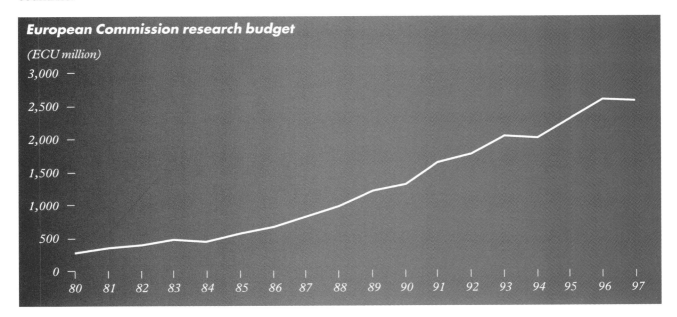

(ECU million)

European cooperation schemes in the field of research and development. Apart from the EU, special bodies such as the European Organisation for Nuclear Research (CERN), the European Molecular Biology Organisation (EMBO) and the European Space Agency (ESA) are responsible for research in specific fields. Organisations such as the European Science Foundation (ESF) and COST (European cooperation in the field of scientific and technical research) actively support cooperation in many different scientific fields. The 22-nation EUREKA programme is more specifically geared to the development of products in response to market demand.

FURTHER READING

Eurostat publications
Research and development –
Annual statistics 1997
A social portrait of Europe

Electronic products
Eurostat Yearbook CD-ROM
Eurostat's New Cronos database

Europe on the move
Europe's science and technology –
towards the 21st century

Other publications
European report on science and
technology indicators 1994
(second report forthcoming)
Community research programmes
– 3rd and 4th framework
programmes
Community policy on research and
technology

8 Spotlight on work
8.1 The labour force

In spring 1997, the EU Labour Force Survey estimated that the EU labour force – those in work plus the unemployed – was 168.2 million people. Some 150 million were in work and over 18.1 million unemployed, an unemployment rate of 10.8%. Women were hit harder than men by unemployment.

Women are becoming more active

The EU's activity rate – the labour force as a percentage of the working age (15 years or over) population of 303.9 million – was 55.4%. The activity rates in USA and Japan were higher, at 67.1% and 63.7%, respectively in the same year. The rate was under 50% in Spain, Italy and Greece, over 61% in the UK and over 65% in Denmark. The extent to which women work is the key factor in explaining these differences.

Women represent only 1 in 3 of the labour force in Spain, Italy and Greece, but in Denmark the activity rate for women is almost as high as the rate for Belgian men. There is a growing number of active women throughout the EU, this is partly attributable to the growth of part-time rather than full-time working. The role of women in the EU labour market has become more and more important, but there remain these big differences between Member States. In Sweden and Finland they form nearly 47% of the labour force; in Luxembourg only 38%. With the exception of the UK and Sweden, the female unemployment rate is higher throughout the EU. This underlines the importance of measures to help women compete for good jobs – working hours matching the school timetable, child-care, retraining, etc. – an approach the EU supports. Women's activity rate peaks between the ages of 25–29. Afterwards, marriage and the birth of a family lead to some fall. But the big dip in women's activity rates

once caused by families has nearly vanished – the rate now only drops significantly for women beyond 54.

In contrast. the activity rates of young people are clearly dropping since they are staying in education longer.

Labour force burgeons

From 1987 to 1997 the EU working age population rose by 16.1% or 42.05 million due mainly to German reunification and the three new Member States of Austria, Finland and Sweden. In 1997 there were 19.2% or 27.1 million more people in the labour market – employed or unemployed – than in 1987. The EU labour force is becoming older. The average age of those in work has risen to 38 years, with the female labour force, on average, two years younger than men.

Activity rate in 1996

(% of population aged 15 and over in the workforce)

	Total	Male	Female
EU-15	55.4	65.9	45.6
B	50.5	60.7	41.0
DK	65.4	72.1	59.0
D	57.7	67.9	48.2
EL	48.9	62.9	36.2
E	49.1	62.3	36.7
F	55.4	63.3	48.2
IRL	55.4	68.5	42.7
I	47.7	61.8	34.8
L	51.2	64.7	38.1
NL	60.9	71.5	50.6
A	58.4	69.1	48.7
P	57.7	67.1	49.4
FIN	60.1	65.9	54.9
S	60.8	65.3	56.5
UK	61.8	70.8	53.2
USA	66.8	74.9	59.3
JPN	63.4	:	:

8.2 Services take the lead

EU employment grew steadily through the 1980s until 1991, but from 1991 to 1994 about 4.8 million jobs were lost. Since then the number of those in work has risen by nearly 2.3 million with most new jobs in the services sector. Women filled around 42% of these new jobs, but many were part-time positions.

Who works in what and where?

Job losses in agriculture are still high: about 3.9 million from 1985 to 1996 (excluding the former East Germany). In the same period employment in EU industry fell by 3.3 million (again excluding the former East Germany). In the EU and beyond most employment growth is in services; this sector now employs 66% of all EU workers. However, patterns vary: in 1997, 1 in 5 Greek workers was still employed in agriculture; Ireland

(1 in 9) and Portugal (1 in 8) also had high proportions.

Industry accounts for some 35% of total workers in Germany. In the Netherlands and Luxembourg the proportion in industry is only 23% with almost three-quarters in services – almost 20 percentage points more than in Greece and Portugal. In the EU as a whole, in 1997, women accounted for 41.9% of all people in work. Only one in three full-time jobs was held by a woman, but women occupied 80.0% of part-time jobs.

Share of economic sectors in employment 1996(1)

	Agriculture		Industry		Services		Total	
	'000	%	'000	%	'000	%	'000	%
EU-15	7,434	5.0	44,059	29.5	98,030	65.6	150,070	100
B	102	2.7	1,057	27.5	2,679	69.8	3,838	100
DK	100	3.7	699	26.2	1,865	70.0	2,675	100
D	1,039	2.9	12,240	34.7	22,021	62.4	35,299	100
EL	765	19.8	866	22.5	2,223	57.7	3,853	100
E	1,055	8.3	3,796	29.9	7,855	61.8	12,706	100
F	1,029	4.6	5,891	26.6	15,229	68.8	22,157	100
IRL	149	10.9	391	28.6	829	60.5	1,373	100
I	1,307	6.5	6,348	31.7	12,377	61.8	20,032	100
L	4	2.3	39	23.3	125	74.3	169	100
NL	251	3.7	1,548	22.9	4,967	73.4	7,186	100
A	249	6.9	1,070	29.6	2,290	63.5	3,609	100
P	601	13.3	1,403	31.0	2,519	55.7	4,523	100
FIN	164	7.8	579	27.4	1,369	64.8	2,120	100
S	127	3.2	1,000	25.6	2,785	71.2	3,917	100
UK	493	1.9	7,133	26.9	18,895	71.2	26,612	100

(1) Data may not always sum to total due to non-response.

8.3 Conditions at work

The average working week for full-time employees in the European Union was 40.4 hours in 1997. It was shorter for women (39.0 hours) than for men (41.3 hours), and also fluctuated, at times substantially, depending on the sector, type of activity and country. The increase in part-time work has continued throughout the EU, reaching significant proportions in some Member States.

The working week

Full-time EU employees worked an average 40.4 hours a week in 1997 – 39.0 for women, 41.3 for men. The working week ranged from 44.0 hours in the UK to 38.3 in Belgium. The difference between men and women was greatest in the UK – five hours.

Across the EU, agricultural employees working full-time had the longest working week – 42.9 hours – compared with 40.6 in industry and 40.2 in services.

Part-time work is mainly women's work

In 11 Member States over 10% of employees worked part-time in 1997. The numbers working part-time were particularly high for women in some countries: 68.1% of all female employees in the Netherlands, 44.1% in UK and 41.9% in Sweden. The proportion of men working part-time is still relatively low.

Contracts

Most EU workers (87.8%) had indefinite employment contracts. The proportion on fixed-term contracts was higher among women and young people. The data show that it is increasingly difficult for young people to start work with a long-term job.

Part-time employment

	Total part-time employees ('000)		Part-time employees as % of all employees		% of women working part-time		% of women working part-time in services	
	1986	1997	1986	1997	1986	1997	1986	1997
EU-15(1)	11,426	21,994	11.9	17.7	26.3	33.1	29.6	35.6
B	293	533	10.3	16.8	25.2	35.2	28.6	38.1
DK	582	572	24.9	23.6	42.6	35.5	45.9	37.9
D	2,880	5,548	12.3	17.6	29.2	35.2	31.8	37.4
EL	75	71	4.2	3.4	7.8	5.8	9.7	6.3
E	:	781	:	8.1	:	17.1	:	18.8
F	:	3,396	11.5	17.6	22.4	31.6	25.1	34.3
IRL	51	149	6.3	13.7	12.4	23.2	14.4	26.4
I	603	997	4.1	7.0	7.7	13.4	7.1	14.1
L	9	13	6.8	8.5	16.4	20.9	17.0	21.2
NL	:	2,412	:	38.4	:	68.1	:	68.1
A	:	459	:	14.8	:	29.5	:	31.0
P	114	173	3.9	5.3	8.1	9.5	9.5	10.3
FIN	:	195	:	10.9	:	15.6	:	17.1
S	:	853	:	25.2	:	41.8	:	43.7
UK	4,757	5,842	22.0	25.3	44.3	44.1	49.3	47.1

(1) EU-12 in 1986.

8.4 Health and safety at work

Health risks

The Single European Act 1986 gave new impetus to EU occupational health and safety measures. A working conditions survey, carried out in 1991 and 1996, revealed 28% of interviewees thought their health and safety at risk through work; this represents around 43 million people EU-wide. For example, in 1996, 43% complained of a high work rate (compared with 35% in 1991) and 32% of 'painful or tiring positions'.

Accidents – construction, agriculture and transport are high-risk branches

In 1994, more than 4.9 million accidents at work leading to over three days' absence were recorded in the EU, affecting around 1 worker in 22; 6,423 accidents were fatal. Workers have more than twice the average risk of being killed in construction, agriculture or transport. Men are ten times more likely to be killed than women. This reflects the sort of jobs they do; in general, these are more high-risk than those of women. There are also relatively more women working part-time, thus reducing their exposure to risk.

Accidents at work in 1994 in the EU by branch of activity

Branch of activity	No. work accidents with more than 3 days' absence		Fatal work accidents	
	number	rate(1)	number	rate(1)
Agriculture, hunting and forestry	348,309	6,496	770	14.0
Manufacturing	1,515,556	5,071	1,330	4.6
Construction	858,129	9,014	1,457	14.7
Wholesale and retail trade and repairs	487,656	2,552	519	2.8
Hotels and restaurants	179,489	4,121	82	1.9
Transport, storage and communication	421,133	6,139	917	13.7
Finance and business services	225,828	1,638	298	2.2
total 8 major branches	4,036,100	4,539	5,373	6.1
other branches	881,966		1,050	
total all branches of activity	4,918,066		6,423	

(1) Number per 100,000 persons in employment.
Source: Eurostat.

8.5 Costs and earnings

Labour costs highs and lows

The cost of employing people – basic salary plus other costs such as social security charges and benefits paid by the employer – varies between countries and activities. In industry, in 1996, it varied from ECU 6.06 in Portugal to ECU 28.82 in Germany. Labour costs were also high in Belgium, Austria, Denmark, France and the Netherlands – ranging from ECU 22.25 to ECU 25.11. In comparison, they were ECU 17.43 in the USA. The EU average was 20.28.

Labour costs in financial institutions are very high, twice those in retailing. Financial institutions in Luxembourg had the highest monthly costs in 1995 – ECU 5,240. The proportion of indirect labour costs varies between countries. Belgium had the highest level of employer social-security contributions per employee in 1996 – an average 32.8% of total costs in industry. They are also very high in France, Italy and Sweden.

What people earn – and keep!

In 1996 Denmark had the highest

Average gross earnings in 1996

(ECU)

	Hourly earnings of manual workers in industry (1)	Monthly earnings of non-manual workers		
		Manufacturing industry	Financial institutions	Retailing
B	10.02	2,700	2,658	1,499
DK	15.86	3,324	3,425	2,845
D (Old Länder)	13.77	3,326	2,747	1,994
D (New Länder)	9.56	2,386	2,100	1,576
EL	4.35	1,122(1)	1,091(2)	589(1)
E	7.01	1,638	1,819	861
F	8.39	2,383	2,241	1,433
IRL	8.38	2,242	:	:
I	6.17	1,751	2,184	1,215
L	12.22	3,539	3,690	1,854
NL	10.63(1)	2,452(2)	2,255(2)	:
A	10.64	2,391	2,397	1,789
P	2.74	901	1,360	561
FIN	10.41	2,259(1)	2,100(1)	1,465(1)
S	11.03	2,555	2,584	2,212
UK	8.72	2,332	2,527	1,535
IS	:	:	:	:
NO	:	:	:	1,986
USA	10.61	:	:	884(1)
JPN	9.19(1)	:	:	:

(1) 1995
(2) 1994
Source : Eurostat, Harmonized statistics of earnings except for Italy (all data) and Denmark (monthly data) where it is Structure of Earnings Statistics, 1995.

gross hourly wage for manual workers in manufacturing industry (ECU 15.86). The lowest were in Portugal (ECU 2.74) and Greece (ECU 4.35). The gross wage of a Portuguese manual worker, expressed in ECU, is barely a fifth of his German counterpart. Workers in retailing in the USA earn less than their opposite numbers in the EU, with the exception of Portugal and Greece.

The gap between gross earnings and what people take home varies between countries. For example, in 1995 an unmarried Danish manual worker in manufacturing on average wages took home little more than half his or her gross pay after tax and social security deductions. But in Spain the same worker had only 19.6% of the gross wage deducted.

Hourly labour costs and their structure – Industry(1)

	Labour costs ECU		Direct costs %		Indirect costs %		Social security % of indirect costs	
	1992	1996	1992	1996	1992	1996	1992	1996
EU-15*	17.7	20.3	76.3	74.8	23.7	25.2	20.9	22.6
EUR-11*	19.1	22.3	73.8	73.2	26.2	26.8	23.4	25.6
B	21.3	25.1	67.9	66.7	32.1	33.3	31.5	32.8
DK	19.3	23.3	93.2	92.0	6.8	8.0	3.4	6.0
D	21.7	26.5	76.7	74.4	23.5	25.6	21.4	23.5
EL	7.0	8.9	79.0	76.9	21.0	23.1	20.0	22.8
E	15.1	14.9	73.6	73.6	26.4	26.4	22.5	25.0
F	19.1	22.5	68.6	66.9	31.4	33.1	28.5	29.2
IRL	12.8	13.9	82.7	82.7	17.3	17.3	14.4	14.4
I	18.7	18.3	70.3	65.9	29.7	34.1	25.2	32.8
L	17.2	20.0	84.1	85.1	15.9	14.9	15.3	14.3
NL	19.3	22.3	74.9	75.6	25.1	24.4	22.6	21.9
A	19.9	24.6	75.5	70.4	24.5	29.6	18.2	25.3
P	5.6	6.1	74.1	75.3	25.9	24.7	20.8	20.2
FIN	17.6	19.7	75.9	75.0	24.1	25.0	21.1	22.7
S	19.0	19.5	68.7	71.5	31.3	28.5	31.3	28.5
UK(2)	13.1	13.4	84.6	84.0	15.4	16.0	12.4	12.8
IS(2)	9.7	9.2	87.6	87.4	12.4	12.6	10.6	11.0
NO(3)	19.4	21.7	83.0	84.3	17.0	15.7	17.0	15.7
USA(4)	15.1	17.4	78.1	77.7	:	:	21.9	22.3
JPN(2)(5)	14.5	19.7	84.4	84.2	15.6	15.8	13.7	14.7

* Eurostat estimates
(1) Industry: mining, manufacturing, energy and construction
(2) 1995 instead of 1996
(3) For 1996: data from National Accounts
(4) Mining, manufacturing and construction. Labour costs exclude vocational training costs, other expenditure and taxes and subsides
(5) 1991 instead 1992; refers to establishements with 5 or more regular employees for the following activities : mining, manufacturing, construction and public utilities

8.6 The problem of unemployment

In 1997, 17.9 million EU people were unemployed. Unemployment is one of the most worrying aspects of the labour market, affecting 10.7% of the active population in that year and hitting women harder than men. Youth and long-term unemployment remained high. The unemployment rate was much lower in the USA (4.9%) and in Japan (3.4%).

Bad for women and young people

The jobless rate in 1997 ranged from Luxembourg's 2.6% to Spain's 20.8%. In several Spanish regions, and in southern Italy, a quarter of the labour force was without work. In contrast, in southern Germany, northern Italy, parts of the Netherlands and all of Austria it was around 5%. For a number of years, women's unemployment has been higher than men's – 12.4% in 1997 compared with 9.3%. The only exceptions to this were UK and Sweden.

Unemployment is also worse among young people. In 1997, 19.7% of the male labour force aged under 25 were jobless; the rate for young women was even higher – 23.0%. In the EU as a whole, almost one in two unemployed persons under 25 are looking for their first job.

The long-term problem

In 1997, over 49% of the unemployed had been jobless for over a year. Only in Denmark (27.2%), Austria (28.7%) and Finland (29.8%) was the percentage of long-term unemployed less than 30% of total unemployment and only in Denmark had the situation improved significantly since 1991. In Belgium (60.5%), Italy (66.3%), Ireland (57.0%), Greece (55.7%) the rate of long-term unemployment has become firmly established at a very high level.

Looking for work

While only 4.3% of all EU unemployed men were seeking part-time work in 1997, 21.3% of unemployed women wanted to work part-time. In Germany,

Unemployment in the EU in 1997

| | Number of unemployed ('000) | | | Unemployment rate (%) | | | | | | Long-term unemployment (% of total unemployed) | | |
| | | | | Total | | | Aged under 25 | | | | | |
	Total	Men	Women	Total	Men	Women	Total	Men	Women	Total	Men	Women
EU-15	17,935	9,015	8,920	10.7	9.3	12.4	21.2	19.7	23.0	49.0	47.5	50.7
B	389	178	211	9.2	7.2	11.9	23.0	19.0	27.8	60.5	59.4	61.5
DK	156	70	86	5.5	4.6	6.6	8.3	6.7	10.3	27.2	26.2	27.9
D	3,910	2,067	1,843	10.0	9.3	10.8	11.0	11.9	9.9	50.1	47.1	53.6
EL	408	162	247	9.6	6.2	14.9	31.0	22.1	40.6	55.7	45.8	62.2
E	3,358	1,582	1,776	20.8	16.1	28.3	39.1	33.2	46.2	51.8	45.8	57.3
F	3,126	1,470	1,656	12.4	10.7	14.4	29.1	26.5	31.9	39.6	38.0	41.0
IRL	155	93	61	10.1	10.0	10.3	15.7	16.4	14.9	57.0	63.3	46.9
I	2,756	1,322	1,434	12.1	9.3	16.6	33.1	28.5	38.9	66.3	66.5	66.2
L	5	2	3	2.6	1.8	3.8	7.7	5.7	10.0	34.7	32.7	36.0
NL	392	171	221	5.2	3.9	6.9	9.2	8.1	10.4	49.1	49.9	48.5
A	164	76	88	4.4	3.6	5.3	6.7	5.6	7.8	28.7	28.9	28.4
P	331	159	172	6.8	6.0	7.8	15.4	12.0	19.7	55.6	53.4	57.7
FIN	326	165	161	13.1	12.6	13.7	25.7	25.0	26.6	29.8	32.3	27.0
S	436	238	198	9.9	10.2	9.5	20.6	21.0	20.1	34.2	35.6	32.5
UK	2,023	1,260	763	7.0	7.8	6.0	14.2	15.9	12.2	38.6	44.9	27.8

France, Sweden, Finland and Spain, roughly 90% of the jobless rely on a public employment office to find a job compared with 30% in UK and Portugal, and 6% in Greece.

FURTHER READING

Eurostat publications

Social portrait of Europe
Unemployment, monthly
Labour force sample survey – Results, yearly
Labour Force Survey – Methods and Definitions 1996
Statistics in Focus (Population and social conditions), several issues per year

Electronic products

Eurostat Yearbook CD-ROM
Eurostat's New Cronos database

Other publications

White Paper on growth, competitiveness and employment, 1993
Employment in Europe, annual
Social Europe: periodical and supplements

9 Lifestyles in Europe

9.1 How we spend our money

A study of household consumption in 1994 covered 11 Member States, representing around 60% of the EU population. Seven were in the north (Belgium, Denmark, Luxembourg, the Netherlands, Finland, Sweden and the United Kingdom) and four in the south (Greece, Spain, Italy and Portugal).

In this study, with the exception of Luxembourg, estimated consumption by 'adult equivalent' varied from 8,400 PPS (see note to chart, right, for definition) in Portugal to 13,700 PPS in Belgium. In Luxembourg it was almost 22,000 PPS.

In all countries except Portugal, expenditure on housing is currently higher than expenditure on food and non-alcoholic beverages; it accounts for between 23% (Spain) and 29% (Belgium and Finland) of total consumption.

On average, housing represents a comparable share of expenditure irrespective of the level of income:

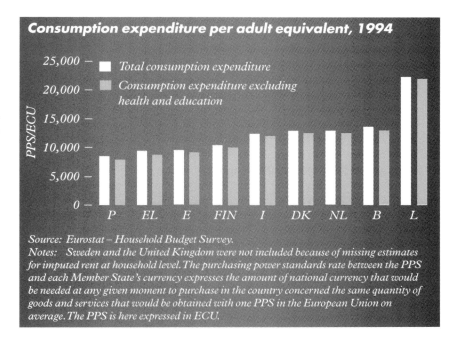

Consumption expenditure per adult equivalent, 1994

■ *Total consumption expenditure*
■ *Consumption expenditure excluding health and education*

Source: Eurostat – Household Budget Survey.
Notes: Sweden and the United Kingdom were not included because of missing estimates for imputed rent at household level. The purchasing power standards rate between the PPS and each Member State's currency expresses the amount of national currency that would be needed at any given moment to purchase in the country concerned the same quantity of goods and services that would be obtained with one PPS in the European Union on average. The PPS is here expressed in ECU.

Structure of total consumption expenditure by country, 1994

(%)

Categories(1)	B	DK	EL	E	I	L	NL	P	FIN	S(2)	UK(2)	Average of 11 countries
1. Housing	29.0	27.9	24.0	23.5	24.1	27.4	27.2	19.9	29.0	25.0	27.9	25.7
2. Food, non alcoholic beverages	12.0	13.5	17.8	22.8	21.1	12.3	12.1	21.2	16.0	18.0	13.0	17.2
3. Transport	10.9	15.5	9.3	11.5	13.1	13.8	9.5	15.7	13.5	13.6	11.2	11.9
4. Recreation and culture	11.0	10.8	3.9	6.7	8.0	11.5	9.5	3.7	9.7	12.8	11.6	9.1
5. Miscellaneous	10.1	8.1	7.9	4.7	7.4	7.3	16.0	6.5	9.1	8.5	6.7	7.7
6. Clothing, footwear	6.2	5.7	12.9	8.0	7.3	8.5	6.0	6.3	4.6	6.2	6.1	7.0
7. Furnishings, equipment, maintenance	6.7	6.3	6.7	6.2	6.2	9.3	7.1	6.7	4.5	5.4	7.7	6.7
8. Hotels and restaurants	5.7	3.3	5.1	8.6	5.1	4.2	6.0	9.2	4.2	3.4	7.7	6.5
9. Alcoholic beverages, tobacco	1.9	4.3	3.4	2.4	2.4	2.2	2.3	2.8	3.3	3.2	3.6	2.9
10. Health	4.2	2.2	5.2	2.8	3.0	1.4	1.5	4.6	4.0	2.1	1.1	2.5
11. Communications	1.8	2.0	1.6	1.5	1.9	1.4	1.7	2.0	2.0	1.7	2.0	1.8
12. Education	0.5	0.4	2.2	1.2	0.6	0.7	1.2	1.3	0.2	0.2	1.3	1.0
Total	100.0	100.0	100.0	100.0	100.0	100.0	100.0	100.0	100.0	100.0	100.0	100.0

(1) For definition of consumption categories, see methodological note at the end of this section.
(2) For Sweden and the United Kingdom, imputed rents have been estimated at national level.
Source: Eurostat – Household Budget Survey.

around 25% (30% including furniture). For the least well-off households (first quartile), the main part of spending in this category is on rent. At the top of the range, the main part is accounted for by the statistically imputed rents of owner occupiers – ie what owner occupiers would notionally be paying in rents to themselves.

In other expenditure, budgetary choices or constraints can differ significantly depending on income. In general, essentials feature less prominently as income rises and luxury goods become more prominent.

Least well off households devote 30% of purchases to spending on food, drink and tobacco. For the richest households, it is 17%. High-income households' spending on recreation, hotels and restaurants accounts for 16% of their budget, compared with just 10% for those with more modest budgets.

Spending on transport averages 14% of total expenditure for the better off, 9% for those less so. In the Netherlands, for example, 90% of better off households have a car, compared with 40% with the lowest income.

Households headed by a manual worker, a farmer or an unemployed person nearly always live below the national average standard of living.

Food accounts for up to 23% of total consumption spending among farmers in Greece, Spain, Italy and Portugal, including their own-consumption. Almost half Greek households said that during the survey period they consumed food from their own holding, private garden or business. The level and structure of consumption depend also on the demographic composition of households. Economies of scale can play a decisive role on expenditure such as housing.

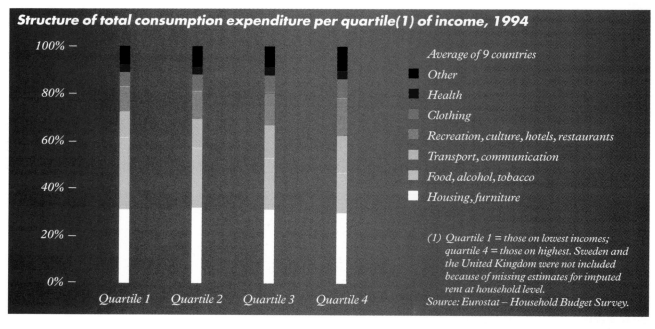

Structure of total consumption expenditure per quartile(1) of income, 1994

Average of 9 countries
- ■ Other
- ■ Health
- Clothing
- Recreation, culture, hotels, restaurants
- Transport, communication
- Food, alcohol, tobacco
- ■ Housing, furniture

(1) Quartile 1 = those on lowest incomes; quartile 4 = those on highest. Sweden and the United Kingdom were not included because of missing estimates for imputed rent at household level.
Source: Eurostat – Household Budget Survey.

Level of consumption by adult equivalent according to socio-economic category of the reference person

(100 = average consumption)

	B	DK	EL	E	I	L	NL	P	FIN	S	UK
Manual worker	90	99	88	87	90	83	98	86	99	94	100
Non-manual worker	108	112	126	118	113	116	113	156	115	108	129
Self-employed person	102	124	117	106	116	122	114	100	122	103	120
Farmer	98	100	86	81	81	81	90	67	94	72	99
Unemployed	78	80	82	75	71	76	77	91	79	.	64
Average consumption	100	100	100	100	100	100	100	100	100	100	100

19/06/98 data
Source: Eurostat – Household Budget Survey.
Note: Without data on imputed rent, for Sweden and the United Kingdom.

Single-person households spend a large portion of their budgets on housing but little on transport. Spending of households of older (65+) people concentrate on absolute essentials such as food, housing and health, at the expense of clothing, transport, recreation and hotels-restaurants. Amongst couples, the share on food increases significantly for each supplementary child. Transport is more prominent in households of couples except for couples over 65 without children.

Structure of total consumption expenditure per household type, 1994

(%; average for nine countries, excluding Sweden and UK)

Categories	Single, 65 years and over	Single, 30 to 64 years	Couple, 65 and over without children	Couple, less than 65 without children	Couple with one child	Couple with two children	Couple with three children	All types
1. Housing	38.3	31.3	30.4	24.8	23.5	22.9	22.4	24.8
2. Food, non alcoholic beverages	20.4	14.1	23.2	16.6	17.2	18.9	22.5	19.0
3. Transport	3.9	10.0	7.8	14.4	14.0	12.9	12.0	12.2
4. Recreation and culture	6.5	7.6	6.1	7.1	7.7	8.4	8.1	7.8
5. Miscellaneous	6.8	8.1	7.3	8.9	8.9	8.2	7.5	8.1
6. Clothing, footwear	5.7	6.9	6.1	6.6	7.7	8.2	7.8	7.4
7. Furnishings, equipment, maintenance	6.5	6.3	6.6	6.9	6.8	6.6	6.6	6.4
8. Hotels and restaurants	3.7	7.8	3.6	6.6	6.4	5.9	5.3	6.2
9. Alcoholic beverages, tobacco	1.5	2.6	2.4	2.7	2.6	2.3	2.4	2.6
10. Health	4.5	2.7	4.6	3.2	2.7	2.8	2.6	3.1
11. Communications	2.2	2.2	1.9	1.8	1.6	1.5	1.5	1.8
12. Education	0.0	0.5	0.0	0.3	0.9	1.4	1.5	0.9
Total	100.0	100.0	100.0	100.0	100.0	100.0	100.0	100.0

Source: Eurostat – Household Budget Survey.
Note: Sweden and the United Kingdom were not included because of missing data on imputed rent.
For definition of consumption categories, see methodological note on the next page.

Survey years and sample sizes

	Collection date	Sample size
Belgium	06/95–05/96	2,724
Denmark	1994	2,936
Greece	10/93–09/94	6,756
Spain	1994	2,876
Italy	1994	33,928
Luxembourg	1993	3,012
Netherlands	1994	2,050
Portugal	1994–1995	10,554
Finland	1994–1995	4,493
Sweden	1992	3,830
United Kingdom	1994	6,928

Methodological note:

Household Budget Surveys are conducted in all the Member States of the European Union. The results presented are obtained from Eurostat's micro-database. In order to guarantee comparability, Eurostat harmonises these data to a predefined Community format. Survey years do not always coincide with the reference year fixed by Eurostat (see table below). When this is the case, data are adjusted for price changes using the general consumer price index of the country concerned. Sample sizes vary significantly according to various factors, including budget constraints and the desired accuracy of the estimates. The categories of consumption used here correspond to the most aggregated level of COICOP-'HBS' (Classification of Individual Consumption by Purpose – Household Budget Survey). This covers 12 functions:

- Food and non-alcoholic beverages;
- Alcoholic beverages and tobacco;
- Clothing and footwear;
- Accommodation, water, electricity and other fuels (including real rents and imputed rents for owner-occupiers);
- Furnishings, household equipment and routine maintenance of the house;
- Health;
- Transport (including public or individual, petrol, etc.);
- Communications (including postal services, telephone, etc.):
- Leisure and culture (including television, photography, personal computers, games, toys, cinemas, museums, books, package tours, etc.);
- Education;
- Hotels, cafés, restaurants;
- Other goods and services (including personal care, personal effects such as jewellery and travels goods, day nurseries, insurance, financial services, etc.).

The purpose of calculating the **imputed rent of owners** is to be able to compare the levels of consumption of households with very different housing patterns. Spending by tenants on rent is included in the survey, whereas the purchase of dwellings by owners is not as this is capital expenditure. The imputed rent of owners-occupiers is thus an evaluation based on the rent that should be paid for similar accommodation rented on the market. In most countries, imputed rent was calculated by the Member States themselves. The exceptions were Sweden and the United Kingdom, for which estimates at national level were produced for the purposes of this study.

- For further information, the reader is referred to the following Eurostat Publications or databases:
  - Household Budget Surveys in the European Union: Methodology and recommendations for Harmonisation (1997).
  - Statistics in focus: Household consumption in the European Union in 1994 (April 1998)
  - Eurostat's New Cronos database
  - Household Budget Survey: Consumption expenditures of private households in the European Union 1994 data

9.2 The homes we live in

In 1994 just over half of all EU households lived in a single-family house, detached or terraced – but with marked national differences. While the vast majority in Ireland, the UK and Belgium live in single-family houses, most German, Spanish, Italian and, to a lesser extent, Greek households are in apartments. Just under 60% of

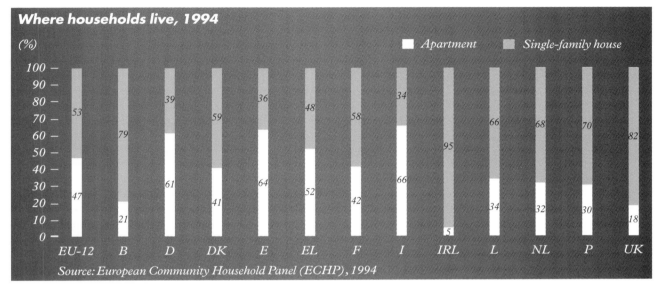

Where households live, 1994

(%)

Apartment — Single-family house

Source: European Community Household Panel (ECHP), 1994

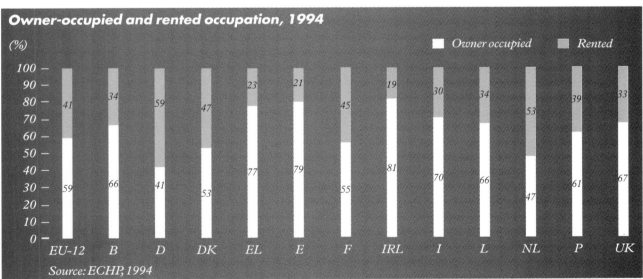

Owner-occupied and rented occupation, 1994

(%)

Owner occupied — Rented

Source: ECHP, 1994

Owner-occupation by type of housing, 1994

(%)

	EU-12	B	DK	D	EL	E	F	IRL	I	L	NL	P	UK
All homes	59	66	53	41	78	79	55	81	70	66	47	61	67
Houses	77	78	78	79	91	85	77	85	83	85	63	67	75
Apartments	38	27	18	17	65	76	24	6	64	30	15	51	27

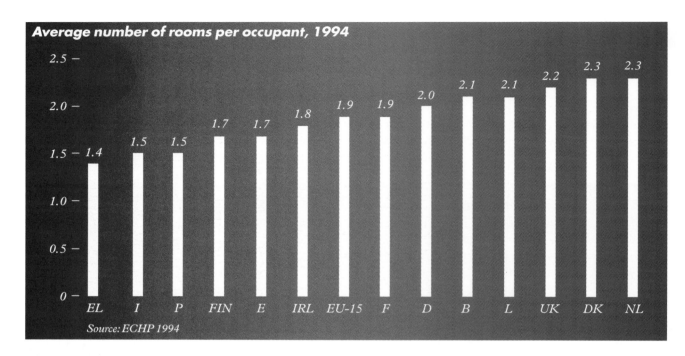

Average number of rooms per occupant, 1994

Source: ECHP 1994

European households owned their accommodation in 1994 – well up on the figure of 45% recorded for 1970. Only in Germany and the Netherlands does the majority rent.

The average number of rooms per EU household stood at 4.8 in 1994 – an average 1.9 rooms per person. Greece, Italy and Portugal are well below the EU average with around 1.5 rooms per person.

Most European households have basic amenities – bathroom or shower, inside toilet and hot running water – but in Portugal and Greece these are less common. Across Europe, 3% of households say they do not have a bath or shower – 18% in Portugal and 9% in Greece.

Just over 70% of EU households possess a car. The highest ownership rates are in Luxembourg, France

and Italy. 9% of households without a car state that they can not afford one. Over a third of Dutch households say they do not want one. Over 90% of EU households have a telephone.

In the EU as a whole, one in five households thought their home too

small in 1994. A significantly higher percentage reported this problem in Portugal and Greece, where the proportion reporting lack of adequate heating is also greater. One in five households also complained of a leaky roof, damp or rot, a particular problem in

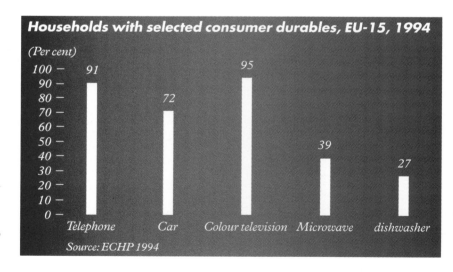

Households with selected consumer durables, EU-15, 1994

(Per cent)

Source: ECHP 1994

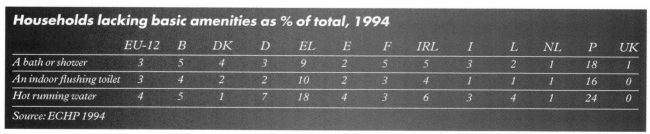

Households lacking basic amenities as % of total, 1994

	EU-12	B	DK	D	EL	E	F	IRL	I	L	NL	P	UK
A bath or shower	3	5	4	3	9	2	5	5	3	2	1	18	1
An indoor flushing toilet	3	4	2	2	10	2	3	4	1	1	1	16	0
Hot running water	4	5	1	7	18	4	3	6	3	4	1	24	0

Source: ECHP 1994

Portugal. One in four households complained about noise from neighbours or outside. This seems to affect Spaniards, Italians and Germans most. One in five reported crime or vandalism in their area: a higher proportion in the UK; Greece and Germany the lowest proportions.

Households declaring specific problems with accommodation as % of total, 1994

	Shortage of space	Lack of adequate heating facilities	Leaky roof, damp or rot	Noise from neighbours or outside	Pollution, grime or other environmental problems	Vandalism or crime in the area
EU-12	19	12	22	27	17	20
B	15	9	22	23	13	19
DK	16	5	13	15	7	14
D	15	6	14	29	14	11
EL	30	38	29	26	21	8
E	23	5	31	33	20	26
F	16	13	26	27	16	25
IRL	16	11	18	11	10	16
I	21	20	15	32	25	18
L	13	6	13	16	17	16
NL	10	7	21	24	16	17
P	35	41	43	18	19	19
UK	21	14	28	22	16	32

Source: ECHP, 1994

9.3 Protection against social ills

EU social protection spending averaged 28.4% of GDP in 1995. Ireland, Greece and Portugal had the lowest ratios (19.9%, 20.7% and 20.7%); Sweden (35.6%) and Denmark (34.3%) the highest. When social protection spending per person is expressed in PPS (see chart, top of next page) the

differences between Member States are more pronounced. In 1995 Luxembourg, Denmark and Sweden spent over 6,000 PPS per head, Greece and Portugal substantially less at 2,250 and 2,313 PPS respectively.

From 1990–1995 there was virtually no change in the ranking of countries in terms of social protection spending as a proportion of GDP. Despite an upturn in GDP in 1994 and 1995, social spending stabilised or even fell slightly in real terms stabilised in Spain, Italy, the Netherlands and Sweden as a result of efforts to curb expenditure.

In most Member States old-age and survivors' (widows and widowers) benefits are the largest item of social protection spending. In Italy these two functions accounted for over

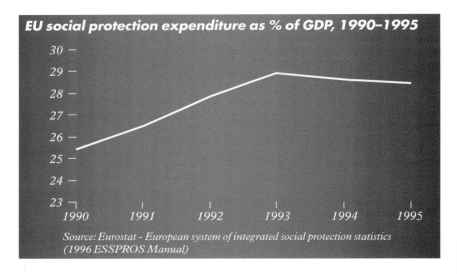

EU social protection expenditure as % of GDP, 1990–1995

Source: Eurostat – European system of integrated social protection statistics (1996 ESSPROS Manual)

Social protection expenditure at constant prices

(1990=100)

	1990	1991	1992	1993	1994	1995
B	100	103	106	112	115	120
DK	100	105	108	113	122	122
D(1)	100	96	103	104	106	110
EL	100	95	91	91	93	95
E	100	109	116	122	118	118
F	100	103	107	111	112	114
IRL	100	106	112	119	123	131
I	100	105	109	109	109	107
L	100	108	112	120	124	129
NL	100	101	103	104	102	101
A	100	104	107	110	115	117
P	100	112	128	143	148	151
FIN	100	108	115	117	119	120
S	100	100	105	104	105	104
UK	100	108	117	125	127	128
EU-15	100	103	109	112	114	115

(1) Excluding the former East Germany for 1990.
Source: Eurostat – ESSPROS (1996 ESSPROS Manual)

Social protection spending in Member States as % of GDP (1990, 1994, 1995)

	1990	1994	1995
B	26.6	29.0	29.7
DK	30.3	35.1	34.3
D(1)	25.4	28.9	29.4
EL	22.6	20.8	20.7
E	19.9	22.4	21.9
F	27.7	30.5	30.6
IRL	19.1	20.3	19.9
I	24.1	25.8	24.6
L	23.5	24.7	25.3
NL	32.4	32.7	31.6
A	26.7	29.7	29.7
P	15.5	21.0	20.7
FIN	25.5	34.7	32.8
S	32.9	37.6	35.6
UK	23.0	28.0	27.7
EU-15	25.4	28.6	28.4

(1) For 1990, excluding the former East Germany.
Source: Eurostat – ESSPROS (1996 ESSPROS Manual)

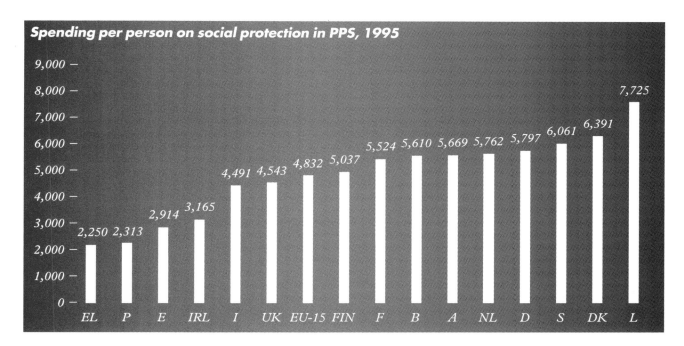

Spending per person on social protection in PPS, 1995

60% of all benefits in 1995. However, in Ireland, the Netherlands, Portugal and Finland, sickness/health care and disability benefits account for the lion's share.

Unemployment-related benefits accounted for over 14% of the total, in 1995, in Belgium, Denmark, Spain, Ireland, and Finland, but less than 3% in Italy and Luxembourg. The variation is partly due to differences in the number of people unemployed and partly to differences in the scale of the benefits. EU-wide, family and child benefits accounted for 7.5% of all benefits in 1995, with Finland spending most (13.3%) and Spain least (1.8%).

Old-age and survivors benefits rose by 14% in real terms between 1990 and 1995 in the EU-15 as a whole. This raised their share of total benefits from 45,8% in 1990 to 44.6% in 1995. Over the same period, the share of total spending on unemployment benefits rose in all Member States except Denmark and Spain, where changes in benefits made them less costly. The proportion of spending on family benefits fell across the EU as a result

of lower fertility in all countries. Throughout the EU, the main sources of funding for social protection are social security

contributions (62.9% of total receipts in 1995); these are mostly from employers (39.3% of the total), except in the Netherlands

Social protection benefits by type as % of total, 1990 and 1995

	Sickness, healthcare, and disability		Old age and survivors		Family and children		Unemploy- ment		Other(1)	
	1990	1995	1990	1995	1990	1995	1990	1995	1990	1995
B	34.4	32.3	40.7	42.5	9.5	8.2	13.9	14.3	1.5	2.7
DK	30.0	28.4	36.8	37.6	11.9	12.4	15.4	14.7	6.0	6.8
D(2)	38.1	38.0	45.8	42.5	7.6	7.5	5.9	9.1	2.7	2.8
El	36.3	34.2	48.8	49.7	5.9	7.0	5.5	5.9	3.5	3.2
E	37.6	37.6	44.0	45.4	1.7	1.8	15.8	14.3	0.9	0.8
F	35.5	34.9	42.7	43.0	9.4	9.0	8.3	8.2	4.1	4.9
IRL	38.3	40.1	30.6	26.0	11.3	11.7	14.6	17.3	5.1	4.9
I	33.7	28.6	59.6	65.7	4.9	3.5	1.7	2.2	0.0	0.0
L	39.1	37.5	45.8	44.7	10.8	13.2	2.6	3.0	1.7	1.6
NL	44.7	44.4	37.4	37.4	5.6	4.7	8.3	10.1	3.9	3.4
A	33.2	33.4	50.0	48.3	10.5	11.3	4.6	5.6	1.8	1.5
P	46.9	44.8	43.1	43.4	7.1	5.8	2.5	5.5	0.4	0.4
FIN	43.7	36.1	34.1	32.8	13.5	13.3	6.1	14.3	2.6	3.6
S	:	33.9	:	37.1	:	11.3	:	11.1	:	6.5
UK	35.9	37.7	42.6	39.4	9.0	9.0	5.7	5.9	6.8	8.1
EU-15(3)	36.6	36.0	45.8	44.6	7.6	7.5	6.9	8.3	3.1	3.6

(1) Housing and social exclusion.
(2) Excluding the former East Germany for 1990.
(3) Excluding Sweden.
Source: Eurostat – ESSPROS (1996 ESSPROS Manual)

and Denmark. The next most important source is tax-funded general government contributions (31.9% in 1995).

Social security contributions are particularly high in France, Germany, and the Netherlands. Here they account for over 68% of total funding. At the other end of the scale, Denmark and Ireland finance their social protection mainly through taxes, which account for a 60%+ share of funding. Sweden and the UK are also heavily dependent on general government contributions: 48.4% and 49.5% respectively.

Methods and concepts

Data on social protection expenditure and receipts for the 15 Member States of the European Union contained in this analysis have been calculated in accordance with the revised methodology for the European System of Integrated Social Protection Statistics (ESSPROS), the 1996 ESSPROS Manual. Data on social protection expenditure are recorded as gross amounts without any deduction of taxes or other compulsory levies applicable to social benefits.

The 1995 data are provisional for Germany, Spain, the Netherlands, Portugal and Finland, and are estimated for Belgium and UK. For the period 1990–1992 the date are estimated for Sweden.

Purchasing Power Standards, or PPS, are obtained by means of a conversion rate (purchasing power parity) based on the relative prices of a basket of comparable products, and express the real purchasing power of the currency within the country concerned.

New data and analyses are available in the following publications:

- *Social protection expenditure and receipts 1980–1996*
- *Statistics in Focus, Population and Social Conditions n°5/99, 'Social protection in the European Union, Iceland and Norway'.*

Trend in spending on social benefits by type in EU-15(1), 1990–95

(1990=100 in constant ecus)

	1990	1991	1992	1993	1994	1995
Sickness, health care & disability	100	103	109	110	111	113
Old age & survivors	100	101	107	109	111	114
Family & children	100	103	108	110	111	111
Unemployment	100	122	137	152	144	137

(1) Data for Sweden and Danmark are not included.
Source: Eurostat – ESSPROS (1996 ESSPROS Manual)

Structure of social protection funding, 1995

(% of total receipts)

	B	DK	D	EL	E	F	IRL	I	L	NL	A	P	FIN	S	UK	EU-15(2)
General government contributions	20.2	71.0	28.6	:	30.5	21.1	62.8	29.8	46.1	16.0	36.4	39.4	44.7	48.4	49.5	31.9
Social security contributions	67.2	23.4	69.0	:	66.7	76.9	36.4	66.8	48.8	68.1	62.8	48.8	48.8	43.2	39.4	62.9
of which:																
by employers	42.3	9.5	40.4	:	51.7	49.4	22.3	49.0	25.3	22.0	36.9	30.0	35.2	38.0	25.5	39.3
by protected persons(1)	24.9	13.9	28.7	:	15.0	27.4	14.1	17.8	23.4	46.1	25.9	18.9	13.6	5.2	13.9	23.6
Other receipts	12.6	5.6	2.4	:	2.8	2.0	0.9	3.4	5.1	16.0	0.8	11.7	6.4	8.4	11.1	5.2
Total	100	100	100	:	100	100	100	100	100	100	100	100	100	100	100	100

(1) Employees, self-employed, pensioners and others
(2) Excluding Greece.

9.4 Our state of health

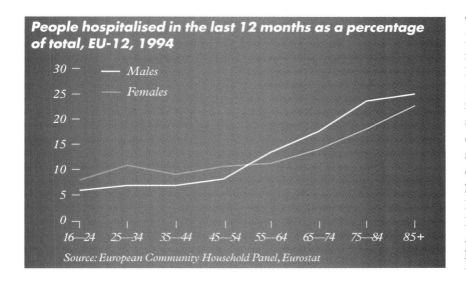

People hospitalised in the last 12 months as a percentage of total, EU-12, 1994

— Males
— Females

Source: European Community Household Panel, Eurostat

The European Community Household Panel (ECHP) in 1994 revealed that two out of three Europeans of 16 years and over (excluding those living in institutions), perceived their health as 'good' or 'very good'. The latter condition was reported by as many as 26% of Danes and as few as 8% of Portuguese. 'Bad' and 'very bad' health was most frequent in Portugal, followed by Spain and Italy.

Almost a quarter report being hampered in daily activities by 'chronic physical or mental health

Self-reported health (16 years and over), 1994, EU-12

(% reporting)

	EU-12	B	DK	D	EL	E	F(1)	IRL	I	L	NL	P(2)	UK
Perceived health													
Very good	23.4	26.6	25.7	18.3	47.9	19.3	19.3	45.5	19.6	27.7	19.6	7.6	36.6
Good	44.0	46.9	26.9	51.1	27.6	45.1	44.7	34.2	39.4	38.8	54.6	45.4	38.1
Fair	23.8	20.7	14.6	23.0	15.2	22.5	28.2	16.5	29.3	25.9	21.3	27.6	19.3
Bad	6.5	4.7	4.4	5.8	6.7	10.3	3.4	2.8	9.5	5.6	3.9	15.4	4.5
Very bad	2.3	1.1	1.4	1.7	2.6	2.8	4.3	0.9	2.2	2.0	0.7	4.0	1.5
Hampered in daily activities because of chronic conditions													
Yes, severely	6.9	6.3	4.8	6.7	6.4	6.0	10.1	3.8	6.8	4.4	6.8	8.7	5.1
Yes, to some extent	14.9	14.7	15.3	17.7	10.3	12.4	9.2	14.3	14.7	19.1	18.5	19.2	17.6
No	78.1	79.0	79.9	75.5	83.4	81.5	80.7	81.9	78.4	76.6	74.7	72.0	77.3
Cutdown of activities in two weeks because of physical and/or mental reasons(3)													
Physical and mental	1.2	1.3	2.7	1.4	0.9	1.0	:	1.6	0.4	1.6	3.6	:	1.5
Physical	10.4	7.7	12.7	13.9	6.5	10.4	:	8.1	4.2	10.9	12.8	12.8	11.8
Mental	1.4	1.8	1.5	1.4	1.1	1.2	:	1.6	0.6	1.6	3.1	4.6	1.3
No	87.0	89.2	83.1	83.4	91.6	87.4	:	88.8	94.8	85.8	80.5	82.6	85.4
Hospitalisation in 12 months (4)													
Yes	10.2	12.0	10.3	13.1	8.0	8.0	9.7	10.8	8.8	14.7	8.1	6.5	10.9
No	89.8	88.0	89.7	86.9	92.0	92.0	90.3	89.2	91.2	85.3	91.9	93.5	89.1
Sample size (=100%)	129,133	8,118	5,903	9,155	12,492	17,908	14,332	9,904	17,729	2,046	9,407	11,622	10,517
Population aged 16+ (m)	280.1	8.2	4.3	67.3	8.5	31.7	44.6	2.6	47.0	0.3	12.3	8.0	45.4

Note: Data for Member States have been standardised to adjust for differences in the age distribution of the population. Data for EU-12 are not standardised.
(1) France: perceived health = satisfaction with health.
(2) Portugal: cutdown of activities: physical includes 'physcial and mental'.
(3) Cutdown of activities: Eur11 (excl. France).
(4) Excl. hospitalisation for child birth.
Source: European Community Household Panel, Eurostat

problem, illness or disability' (8% 'severely', 16% 'to some extent'). Those who had been in hospital in the last 12 months in 1994 (excluding childbirth) ranged from 7% in Portugal to 13% in Germany and 15% in Luxembourg. Up to their mid-50s, women have higher hospitalisation rates than men; the position then reverses.

After peaking in 1994–1995, the annual incidence of AIDS (adjusted for reporting delays) fell for the first time in 1996 and fell again in 1997. By 31 December 1997, a cumulative total of 193,630 cases had been reported in the 15 Member States. Although 1997 saw a significant decrease in Spain (–22%), it remains the country with the highest rate in the EU. In Portugal, where AIDS has risen rapidly, and Greece the epidemic did not appear to have levelled off in 1996–97 to the same degree as in

the rest of Member States (although in Greece the incidence of new cases did fall in 1997). In the EU as a whole, the biggest fall was estimated for homo/bisexual men (–37% in 1997 compared with –21% in 1996 and –8% in 1995). Women account for 21% of adult/adolescent cases diagnosed in 1997, compared with 11% in 1986.

Cancer is the second most frequent cause of death (following cardio-

vascular diseases). An average 840,000+ people (1 in 4) die this way every year. Since the 1980s fewer men have been dying of lung cancer.

Tuberculosis remained an important health problem in Portugal with 52.9 cases per 100,000 people in 1996; this compared with under 22 for all the other Member States. For Austria, England/Wales/Scotland, Spain,

People with perceived health 'bad or very bad' by level of education (standardised according to age) as a percentage of total, EU-12, 1994

Males / Females

■ Primary and lower secondary education
■ Upper and post-secondary education

Source: European Community Household Panel, Eurostat

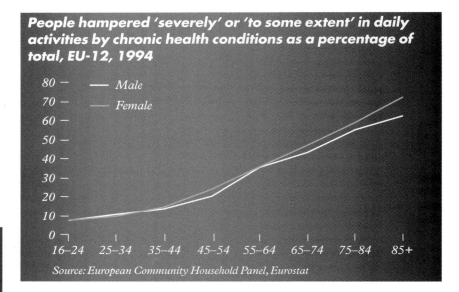

People hampered 'severely' or 'to some extent' in daily activities by chronic health conditions as a percentage of total, EU-12, 1994

— Male
— Female

16–24 25–34 35–44 45–54 55–64 65–74 75–84 85+

Source: European Community Household Panel, Eurostat

AIDS cases per million people by year of diagnosis

	1985	1990	1991	1992	1993	1994	1995	1996	1997
EU-15	4.4	31.7	36.4	39.2	44.3	47.6	47.5	42.4	31.3
B	6.8	20.6	25.7	24.6	25.2	25.0	23.4	17.4	18.2
DK	7.4	38.3	40.8	40.5	46.3	45.4	41.3	30.1	21.0
D	4.8	18.8	21.0	22.2	23.0	22.8	20.7	18.2	10.7
EL	1.5	14.1	17.6	18.3	15.6	20.2	21.1	26.0	18.5
E	4.5	97.6	112.8	124.4	134.7	178.9	174.1	163.5	127.5
F	10.6	75.9	79.5	87.9	93.0	96.1	88.8	68.5	38.9
IRL	2.0	18.5	20.5	19.9	21.3	20.3	15.2	18.4	5.1
I	3.5	54.4	67.0	74.6	84.3	96.6	99.4	89.2	59.0
L	5.5	23.6	31.2	30.8	50.6	32.4	36.9	29.3	24.2
NL	4.6	28.0	29.6	33.5	30.7	30.3	32.2	26.4	19.6
A	3.4	21.0	25.5	24.3	29.3	20.9	25.7	17.8	11.1
P	2.9	25.3	30.0	40.5	55.0	64.2	74.4	87.1	82.5
FIN	0.8	3.0	5.2	4.2	4.9	8.5	7.8	4.3	3.7
S	4.1	15.4	15.9	14.7	20.9	21.2	21.6	15.3	8.3
UK	4.3	21.6	24.0	27.1	30.2	31.1	30.2	24.7	21.4

Further reading: Surveillance in Europe, quarterly reports on AIDS, European Centre for Epidemiological Monitoring of AIDS, Paris

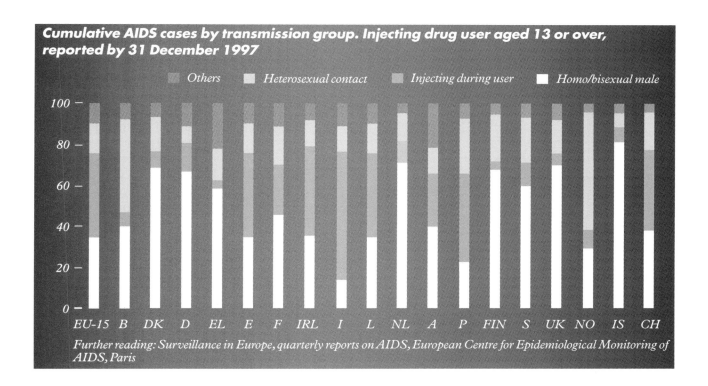

Cumulative AIDS cases by transmission group. Injecting drug user aged 13 or over, reported by 31 December 1997

Others · Heterosexual contact · Injecting during user · Homo/bisexual male

Further reading: Surveillance in Europe, quarterly reports on AIDS, European Centre for Epidemiological Monitoring of AIDS, Paris

Incidence of cancer in EU-12, 1990 – Age standardised rate per 100,000 people using standard world population

	Males	Females
All sites but skin	268.4	196.4
Lung	55.6	10.3
Colon / rectum	33.8	23.7
Breast	–	61.0
Prostate	28.5	–
Stomach	16.7	7.5
Oeosophagus	6.1	1.2
Bladder	18.8	3.4
Larynx	8.8	0.5
Testis	4.8	–
Cervix uteri	–	10.2
Ovary	–	9.6
Corpus uteri	–	10.7
Leukaemias	8.3	5.5
Liver	5.8	2.0
Non Hodgkins Lymphoma	9.5	5.9
Hodgkin's disease	2.7	1.7
Pancreas	6.1	3.9
Lip, oral cavity, pharinx	16.7	2.6
Kidney	8.6	3.9
Melanoma of skin	4.6	6.5
Myeloma multiple	2.6	1.9
Brain, nervous system	6.0	4.5
Thyroid	1.3	2.4

Source: International Agency on Research on Cancer, Lyon

Incidence of tuberculosis, total per 100,000 people

	1985	1990	1993	1994	1995	1996
EU-15	19.5	15.1	15.6	15.3	14.3	13.6
B	19.8	15.8	14.9	15.0	13.6	13.3
DK	6.1	6.8	8.1	9.7	8.7	9.2
D	19.5	18.5	17.4	15.9	14.9	14.3
EL	15.7	8.7	9.6	8.8	9.0	:
E	27.9	19.5	24.2	24.1	22.4	21.2
F	20.5	15.6	16.9	16.7	:	:
IRL	22.7	17.5	16.7	14.6	12.7	12.0
I	7.2	7.3	8.3	9.1	9.4	7.2
L	11.5	12.6	9.6	10.7	8.3	9.9
NL	9.4	9.2	10.4	11.8	10.5	10.8
A	19.0	19.7	15.9	15.7	13.4	17.1
P	68.8	62.8	55.2	56.8	49.6	52.9
FIN	37.1	15.5	10.6	13.4	10.4	12.6
S	8.4	6.5	7.1	6.0	5.7	5.6
UK	11.8	10.3	11.3	10.7	10.5	10.6

Source: World Health Organisation, Health for All Database, 1998

Distribution of mortality (males) by cause in 1994 (EU-15)

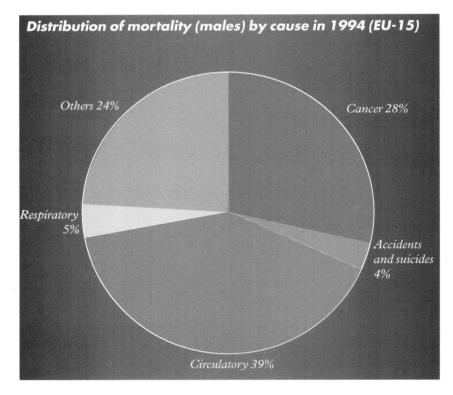

Netherlands and Switzerland, 55,911 cases of salmonellosis (transmission diseases) were reported in 1995, a fall of 6.8% on 1993.

A total of 919 cases of travel-associated legionnaires' disease were reported from 1987 to 1995. Almost a third in 1995 were in people aged 55 to 64, three-quarters of people affected were male and 60% were British citizens. The incidence of meningococcal infection in 1994 varied from 0.19 (Italy) to 11.32 (Iceland) per 100,000 population. Overall mortality has dropped over the past decades. In general it is dominated by four main groups of causes of death: cardio-vascular (circulatory) diseases, cancer, respiratory diseases and such things as accidents and suicide. Together these account for over 80% of deaths.

Damage to public health caused by smoking is considerable: about 500,000 EU deaths a year from its effect. Of the population aged 15 and over, 29% smoke daily, even more in the 15–34 age group – 41% of men and 34% of women. However, the trend is downwards. The heaviest young smokers are in Denmark, France, the Netherlands, Spain and the UK.

The health risks of alcohol are well known. It is strongly associated with cardiovascular disease and primary liver cancer. In terms of alcohol drunk, Sweden, Finland and the UK are at the lower end of the scale with 6–9 litres per person a year. France and Luxembourg lie at the top with about 15 litres. Other Member States are between 10 and 13 litres.

In 1996 EU Member States spent between 6% and 10% of GDP on health care. France and the Netherlands were at the top end, Greece and Denmark at the bottom.

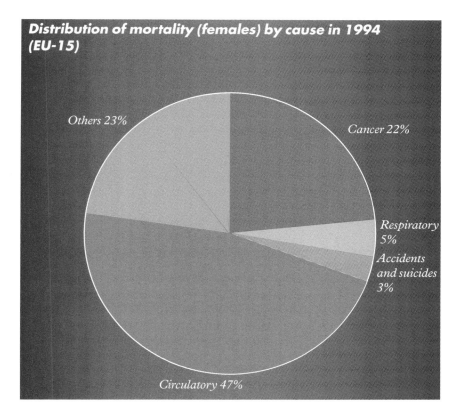

Distribution of mortality (females) by cause in 1994 (EU-15)

Others 23%

Cancer 22%

Respiratory 5%

Accidents and suicides 3%

Circulatory 47%

Between 1980 and 1996, the average annual growth rate of total health expenses exceeded GDP growth almost everywhere in the EU. In 1993, public spending accounted on average for three-quarters of total spending on health care. From 1980–1996 public spending rose more slowly than total spending in all Member States apart from Belgium, the Netherlands and Finland as some financial responsibility shifted to households themselves. Expressed in PPS, Germany and Luxembourg spend almost 50% more per person on health care than the EU average and over four times as much as Greece.

From 1980–1996 the number of physicians, dentists, nurses and pharmacists rose in all Member States. In 1996 the number of

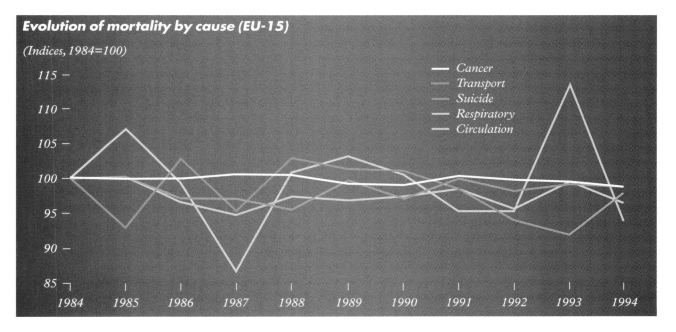

Evolution of mortality by cause (EU-15)

(Indices, 1984=100)

— Cancer
— Transport
— Suicide
— Respiratory
— Circulation

115 —
110 —
105 —
100 —
95 —
90 —
85 ¬

1984   1985   1986   1987   1988   1989   1990   1991   1992   1993   1994

Cigarette and pure alcohol consumption

	Cigarette consumption: number per person per year						Pure alcohol consumption: litres per person aged over 15 per year					
	1985	1990	1994	1995	1996	1997	1985	1990	1991	1992	1993	1994
EU-15	1,852	1,816	1,747	1,713	1,641	1,646	:	:	:	:	:	:
B	1,671	1,534	1,526	1,585	1,573	1,568	12.9	12.1	:	:	:	:
DK	1,717	1,566	1,558	1,702	1,800	1,791	12.1	11.7	11.7	12.0	12.1	12.1
D	2,062	2,025	1,840	1,859	1,835	1,841	12.7	12.5	12.4	12.2	11.8	:
EL	2,866	2,864	3,012	2,937	2,959	3,020	11.2	10.6	11.1	10.9	10.6	10.4
E	2,023	2,122	2,119	1,989	1,902	1,929	15.1	13.5	12.0	11.7	11.4	:
F	1,744	1,689	1,556	1,519	1,476	1,443	16.7	15.6	14.2	14.1	:	:
IRL	1,808	1,770	1,729	1,723	1,751	1,784	9.6	10.5	11.2	11.5	:	:
I	1,986	1,662	1,688	1,531	1,516	1,541	13.2	11.0	10.4	10.1	9.4	:
L	1,967	1,671	2,140	:	:	:	14.6	14.8	15.3	15.0	14.8	14.5
NL	1,074	1,555	1,685	2,322	1,216	1,245	10.6	9.9	9.7	9.7	9.8	:
A	2,141	1,791	1,784	1,568	1,578	1,685	12.1	12.6	12.3	11.9	11.9	11.9
P	1,373	1,569	1,777	1,638	1,627	1,681	17.1	12.7	13.2	13.2	13.4	13.6
FIN	1,393	1,436	1,055	1,019	882	817	8.1	9.5	8.4	8.2	8.4	:
S	1,356	1,254	992	920	933	893	6.4	6.7	6.5	6.7	6.4	:
UK	1,711	1,710	1,621	1,552	1,531	1,515	9.2	9.4	9.1	9.3	9.1	9.4

Source: World Health Organisation, Health for All Database, 1998

Total health expenditure as a % of GDP

	1985	1990	1991	1992	1993	1994	1995	1996
EU-15	:	:	:	:	:	:	:	:
B	7.4	7.6	8.0	8.1	8.2	8.1	8.0	7.9
DK	6.3	6.5	6.5	6.6	6.8	6.6	6.4	6.4
D	8.5	8.9	9.1	9.3	8.4	7.9	7.7	7.5
EL	4.0	4.2	4.2	4.5	5.0	5.5	5.8	5.9
E	5.7	6.9	7.1	7.2	7.3	7.3	7.6	:
F	8.5	8.9	9.1	9.4	9.8	9.7	9.9	9.6
IRL	7.8	6.6	6.8	7.1	7.1	7.6	:	:
I	7.1	8.1	8.4	8.5	8.6	8.4	7.7	7.6
L	6.1	6.6	6.5	6.6	6.7	6.5	7.0	:
NL	7.9	8.3	8.6	8.8	8.9	8.8	8.8	8.6
P	6.3	6.5	7.2	7.4	7.7	7.8	8.2	8.2
UK	5.9	6.0	6.9	6.9	6.9	6.9	6.9	6.9
A	6.7	7.1	7.2	7.5	7.9	7.8	7.9	7.9
FIN	7.3	8.0	9.1	9.3	8.4	7.9	7.7	7.5

Source: OECD, Ecosanté Health Data 1997

physicians per 100,000 people ranged from 175 and 211 in the UK and Ireland respectively to 422, 389 and 379 in Spain, Greece (for 1995) and Belgium respectively. Belgium, Finland and Spain have the largest number of pharmacists per 100,000 people. Nurses range from 2,130 per 100,000 in Finland to 348 in Portugal. Dentists range from 28 per 100,000 in Portugal and 38 in Spain to around 104 in Greece and Sweden.

In Luxembourg and the Netherlands there are over 11 hospital beds for every 1000 people – twice as many as in Spain, Portugal or Greece. The average length of stay per person in hospital in 1980 was between 14.4 days in Portugal and 34.7 in the Netherlands. In 1995 the range had fallen to between 11 days in Spain and 32.8 in the Netherlands. EU pharmaceutical spending represents between 10% and 20% of total health care spending. This rose more quickly than total health

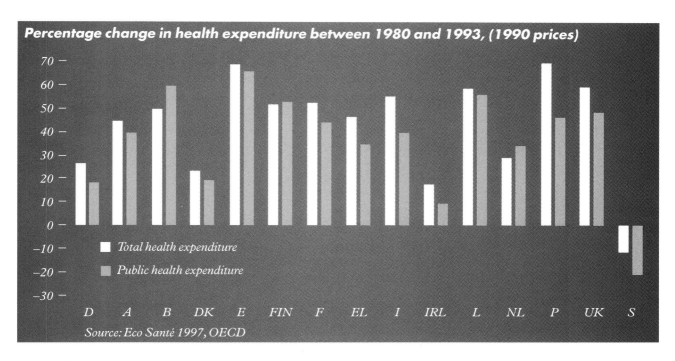

Percentage change in health expenditure between 1980 and 1993, (1990 prices)

■ Total health expenditure

■ Public health expenditure

Source: Eco Santé 1997, OECD

Trends in health care personnel

(No. per 100,000 inhabitants)

	B	DK	D	EL	E	F	IRL	I	L	NL	P	UK	FIN	S	A
Physicians															
1985	292.4	253.9	255.9	293.4	331.7	:	162.2	380.3	181.0	222.7	243.7	151.2	:	:	257.4
1991	343.2	:	306.2	365.1	394.4	271.7	170.3	504.5	202.9	:	286.9	161.4	247.2	289.9	308.7
1994	364.5	290.6	328.5	388.9	414.4	281.7	199.7	547.4	228.2	:	293.6	164.5	269.8	:	339.0
1996	378.3	:	341.4	393.0	421.9	:	210.8	569.7	:	:	301.4	174.5	284.9	:	:
Dentists															
1985	60.0	92.7	62.6	88.1	13.4	64.0	33.0	:	45.9	49.2	12.6	37.3	:	:	40.7
1991	71.4	88.9	68.9	100.6	28.9	68.8	38.3	:	51.5	:	17.1	38.3	91.3	103.9	43.0
1994	69.0	88.1	72.8	104.4	33.9	:	41.9	59.9	49.6	:	23.3	40.7	92.3	:	45.0
1996	69.9	:	75.0	:	37.9	:	44.5	:	:	:	28.0	41.7	93.7	:	47.1
Pharmacists															
1985	107.6	:	46.3	60.4	79.7	41.2	58.3	:	69.4	13.1	41.6	34.1	144.8	52.4	41.5
1991	123.5	:	52.2	75.2	96.9	45.3	62.3	:	82.2	15.2	59.9	36.5	138.5	:	46.0
1994	132.3	:	53.9	78.3	103.1	46.3	65.4	:	:	:	63.9	:	140.1	:	50.0
1996	137.3	50.4	55.7	:	110.1	:	70.5	:	:	:	68.4	:	141.7	:	:
Nurses															
1985	:	601.8	581.7	:	:	:	:	:	:	:	239.7	:	1,623.2	:	630.5
1991	:	704.6	887.7	:	:	:	:	:	:	:	298.0	:	1,879.0	:	761.7
1994	:	710.6	:	:	:	:	:	:	:	:	323.5	:	2,071.1	:	845.9
1996	:	:	:	:	:	:	:	:	596.4	:	347.8	:	2,129.9	:	:

Source: Eurostat

spending in the 1980s and early 1990s. The proportion of prescription costs paid by publicly-financed schemes rose steadily. Expressed in PPS, France has the largest EU consumption per person of medical and other pharmaceutical products, the UK the lowest.

Per million population, 9.1 hospitals in France provide kidney dialyses. In Germany and the Netherlands it is 3.1. Austria (45.6 per million people) and Spain (44.2) take the lead in kidney transplants while Greece (10.1) has the lowest rate.

Indicators of provision and use of hospital and in-patient resources

	B	DK	D	EL	E	F	IRL	I	L	NL	P	UK	FIN	S	A
Hospital beds per 1,000 habitants															
1985	7.1	:	:	5.5	4.6	10.5	8.3	8.3	12.5	11.9	4.4	7.4	12.7	13.7	10.9
1990	6.2	5.7	:	5.1	4.3	9.8	6.3	7.2	11.8	11.6	4.3	5.9	12.5	11.5	10.3
1993	5.9	5.1	7.8	5.0	4.1	9.3	:	6.7	11.5	11.3	4.2	:	10.1	6.1	9.5
1995	5.8	:	7.5	:	:	:	:	6.2	:	:	4.1	:	9.3	:	9.3
In patient admission rates (% of population)															
1985	14.9	19.9	19.9	11.9	9.3	21.1	17.0	17.0	18.8	11.4	8.5	15.5	22.6	20.0	21.6
1990	18.6	21.2	19.0	12.8	9.7	23.2	15.1	15.5	19.9	10.9	10.8	18.4	22.4	19.5	23.4
1993	19.7	21.5	19.7	13.5	10.0	23.3	15.5	15.9	19.6	11.0	11.0	20.8	24.4	19.5	24.1
1995	:	:	20.7	:	10.0	22.7	15.5	:	:	11.1	11.3	23.0	25.4	18.5	24.7
Average length of stay (in days)															
1985	16.9	10.7	18.0	11.6	13.4	15.5	8.6	12.2	20.4	34.3	13.9	15.8	19.9	21.3	14.1
1990	13.8	8.0	16.7	9.9	12.2	13.3	7.9	11.7	17.6	34.1	10.8	15.6	18.2	18.0	13.0
1993	12.0	7.6	15.0	8.8	11.5	11.7	:	11.1	15.7	33.3	9.9	10.2	14.8	9.4	11.5
1995	11.5	7.5	14.2	8.2	11.0	11.2	7.2	10.5	15.3	32.8	9.8	9.9	11.8	7.8	10.9

Source: EUROSTAT and OCDE

Solid organ transplants per million population

	A	B/L	DK	FIN	F	D	EL	I	NL	P	E	S	UK/IRL
Kidney													
1995	38.1	33.2	29.4	32.5	27.1	25.7	12.5	20.0	31.9	37.5	46.7	31.4	30.9
1996	45.6	42.0	32.1	34.9	28.3	24.3	10.1	21.5	32.8	40.5	44.2	34.8	27.3
Heart													
1995	13.5	9.6	5.7	5.1	7.0	5.7	0.9	6.7	3.1	0.5	7.1	2.4	5.5
1996	12.9	10.2	6.1	5.7	6.9	5.9	0.7	6.0	3.9	0.9	7.2	2.5	4.5
Liver													
1995	13.8	14.6	6.9	6.1	11.3	7.1	0.7	6.9	6.0	7.1	17.8	9.9	11.2
1996	16.4	13.9	7.8	5.7	11.2	8.4	0.9	7.4	4.9	11.6	17.9	8.4	10.3
Lung													
1995	3.6	1.5	3.4	0.8	1.4	0.7	0.1	0.7	1.3	0.0	1.1	1.8	1.8
1996	2.1	1.9	5.4	1.0	1.1	1.0	0.3	1.0	1.3	0.0	2.2	2.6	1.9

Sources: European Transplant Coordination Organisation (ETCO) and International Transplant Coordinators Society (ITCS)

10 Agriculture

The Common Agricultural Policy

The aims of the Common Agricultural Policy (CAP) are to increase agricultural productivity, thus helping to ensure a fair standard of living for the agricultural community, to stabilize markets, to assure the availability of supplies and to ensure that supplies reach consumers at reasonable prices.

Since the CAP began, there has been a spectacular rise in production, productivity and trade in agricultural produce. Consumers have more variety than ever while prices have risen less than those of other things people buy. The CAP aim of food self-sufficiency has been broadly achieved for most non-tropical agricultural products. Indeed, there have been considerable production surpluses for some products. The EU therefore faced a new challenge: stabilising supplies at a cost-effective level. This began with the imposition of milk quotas in the eighties. Regulation of major crops followed, culminating in compulsory set-aside of agricultural land in 1993. Further reform of the CAP is envisaged. The Commission is proposing reductions in prices of cereals, beef and, to a minor extent milk, compensated for by direct payments to farmers. It also wants to spend more on farming-related environmental activities and socio-economic development in rural areas.

Meeting our need for food

Of the 139 million hectares of EU agricultural area, 67 million is used for stock farming. This is either permanent pasture and meadows or fields for fodder crops. Around half of cereals output is eaten by livestock. The share of stock farming varies substantially between Member States – from 87% in Ireland to only 31% in Greece. Milk and meat are still the two main Community products. Milk accounts for over 18% of total agricultural output. Beef and veal make up about 12% and pork 11%.

In 1995 the EU cattle herd totalled 85 million. The dairy herd has declined by nearly 25% since milk quotas were introduced in 1984. Of 34 million cattle, 11 million are exclusively for meat production. In 1995 the EU produced 7.2 million tonnes of beef from 23 million adult animals. Veal production, 79% of which is concentrated in France, Italy and the Netherlands, came to 800,000 tonnes. Cattle farming was shaken by the Bovine Spongiform Encephalopathy (BSE or mad cow disease) crisis in 1996 and UK production fell dramatically.

Despite a big fall in output since 1983, dairy produce is still the key element of Community agriculture. In 1995 over one farm in ten was producing milk although milk quotas to cut surpluses have led to far-reaching reductions in the number of dairy cows. There have been incentives for many small producers to abandon dairy farming altogether. Thanks to technical advances, average dairy cow productivity rose between 1992–1996 from 5,000 kg of milk a year to 5,445 kg.

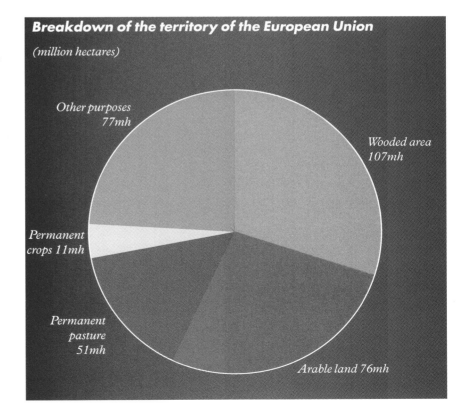

Breakdown of the territory of the European Union

(million hectares)

Other purposes 77mh

Wooded area 107mh

Permanent crops 11mh

Permanent pasture 51mh

Arable land 76mh

Production of butter, milk powder and cheese

(1 000t; EU-12, excl. former East Germany until 1990, EU-15 from 1991)

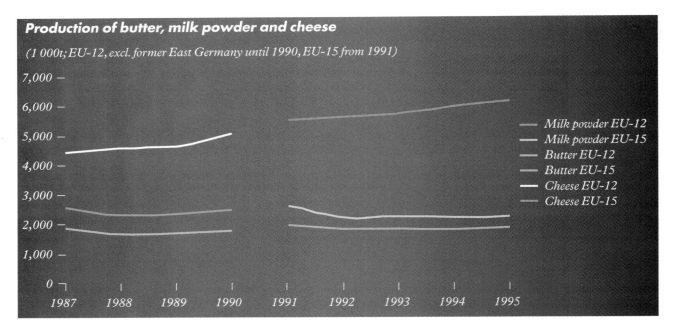

Milk powder EU-12
Milk powder EU-15
Butter EU-12
Butter EU-15
Cheese EU-12
Cheese EU-15

Meat production

(1 000t carcass weight)

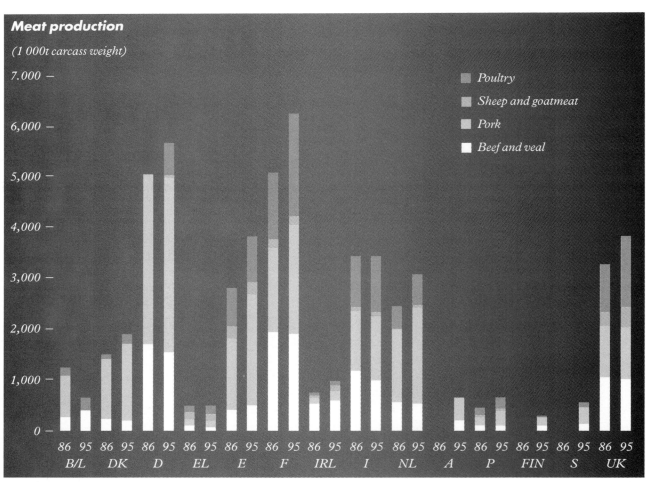

Poultry
Sheep and goatmeat
Pork
Beef and veal

In 1995 the EU produced 125 million tonnes of raw milk. Dairies turned out 29.8 million tonnes of processed milk, 6.2 million tonnes of cheese, 4.6 million tonnes of acidified milk (yoghurt etc), 2.2 million tonnes of milk powder and 1.9 million tonnes of butter. Consumer preferences have led dairies to turn increasingly to cheese and products such as yoghurts and dairy desserts. Sales of processed milk are stable. Butter and milk powder production have been falling for 10 years.

Eating habits are also reflected in meat production. Pork is top of the menu in every country and demand is constantly rising. To meet this, the EU had 117 million pigs in 1995. Its annual pork output of 16 million tonnes is second in the world after China. Germany produces nearly a quarter of the EU's pork and the average German eats 57 kg a year. The Danes eat even more – 65 kg.

Poultry farming is also booming, with consumption up 25% in 10 years. As with pork, production is increasingly intensive in order to slash costs and win market shares. EU poultry production was about 8 million tonnes in 1996. The Spaniards eat most – 21 kg per head. France is by far the main producer, followed by UK and Italy. France also leads the field in egg production. The EU produces 87,000 million eggs a year, 13% of world output.

In 1997, 48% of EU agricultural output was crops and 52% animals. The value of crop production was 104,792 million ECU. Crops are most important in southern Member States. In Greece and Italy they account for 60% or more agricultural output by value, in Spain 58%.

In the EU as a whole, 76 million of

Final agricultural output in 1997

(as % of each Member State's final output at current prices)

	EU-15	B	DK	D(1)	EL	E	F	IRL	I	L	NL	A	P	FIN	S	UK
Final crop output	48.2	36.1	28.2	39.7	69.8	57.8	52.1	12.4	59.7	15.7	49.7	33.8	47.7	29.2	30.6	36.4
Cereals excluding rice	9.3	3.4	11.2	10.6	6.2	8.0	14.4	3.7	6.9	5.2	1.0	5.0	3.1	10.3	11.8	13.8
Root crops	4.6	7.6	3.7	6.6	4.7	3.0	4.5	2.9	3.2	1.7	5.5	4.9	3.9	6.7	6.9	4.9
Industrial crops	2.5	0.7	1.0	2.1	13.8	2.7	3.1	0.0	2.0	0.8	0.0	1.8	0.6	1.0	0.8	2.0
Fresh vegetables	8.9	11.2	1.9	3.7	12.5	13.0	6.4	3.7	14.8	0.7	12.3	3.5	12.0	4.5	3.6	7.9
Fresh fruit (excluding citrus fruit, grapes, olives and tropical fruit)	4.3	5.8	0.4	5.1	7.5	6.4	3.6	0.5	5.4	1.8	2.0	6.1	8.2	1.2	1.1	1.4
Citrus fruit	1.3	0.0	0.0	0.0	2.2	5.6	0.0	0.0	3.1	0.0	0.0	0.0	1.8	0.0	0.0	0.0
Grape must and wine	6.1	0.0	0.0	4.0	1.8	5.2	14.0	0.0	8.8	5.3	0.0	5.9	10.8	0.0	0.0	0.0
Olive oil	2.2	0.0	0.0	0.0	12.7	7.1	0.0	0.0	4.8	0.0	0.0	0.0	2.7	0.0	0.0	0.0
Flowers and ornamental plants (including Christmas trees)	3.9	4.1	5.9	4.3	1.1	1.9	2.1	0.0	5.4	0.0	14.0	3.0	0.0	4.0	3.8	2.5
Final animal output	51.5	63.6	71.8	60.2	30.1	41.5	48.1	87.6	39.0	83.8	50.3	66.2	50.5	70.8	69.4	63.6
Cattle (including calves)	9.9	12.7	5.9	10.7	2.8	6.4	12.2	33.2	8.8	25.1	8.9	14.3	7.5	9.3	9.8	8.5
Pigs	12.2	27.1	36.2	17.6	3.5	14.2	7.8	7.7	6.9	11.6	11.4	21.8	17.8	11.3	15.2	8.8
Sheep and goats	2.1	0.1	0.1	0.6	7.2	4.5	1.2	5.7	0.6	0.0	0.4	0.7	4.9	0.1	0.3	6.2
Poultry	5.5	5.4	2.5	2.8	3.0	4.6	7.9	3.9	5.4	0.1	4.5	3.3	4.4	2.6	2.8	11.2
Milk (untreated)	17.5	14.0	21.6	24.6	10.3	7.5	16.2	33.6	12.2	45.1	21.4	21.1	12.8	35.5	33.4	24.2
Eggs	2.5	2.8	1.2	3.3	2.3	2.6	1.7	0.6	2.7	1.1	3.0	2.8	1.5	1.8	2.9	3.3
Final output as % all EU output	100.0	3.1	3.2	15.3	3.9	12.4	21.6	2.0	16.1	0.1	7.3	1.6	2.1	1.0	1.6	8.7

(1) Including West Germany since 1991.

the 139 million hectares of utilised agricultural area were arable in 1994–96, 11 million were devoted to permanent crops and the rest were permanent grassland and minor areas.

Cereals covered nearly half of arable land in most countries. The EU is the fourth largest cereals producer in the world – still way behind USA and China but almost level with India. France is Europe's biggest granary, followed by Germany and UK. It grows 30% of EU production and exports about half. Germany is the main barley producer.

Faced with constantly growing cereal output until 1992, the EU had to export on a massive scale – one in every five quintals of cereals produced. Regulations to reduce accumulating stocks were set up from the early 1980s. A key step was the compulsory set-aside of arable land, a system used for several years in the USA to match cereal production to demand. Under this, farmers are compensated for not using land previously under crops.

The EU is still a net importer of oilseed – 18.5 million tonnes in 1995–96. It is the world's biggest sugar beet producer with 42% of the total, grown mainly in northern Europe. The north is also the home of the potato: Germany, the Netherlands and UK are the main producers. EU production of 46 million tonnes (1994–1996 average) covers its needs for food and other purposes. Fresh vegetable production, around 50 million tonnes, is largely concentrated in the southern countries with half of the total produced by Spain and Italy. Greece and Spain export vegetables to the north of the EU, but those grown in greenhouses make the Netherlands the second largest exporter by volume.

The EU imports fruit, as demand

Livestock and milk production

1 000 head

	Cattle	Pigs	Sheep	Goats	Laying hens	'000 tonnes Milk production
EU-15	83,243	118,650	98,539	12,224	346,374(1)	121,336
B	2,977	7,498	118	11	12,300	3,416
DK	2,026	11,494	90	0	4,725	4,630
D	15,227	24,795	2,302	93	50,600	28,779
EL	542	938	9,312	5,878	14,681	741
E	5,825	19,269	24,512	2,690	44,351	6,084
F	20,154	15,473	9,824	1,110	63,700	25,084
IRL	6,992	1,717	5,634	0	2,873	5,360
I	7,345	8,155	10,940	1,379	47,774	10,746
L	205	74	7	1	61,855	266
NL	4,287	11,437	1,340	130	39,579	11,013
A	2,198	3,680	384	58	5,752	3,034
P	1,285	2,365	3,414	785	7,747	1,785
FIN	1,125	1,444	103	7	5,229.6	2,431
S	1,708	2,353	442	5	5,708.5	3,316
UK	11,347	7,959	30,118	77	41,292	14,651

(1) 1996.

Wine production

(1 000 hectolitres)

	1993	1994	1995	Average 1993–95
EU-15	161,628	155,481	151,986	156,365
B	2	2	2	2
D	9,920	10,406	8,361	9,562
EL	3,378	3,051	3,875	3,435
E	26,495	20,995	20,045	22,512
F	52,059	53,325	54,354	53,246
I	62,068	58,776	55,702	58,849
L	170	175	150	165
A	2,647	2,212	2,219	2,363
P	4,871	6,521	7,255	6,216
UK	18	18	13	16

exceeds supply by 25%. The deficit is mainly in citrus fruits and, of course, tropical produce, which is consumed in increasing amounts. Vulnerable to climate, the total harvest of EU table fruit fluctuates around 34 million tonnes a year. Thirty per cent of the total is citrus. After citrus fruit, apples are the second most commonly produced

fruit (9.5 million tonnes a year on average during 1994–1996). Greece and Italy eat the most fruit per person.

About 3.3 million hectares are under vine in the EU. Output for the 1995/96 wine year was an estimated 151 million hectolitres – around 56% of world output. The bulk is produced in France, Italy and

Spain, which are also major wine consumers and exporters. They export mostly within the EU, where consumption is going up, and to the USA.

A falling share of GDP

Agricultural production accounted for only 1.7% of EU GDP in 1996; in 1973 it had been about 5%. Only in Greece, in 1996, did agriculture's share of total output exceed 5%.

Agriculture accounted for an estimated 5% of total EU employment in 1996, including self-employment and hired labour. In the early 1970s it had been as high as 11–12%. But in Greece 20% of the workforce was still estimated to be in agriculture in 1996, and in Portugal and Ireland 11–12%. In the UK it was only 2%.

In external EU trade – excluding that between Member States – imports of agricultural products were an estimated 11.4% of the

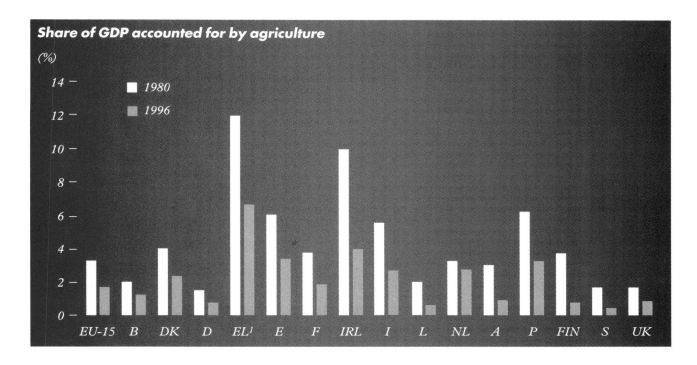

Share of GDP accounted for by agriculture

(%)

■ 1980
■ 1996

EU-15   B   DK   D   EL¹   E   F   IRL   I   L   NL   A   P   FIN   S   UK

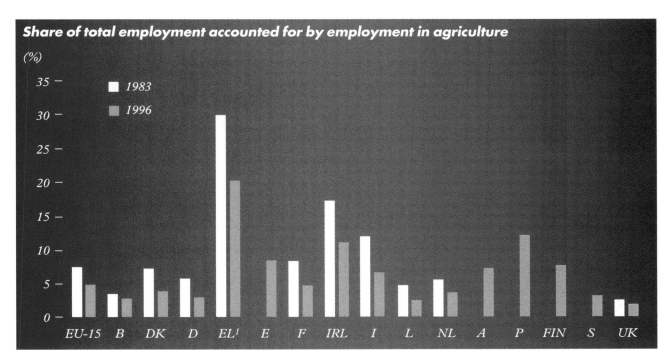

Share of total employment accounted for by employment in agriculture

(%)

■ 1983
■ 1996

EU-15   B   DK   D   EL¹   E   F   IRL   I   L   NL   A   P   FIN   S   UK

value of all EU imports in 1996. Agricultural exports accounted for about 7.9% of the value of all EU exports to non-EU countries.

People leaving the land

Since the beginning of the 1980s, the total income from EU-15 agricultural activity has fallen by about 20% in real terms, after allowing for inflation. The main reason for this has been falling real prices for agricultural products. But income has fallen less sharply than the volume of agricultural labour (measured in full-time equivalents because of the large amount of part-time work); thus income from agricultural activity per unit of agricultural labour has risen by about 30% in real terms.

In 1980 there were an estimated 11.9 million full-time labour equivalents in agriculture in the present 15 Member States. By 1997 the number had fallen to 6.9 million, despite additions from the former East Germany.

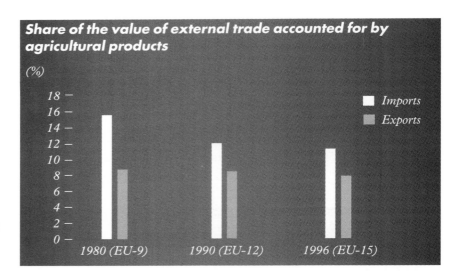

Share of the value of external trade accounted for by agricultural products

Far-reaching changes

Far-reaching changes in agriculture caused more than a million farmers in EU-12 to give up their agricultural holdings from 1990–1995. The agricultural labour force fell by over 2.2 million in this period.

Smallholdings still predominate in the south. In Greece, Italy and Portugal the average size is between 5 and 9 ha of utilised agricultural area. In contrast, the biggest holdings, averaging 70 ha, are in the UK. Around 17% of holdings are bigger than 100 ha in UK but under 1% in Greece, Italy, the Netherlands and Finland. Over half of all EU farmers are over 55. This means many decisions about whether or not to continue operating a holding are imminent. Almost two-thirds of

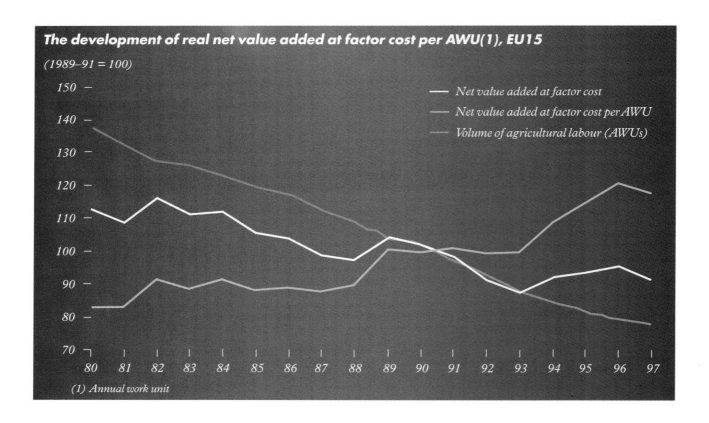

The development of real net value added at factor cost per AWU(1), EU15

(1) Annual work unit

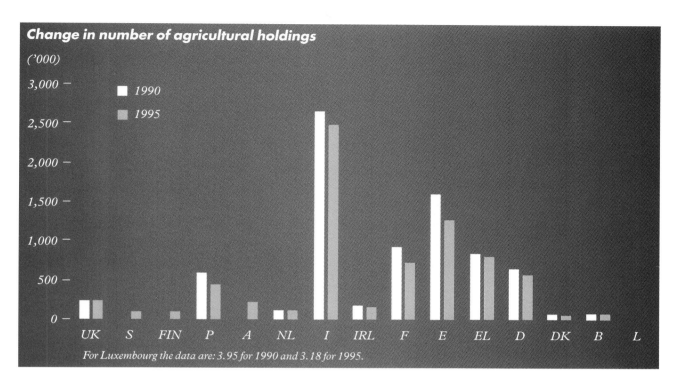

Change in number of agricultural holdings

('000)

For Luxembourg the data are: 3.95 for 1990 and 3.18 for 1995.

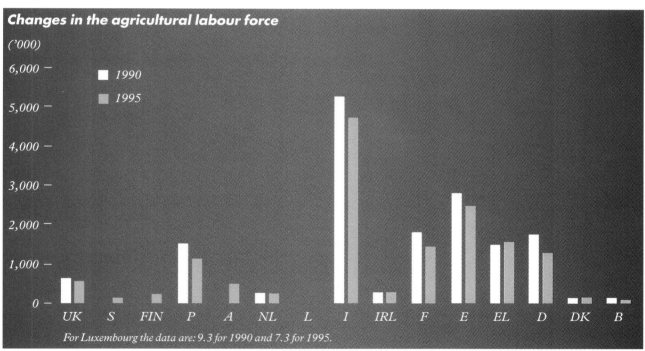

Changes in the agricultural labour force

('000)

For Luxembourg the data are: 9.3 for 1990 and 7.3 for 1995.

farmers in the southern Member States are over this age.

In 1995 an estimated 15.3 million people were regularly working in agriculture in the EU, the vast majority being farmers and members of their families. Of these, 4.8 million were in Italy and 2.5 million in Spain. Manpower requirements vary greatly. In UK it takes little more than two full-time workers to farm 100 ha; in Greece nearly 16 people are needed on average. The EU average is five. Field crops are an important type of EU farming. In 1995, some 57% of utilised agricultural area was used this way. Out of approximately 7.3 million holdings in 1995, around 3.9 million kept livestock. The proportion of farms with livestock is highest in Ireland, where almost every agricultural holding is involved in animal production. In contrast, in Italy and Spain only about a third of holdings keep livestock.

France has 24% of the EU's total bovine population, Germany 19% and the UK 14%. The UK has about 41% of the EU's total sheep population. Pig farming is concentrated mainly in Germany, the Netherlands and France, which together have almost half of the EU pig population. France is the most important poultry producer, with more than a quarter of total poultry in the EU.

Boost to forestry through enlargement

In 1995, the total wooded area in the EU was 133 million ha – 42% of the total land area. Forest land totalled 102 million ha and other wooded land 31 million ha. Wooded land in the EU represents less than 3% of the world total. For several decades now, EU forest resources have been slowly expanding, and this trend is expected to continue.

Number and size of agricultural holdings, 1995

	Holdings (1 000)	Total agricultural area (1 000 ha)	Average size of holding (ha)	Distribution of holdings (%) under 5 ha	over 100 ha
EU-15	7,370.0	128,497.3	17.4	56.4	2.9
EU-12	6,958.5	119,820.7	17.2	58.2	3.0
B	71.0	1,354.4	19.1	31.1	1.3
DK	68.8	2,726.6	39.6	2.7	7.3
D	566.9	17,156.9	30.3	31.2	3.5
EL	802.4	3,578.2	4.5	74.8	0.1
E	1,277.6	25,230.3	19.7	54.3	3.6
F	734.8	28,267.2	38.5	26.7	9.6
IRL	153.4	4,324.5	28.2	9.3	2.7
I	2,482.1	14,685.5	5.9	77.9	0.5
L	3.2	126.9	39.9	24.5	6.6
NL	113.2	1,998.9	17.7	31.3	0.8
A	221.8	3,425.1	15.4	38.1	1.3
P	450.6	3,924.6	8.7	76.4	1.2
FIN	101.0	2,191.7	21.7	10.0	0.8
S	88.8	3,059.7	34.4	11.9	6.3
UK	234.5	16,446.6	70.1	13.0	16.7

Agricultural labour force, by time worked on the holding, 1995

	Total labour force Total 1,000	of which: full time employed %	Family labour force Total 1,000	of which: full-time employed %
EU-15	15,243.6	21.6	14,258.9	18.6
EU-12	14,300.1	21.5	13,368.8	18.5
B	122.0	44.8	112.7	43.6
DK	141.1	52.2	103.2	41.3
D	1,325.2	33.0	1,147.1	25.3
EL	1,566.7	9.1	1,557.5	8.8
E	2,543.1	19.3	2,384.8	16.2
F	1,507.4	39.2	1,337.3	36.4
IRL	293.3	52.3	277.9	52.5
I	4,773.2	11.9	4,695.6	11.3
L	7.3	41.0	6.6	36.3
NL	276.2	49.6	212.8	47.7
A	547.3	15.6	525.7	14.2
P	1,172.8	14.2	1,111.0	11.8
FIN	232.1	34.3	229.4	34.3
S	164.2	27.5	135.0	24.4
UK	571.7	45.6	422.4	40.5

Sweden, Finland, France, Germany and Spain have forest land area over 10 million ha. The three new Member States are the ones with the highest forest cover: Finland (66% of land area), Sweden (59%) and Austria (47%).

The total volume of the growing stock in EU forests is estimated at around 13,300 million m³. Two thirds are coniferous, mostly spruce. Two thirds of the total EU wooded area are privately owned with approximately 12 million forest owners.

EU removals correspond to around 10% of the world total. For industrial roundwood, the EU's share is larger; for fuel wood, significantly lower. In 1996, a total of 246 million m³ of roundwood was harvested from Community forests. With the inclusion of the new Member States, EU removal quantities were nearly doubled.

In 1996, 19 million m³ of roundwood was imported into the EU. Despite their extensive forests, Finland and Sweden are the major net importers due to the size of their wood manufacturing industries. EU exports of roundwood remained at around 2 million m³. The EU self-sufficiency in roundwood was 94% in 1996.

The EU entry of the new Member States gave a dramatic boost to forest industries. For example, the production of sawnwood was almost doubled, and the manufacture of woodpulp was more than tripled. EU self-sufficiency rates in the major forest industry products increased considerably, as Finland and Sweden in particular are key market players in coniferous sawnwood, woodpulp, paper and paperboard products. Their exports are mainly within the single market, increasing its self-sufficiency.

In 1996, the EU Member States produced 67 million m³ of

Number of farmholders(1) by age

(1995; 1 000)

	under 35 years	35 to 54 years	55 to 64 years	65 years and over	Total
EU-15	570.7	2,682.0	1,994.5	2,022.0	7,269.2
EU-12	507.5	2,472.7	1,911.9	1,975.9	6,867.9
B	10.9	29.0	17.8	11.8	69.5
DK	6.6	29.8	16.3	15.7	68.4
D	98.2	268.6	152.8	41.8	561.4
EL	49.0	277.5	227.2	248.5	802.2
E	76.6	426.0	367.5	371.4	1,241.4
F	92.3	341.5	174.5	110.2	718.4
IRL	20.9	64.3	35.3	32.5	153.0
I	110.2	747.1	701.0	912.3	2,470.6
L	0.4	1.5	0.7	0.6	3.1
NL	10.3	50.2	30.3	19.0	109.8
A	39.7	109.6	46.8	20.9	217.1
P	18.5	140.2	129.5	157.0	445.2
FIN	16.1	59.6	18.0	7.1	100.8
S	7.5	40.1	17.9	18.0	83.4
UK	13.7	97.0	59.1	55.2	224.9

(1) Holders who are a natural person.

Production and trade of roundwood and the major forest industry products in 1996, EU-15

	Unit (1 000)	Production	Imports from extra EU-15	Exports to extra EU-15
Industrial roundwood	m3	211,388	18,225	2,412
Fuelwood	,,	34,860	509	18
Sawnwood total	,,	67,022	12,317	6,051
coniferous	,,	59,562	8,145	5,785
non-coniferous	,,	7,460	4,171	266
Wood-based panels total	,,	34,037	5,237	2,452
veneer sheets and plywood	,,	4,422	3,654	611
particle board	"	25,162	831	1,113
fibreboard	,,	4,453	750	729
Woodpulp total	metric tonne	30,112	7,782	1,283
chemical	,,	19,261	7,301	1,161
mechanical and semi-chemical	,,	10,851	480	122
Newsprint	,,	8,068	1,516	1,161
Printing and writing paper	,,	25,862	1,095	5,027

Source: Eurostat forestry statistics 1992–1996

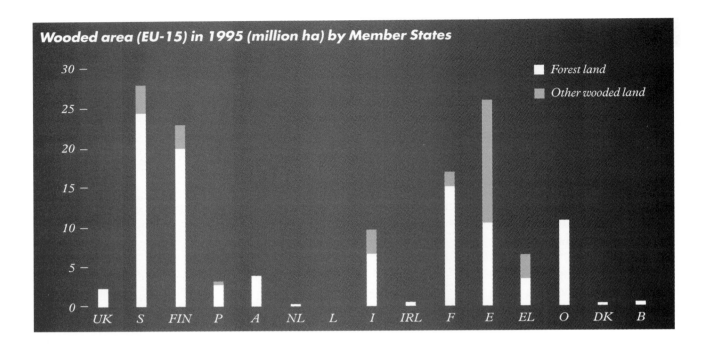

Wooded area (EU-15) in 1995 (million ha) by Member States

Forest land
Other wooded land

sawnwood, 16% of the world total. Sweden, Finland and Austria are the main exporting countries of sawnwood. The biggest net importers include Italy and the UK. In 1996, the EU was 91% self-sufficient in sawnwood.

In the pulp and paper industries, the EU plays a very significant role in printing and writing paper. The total EU production of 26 million tons in 1996 constituted one third of the world total. Newsprint production totalled 8.1 million tons, which accounted for 23% of the worldís total. The EU-15 is 96% self-sufficient in newspaper, and 118% in printing and writing paper.

11 Fishing

Fishing is a key activity in the EU, even though it employs only around 300,000 fishermen directly or 0.2% of the total working population. Perhaps four or five times as many – working in boat-building or fish processing – depend on it for their employment. It is often important in many less well-developed regions with few alternative jobs. Outside the EU itself, it is significant in the European Economic Area (EEA) countries of Norway and Iceland.

The annual EEA fish catch is 11.2 million tonnes – 13.2% of the world total of 85 million tonnes. Thus the EEA leads the world in front of Peru (8.9 million tonnes) and Chile (7.4 million tonnes). The leading EEA fishing country is Norway with 2.5 million tonnes followed by Denmark (2.0 million tonnes), Iceland (1.6 million tonnes) and Spain (1.2 million tonnes). The North-East Atlantic accounts for 85% of catches. However, EEA fishermen, largely excluded from traditional distant water fisheries in the North Atlantic that now fall within the extended economic zones of other countries, have increasingly headed for the more distant waters of the South Atlantic, Indian Ocean and Pacific Ocean.

The EEA fishing fleet consists of an estimated 110,000 motor vessels with a total tonnage of 2.3 million gross tonnes. 85% of vessels have a gross tonnage of under 25 tonnes and these more adaptable smaller boats are on the increase. The most commonly caught EEA fish are herring (1,739 thousand tonnes), sandeels and capelin (1,125 thousand tonnes and 743 thousand tonnes for industrial use), cod (849 thousand tonnes) and mackerel (638 thousand tonnes). Europeans eat 22 kg of fish per capita per annum; the Japanese eat 68 kg. Fish farming is of increasing importance. The EEA produces 1.3 million tonnes, some 10% of total fish production and approximately 5% of world fish-farming output. Fish farms produce more salmon than are caught by fishermen. There are high hopes that better techniques will lead to the viable farming of more mundane species such as cod.

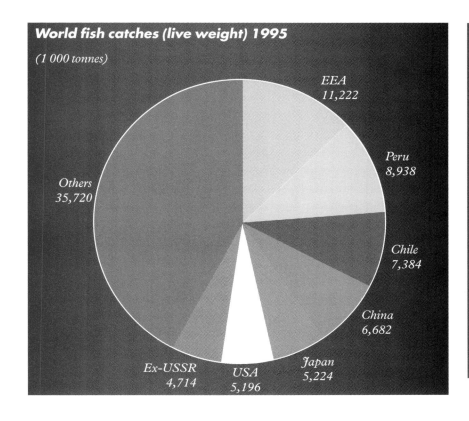

World fish catches (live weight) 1995

(1 000 tonnes)

- EEA 11,222
- Peru 8,938
- Chile 7,384
- China 6,682
- Japan 5,224
- USA 5,196
- Ex-USSR 4,714
- Others 35,720

EEA Fishing fleet, 1995

	Number	Tonnage (1 000 gt)
EU-15	100,085	2,107
B	155	23
DK	5,200	97
D	2,392	77
EL	20,343	116
E	18,483	658
F	6,593	178
IRL	1,389	62
I	16,352	260
NL	1,006	180
P	12,101	125
FIN	4,106	24
S	2,513	51
UK	9,452	255
IS	953	120
NO	8,318	112
EEA	109,356	2,340

EEA total catches by fishing region, 1995

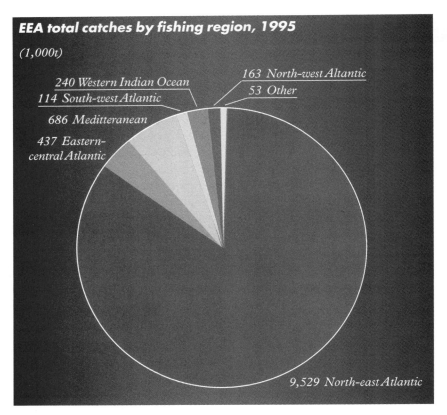

(1,000t)

240 Western Indian Ocean

114 South-west Atlantic

686 Meditterranean

437 Eastern-central Atlantic

163 North-west Altantic

53 Other

9,529 North-east Atlantic

FURTHER READING

Eurostat publications
Fisheries: annual statistics
Agriculture, forestry and fisheries,
   Rapid Reports and Statistics in
   Focus

Electronic products
Eurostat Yearbook CD-ROM
Agriculture and Fisheries in the
   European Union: CD
Eurostatis New Cronos database
   (Eurofarm)

Glossary
Gross tonne (gt) 1 gt = 100 cubic
feet or 2.83 m³

EEA fish-farming output, 1995

(tonnes, live-weight)

	Fish	Molluscs and crustaceans	Total
EU-15	389,071	626,685	1,015,756
B	846	–	846
DK	42,205	–	42,205
D	39,218	19,046	58,264
EL	21,755	10,889	32,644
E	28,518	109,742	138,260
F	65,488	215,197	280,685
IRL	13,284	18,623	31,907
I	59,040	160,825	219,865
NL	2,604	80,681	83,285
A	4,055	3	4,058
P	1,734	3,247	4,981
FIN	17,345	–	17,345
S	6,040	1,533	7,573
UK	86,939	6,899	93,838
IS	3,451	–	3,451
NO	282,463	–	282,463
EEA	674,985	626,685	1,301,670

12 Energy
12.1 Challenges for the EU

Energy has a significant influence on the environment and is important in geopolitics, as well as affecting the whole of economic and social life. It is the driving force of industry, transport and heating; indeed there are few aspects of daily life which are not in some way dependent on energy in one form or another. Energy shortages, and fluctuations in the price of oil, have repercussions on the whole economy and can lead to economic crises and recessions. Therefore, energy policy is one of the European Union's priorities.

The major challenges facing the Union in the energy field are:

- Increasing dependence on outside supplies, up from 50% to 70%;
- The need to ensure more competitive energy prices in the context of economic globalization, notably by liberalizing the electricity and gas sectors and developing trans-European energy networks;
- The pressing need to make energy markets more compatible with environmental objectives, in particular in the context of the recent commitments made by the European Union on climate change.

Eurostat has developed a coherent, harmonised system of energy statistics to meet the need for energy monitoring, and to quantify factors relevant to energy policy.

Total primary energy production in the world increased significantly between 1985 and 1990. Since 1990, however, energy production has increased only slightly, due to the sharp fall in output in the NIS that has counter-balanced the gradual rise in production of almost all other world regions. The European Union contributes 8.3% of the world's energy production; its gross consumption per capita was stable between 1990 and 1994 at 3.6 tonnes of oil equivalent (toe) per head per year rising to 3.7 toe/head in 1995 and 1996.

World primary energy production

(Mtoe)	1985	1990	1993	1994	1995	1996
World	7,531	8,545	8,587	8,723	8,887	9,065
Western Europe	816	841	875	907	936	955
EU-15(1)	732	710	709	724	740	767
EFTA	83	131	166	183	195	199
Rest of OECD	2,222	2,381	2,412	2,501	2,533	2,583
NAFTA	1,998	2,111	2,112	2,198	2,208	2,252
OECD Pacific	202	245	275	277	299	304
Mediterranean	22	26	26	26	26	27
Central and Eastern Europe	285	235	211	206	204	208
NIS(2)	1,513	1,630	1,288	1,177	1,140	1,163
Africa	530	617	658	659	680	694
Middle East	605	955	1,072	1,103	1,116	1,139
Asia	1,203	1,466	1,611	1,683	1,758	1,794
Latin America	357	421	459	487	519	529
of which (%)						
European Union	10	8	8	8	8	8
OECD	40	38	38	39	39	39

(1) Including the former East Germany before 1991.
(2) Including Baltic countries for statistical reasons.

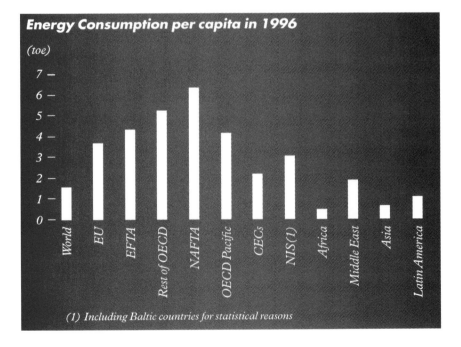

Energy Consumption per capita in 1996

(toe)

(1) Including Baltic countries for statistical reasons

12.2 Energy supply

Primary energy production

Primary energy production in the 15 Member States of the European Union reached a high point of 750 million tonnes of oil equivalent (Mtoe) in 1986 after which it fell to 705Mtoe in 1990 and a low point of 700Mtoe in 1992. At present output is rising, reaching 767Mtoe in 1996. It is worth noting the boom in crude oil production since 1994, which has been driven by more efficient and economical methods for off-shore exploitation.

Europe's main energy sources are nuclear energy, accounting for 28% of total production in 1996, and

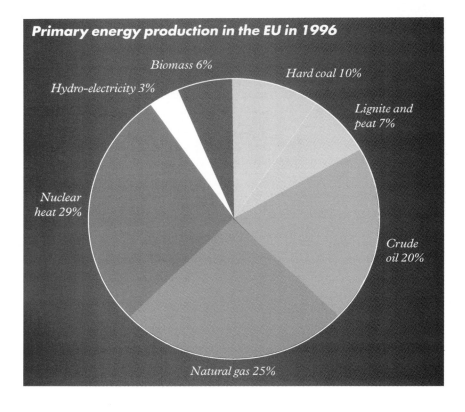

Primary energy production in the EU in 1996

- Biomass 6%
- Hydro-electricity 3%
- Nuclear heat 29%
- Hard coal 10%
- Lignite and peat 7%
- Crude oil 20%
- Natural gas 25%

Primary energy production in the European Union(1)

(Mtoe)	1985	1990	1993	1994	1995	1996
Total	732	705	708	724	740	767
of which:						
Hard coal	134	119	95	79	81	77
Lignite and peat	103	90	60	58	55	54
Crude oil	149	115	125	153	156	155
Natural gas	132	133	158	160	167	189
Nuclear heat	148	182	198	199	205	214
Hydro-electricity	24	22	25	26	25	25
Biomass	40	40	43	44	45	47

(1) including former East Germany before 1991.

natural gas, which has a growing
share of total output (25% in 1996).
Other primary fuels used for energy
production are solid fuels (20%),
crude oil (20%) and hydropower
(3%).

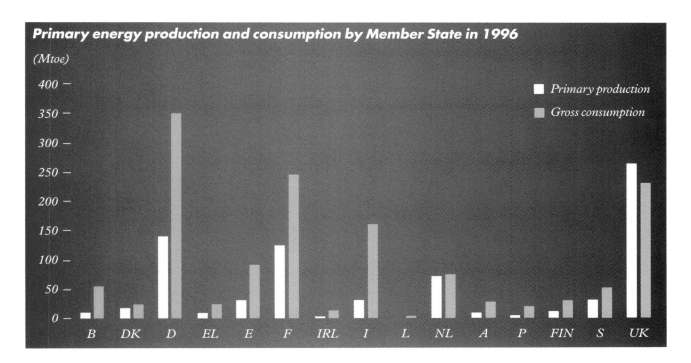

Primary energy production and consumption by Member State in 1996

12.3 Electricity generation

Electricity generation in the European Union has increased steadily, by almost 2% per year, for the last 10 years despite a very limited increase in installed capacity. In 1996, electricity generation reached 2,409 terawatt-hours (TWh), 51.0% of which was produced by thermal power stations using mainly hard coal and lignite, natural gas and petroleum products. The remainder was generated by nuclear power (35.3%) and from renewable energy, including hydro.

Since 1985, the use of natural gas and nuclear energy in electricity generation has increased faster than solid fuels and petroleum products. The share of natural gas has grown from 6.2% of the total in 1985 to 11.1% in 1996, while nuclear

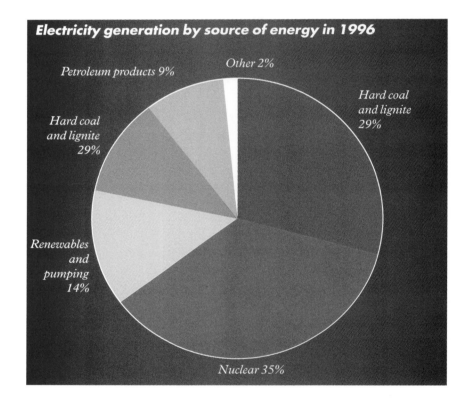

Electricity generation by source of energy in 1996

Other 2%

Petroleum products 9%

Hard coal and lignite 29%

Hard coal and lignite 29%

Renewables and pumping 14%

Nuclear 35%

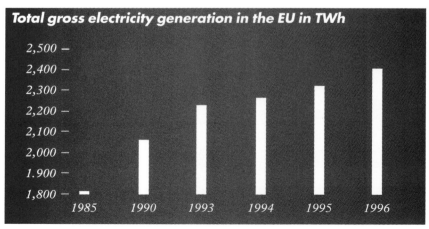

Total gross electricity generation in the EU in TWh

2,500 —
2,400 —
2,300 —
2,200 —
2,100 —
2,000 —
1,900 —
1,800 —

1985   1990   1993   1994   1995   1996

electricity increased from 31.6% to 35.3% over this period. In contrast, the share of hard coal and lignite decreased from 33.4% in 1985 to 29.4% in 1996 and the use of petroleum products decreased from 10% to 8.8% in the same period.

Electricity generation by source of energy

(TWh)

	1985	1990	1993	1994	1995	1996
Total gross generation	1,818	2,062	2,232	2,269	2,326	2,409
Hard coal and lignite	607	676	696	705	707	709
Nuclear	574	720	794	792	810	850
Renewables and pumping	304	291	316	321	320	329
Natural gas	112	142	184	208	237	267
Petroleum products	181	194	196	194	205	212
Other	40	39	46	50	47	42

12.4 Energy dependency

The European Union cannot meet its energy requirements; it imports almost half the energy it consumes. In addition, there has been an upward trend in EU imports over the last 10 years.

The main fuels imported in 1996 were crude oil and petroleum products, and natural gas. The former came mainly from OPEC countries and the Near and Middle East and the latter from the NIS, Norway and Algeria. There are also

some exports of crude oil and petroleum products mainly to the USA, Switzerland and Norway. The United Kingdom is the only EU country that produces more energy than it consumes, due to its off-shore reserves.

Energy imports of the European Union

(Mtoe)	1985	1990	1993	1994	1995	1996
Total imports	786	908	966	967	977	1,021
of which:						
Hard coal	81	92	87	89	93	94
Crude oil and feedstocks	412	488	536	542	532	550
Petroleum products	181	193	192	185	187	195
Natural gas	94	115	130	131	143	160
Electricity	8	13	13	13	14	15

Energy exports of the European Union

(Mtoe)	1985	1990	1993	1994	1995	1996
Total exports	277	282	313	333	326	350
of which:						
Crude oil and feedstocks	88	68	77	99	97	103
Petroleum products	135	165	183	182	175	185

Energy imports-exports in the European Union

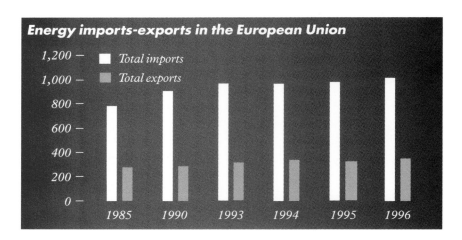

12.5 Renewable energy

πIncreasing the contribution of Renewable Energy Sources in the EU energy balance is one of the main goals of EU energy policy. With the ALTENER programme in 1993, the Council adopted, for the first time, a specific financial instrument for the promotion of renewable energy. In 1996, with renewable sources supplying 5.3% of the EU's total energy demand, ALTENER II has set a target of a 12% renewable contribution by 2010, while the European Parliament has pleaded for the establishment of a Community action plan in order to increase the share of renewable sources to the EU energy mix.

To assist the EU's political aims, Eurostat established a methodology, which has been used since 1989, for the collection of detailed Renewable Energy Sources statistics. This covers commercially mature renewable energy technologies and is a successful and cost-effective tool for assessing the EU's quantitative objectives on Renewable Energy.

The data, collected by means of annual surveys in the Member States, cover hydro, wind, solar and geothermal energy, as well as biomass and municipal wastes, giving detailed information on thermal and electrical installed capacities, primary energy consumption and electricity and heat production. Statistics are published yearly alongside those on conventional energy sources.

Production from Renewable Energy Sources

(ktoe)	1989	1990	1991	1992	1993	1994	1995	1996
Total	64,241	64,960	67,490	69,065	71,337	72,135	72,692	75,051
of which:								
Hydro	21,600	22,257	23,083	24,587	24,882	25,535	25,033	24,910
Wind energy	43	61	93	138	202	302	350	418
Solar energy	131	142	154	165	182	208	265	299
Geothermal energy	2,215	2,215	2,204	2,377	2,613	2,497	2,518	2,741
Biomass	40,252	40,285	41,956	41,798	43,458	43,593	44,570	46,727

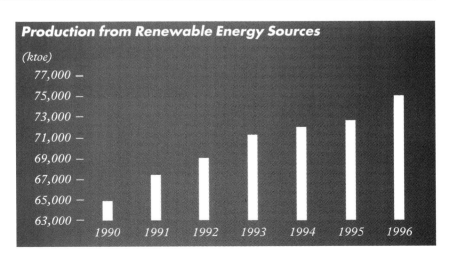

Production from Renewable Energy Sources

(ktoe)

Member States' contributions differ according to geographic location, the availability of natural resources and existing renewable energy policy. In 1996, 75.1 Mtoe of renewable energy were produced and consumed in the EU, 62% of which came from biomass, 33% from hydro, 4% from geothermal energy, 0.6% from wind and 0.4% from solar energy. In 1996, 13.5% of total electricity, i.e. 325 TWh, was generated using renewable sources, hydropower being the main contributor with a 89.2% share. It is, however, worth noticing the rapid evolution of certain technologies such as wind energy, where the installed capacity from rose from 354 MW in 1989 to 3,429 MW in 1996.

Renewable energy contribution as a percentage of total in 1996

	To total electricity generation	To total inland consumption
EU-15	13.5	5.3
B	1.1	1.2
DK	4.5	4.9
D	4.4	1.8
EL	10.3	5.7
E	24.0	7.3
F	13.4	6.9
IRL	4.0	1.6
I	19.0	5.9
L	7.6	1.2
NL	3.1	1.7
A	67.1	22.5
P	46.0	19.6
FIN	25.4	19.8
S	40.4	22.8
UK	1.6	0.6
NO	99.7	42.6

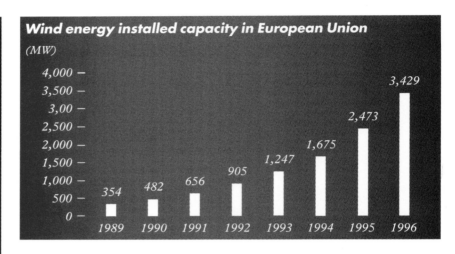

Wind energy installed capacity in European Union

12.6 Final energy consumption

This section looks at final energy consumption—that is the use of energy after it has been transformed into a useable state, for example into electricity. In the process of conversion much energy is lost; thus final consumption is much less than gross consumption.

Data for 1985 to 1996 show that most of the increase in final energy consumption in the EU was concentrated in southern European Member States, where economic growth has been faster than the European Union average, and especially in Portugal, Spain and Greece. Total final consumption of 943 Mtoe in 1996 was made up of 45.8% from petroleum products, 23.9% from natural gas, 18.5%

from electricity and 5.0% from solid fuels. Comparing this fuel mix with that of 1985, it is noted that the use of solid fuels was reduced by 4%, while natural gas and electricity increased their share by 2.9% and 2% respectively. The contribution of petroleum products decreased by as little as 0.8%.

Including former East Germany before 1991, final consumption increased by 14% from 1985 to 1996, mainly due to the 40% increase in consumption of the transport sector; a sector which accounted for 30% of the total final energy use in 1996. It is worth noting that the share of diesel oil reached 41% of total road consumption in 1996. The services

Final energy consumption by sector and by fuel

(Mtoe)	1985	1990	1993	1994	1995	1996
Total	769	817	887	881	899	943
of which:						
Petroleum products	366	388	417	416	420	432
Natural gas	144	165	190	184	197	225
Solid fuels	73	58	55	52	49	47
Electricity	130	150	162	165	170	174
Industry	245	252	248	253	257	266
of which:						
Residual fuel-oil	33	26	24	25	23	20
Natural gas	53	66	68	69	73	86
Solid fuels	51	46	41	40	39	37
Electricity	59	67	68	69	71	72
Transport	197	247	271	272	276	283
of which:						
Motor spirit	103	118	126	122	121	123
Diesel oil	66	94	106	110	113	117
Services, households etc	327	318	369	357	366	394
of which:						
Gas oil	95	79	84	80	81	88
Natural gas	91	99	121	115	123	139
Heat	6	7	15	15	16	16
Electricity	68	79	90	91	93	97

and households sector accounted for 42% of the total, up by 11% since 1985. The fuels used in the services and households sector shifted from gasoil to natural gas and electricity, while district heating where energy use is more efficient, doubled its contribution. Industrial consumption accounted for 28.2% of total final consumption in 1996. With increased use of natural gas and less residual fuel-oil and solid fuels being used, industry was able to reduce its share of total consumption from 1985 onwards, reaching a low point in 1993 before the most energy intensive sectors, the iron and steel and chemical industries (accounting for 38.9% of industry's total in 1996) showed signs of revival.

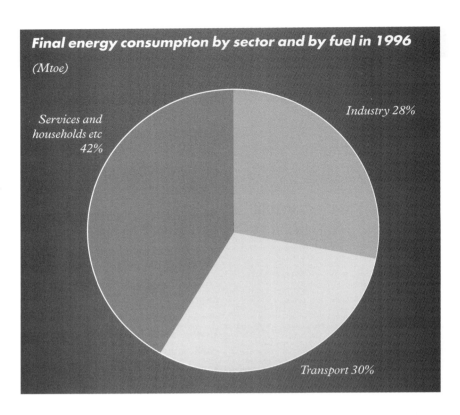

Final energy consumption by sector and by fuel in 1996

(Mtoe)

Services and households etc 42%

Industry 28%

Transport 30%

European Union energy indicators

	1985	1990	1993	1994	1995	1996
Degree of self-sufficiency in energy supply (%)						
Total Production/Gross Consumption	*57.3*	*52.2*	*53.2*	*54.2*	*54.1*	*54.4*
Degree of self-sufficiency in energy supply (%)						
Total Production/Gross Consumption	*57.3*	*52.2*	*53.2*	*54.2*	*54.1*	*54.4*
Energy dependency (%)						
Net energy imports/(G.I.C.+Bunkers)	*43.2*	*49.1*	*47.7*	*46.3*	*46.5*	*46.7*
Energy intensity (kgoe/1000ECU)						
Gross inland consumption/GDP	*258.9*	*238.7*	*247.2*	*240.7*	*240.4*	*245.0*
Final energy consumption/GDP	*172.9*	*157.3*	*164.7*	*158.8*	*158.1*	*163.2*
Importance to imports (%)						
Fuel imports/Total imports	*17.2*	*7.3*	*6.4*	*5.9*	*5.2*	*6.9*
Oil imports/Fuel imports	*85.0*	*84.3*	*81.3*	*80.9*	*79.8*	*78.9*
Personnel employed in coal mines underground						
(annual mean, '000)	*311*	*187*	*125*	*103*	*94*	*93*
Number of active hard coal mines						
(end of year)	*465*	*317*	*184*	*169*	*164*	*158*
Total energy consumption per capita						
(toe/head)	*3.4*	*3.6*	*3.6*	*3.6*	*3.7*	*3.7*
Electricity consumption per capita						
(MWh/head)	*4.6*	*5.2*	*5.3*	*5.4*	*5.4*	*5.4*

12.7 Energy prices

Trends in gas and electricity prices in the EU between 1980 and 1998

Electricity prices for industrial users rose appreciably between 1980 and 1985, stabilised for a while, fell sharply between 1986 and 1988, were relatively stable between 1992 and 1995, and dropped slightly in 1996, 1997 and 1998.

Price variations for domestic users have been less marked. Prices rose slowly but steadily until 1995, decreasing slightly or stabilising between 1996 and 1998. There is little difference in the price levels in the different countries.

There was a steep and steady rise in gas prices for industrial users between 1980 and 1986, followed by a sharp fall which lasted until 1989 and was most pronounced in 1986 and 1987. Prices started to rise again slightly in 1991 before

Gas and electricity prices on 1 January 1998

ECUS/GJ

		Taxes excluded	Specific taxes	VAT
B	a.	7.03	0.34	1.55
	b.	4.25	0.00	0.89
	c.	3.48	0.00	0.73
DK	a.	0.00	0.00	0.00
	b.	3.59	0.47	1.01
	c.	2.95	0.47	0.85
D	a.	7.00	0.51	1.13
	b.	4.98	0.51	0.83
	c.	4.15	0.51	0.70
EL	a.	:	:	:
	b.	:	:	:
	c.	:	:	:
E	a.	9.09	0.00	1.46
	b.	3.67	0.00	0.59
	c.	3.50	0.00	0.56
F	a.	7.67	0.00	1.58
	b.	3.62	0.19	0.78
	c.	2.97	0.31	0.68
IRL	a.	7.23	0.00	0.90
	b.	2.96	0.00	0.37
	c.	0.00	0.00	0.00
I	a.	8.31	4.58	2.58
	b.	4.20	0.40	0.46
	c.	3.51	0.40	0.39

ECUS/GJ

		Taxes excluded	Specific taxes	VAT
L	a.	5.76	0.00	0.35
	b.	5.03	0.00	0.30
	c.	4.82	0.00	0.29
NL	a.	6.16	1.08	1.27
	b.	3.72	0.45	0.73
	c.	3.05	0.28	0.58
A	a.	7.72	1.07	1.76
	b.	4.23	1.07	1.06
	c.	3.67	1.07	0.95
P	a.	0.00	0.00	0.00
	b.	0.00	0.00	0.00
	c.	0.00	0.00	0.00
FIN				
	b.	3.62	0.37	0.88
	c.	3.22	0.37	0.79
S	a.	7.24	3.02	2.56
	b.	4.59	1.06	1.41
	c.	0.00	0.00	0.00
UK	a.	6.45	0.00	0.32
	b.	3.41	0.00	0.60
	c.	3.01	0.00	0.53
NO	a.	:	:	:
	b.	:	:	:
	c.	:	:	:

ECUS/100kWh

		Taxes excluded	Specific taxes	VAT
B	d.	11.86	0.14	2.51
	e.	11.66	0.00	2.45
	f.	5.64	0.00	1.18
DK	d.	6.74	7.65	3.59
	e.	5.41	0.79	3.04
	f.	4.72	0.78	2.88
D	d.	12.34	0.00	1.85
	e.	11.53	0.00	1.73
	f.	6.14	0.00	0.92
EL	d.	6.27	0.00	1.13
	e.	7.96	0.00	1.44
	f.	4.94	0.00	0.89
E	d.	9.46	0.48	1.59
	e.	7.43	0.38	1.25
	f.	5.22	0.27	0.87
F	d.	9.61	1.01	2.19
	e.	8.43	0.33	1.80
	f.	5.15	0.00	1.06
IRL	d.	7.96	0.00	0.99
	e.	10.89	0.00	1.36
	f.	5.31	0.00	0.66
I	d.	16.69	3.45	2.02
	e.	9.46	2.35	1.18
	f.	5.95	1.12	0.71

ECUS/100kWh

		Taxes excluded	Specific taxes	VAT
L	d.	10.60	0.00	0.63
	e.	10.49	0.00	0.63
	f.	4.64	0.00	0.28
NL	d.	9.08	1.02	1.77
	e.	10.70	0.41	1.95
	f.	4.86	0.00	0.86
A	d.	9.69	0.72	2.08
	e.	11.54	0.72	2.45
	f.	6.28	0.72	1.40
P	d.	12.51	0.02	0.63
	e.	9.44	0.00	0.47
	f.	5.82	0.00	0.29
FIN	d.	7.05	0.57	1.67
	e.	5.41	0.35	1.27
	f.	3.56	0.35	0.85
S	d.	6.75	1.66	2.11
	e.	5.92	0.00	1.48
	f.	3.29	0.00	0.82
UK	d.	10.33	0.00	0.52
	e.	8.50	0.00	1.49
	f.	0.00	0.00	0.00
NO	d.	9.29	0.69	2.30
	e.	5.24	0.00	1.21
	f.	2.55	0.00	0.57

a. Gas: Household 83.7 GJ/year
b. Gas: Industrial consumer 41 860 GJ/year (200 days, 1600 hours)
c. Gas: Industrial consumer 418 600 GJ/year (250 days, 4000 hours)
d. Electricity: Household 3 500 kWh/year (of which 1300 night)
e. Electricity: Industrial consumer 0.160 GWh/year (100 kW, 1600 hours)
f. Electricity: Industrial consumer 24 GWh/year (4000 kW, 6000 hours)

Gas prices on 1 January 1998

(ECUS/GJ)

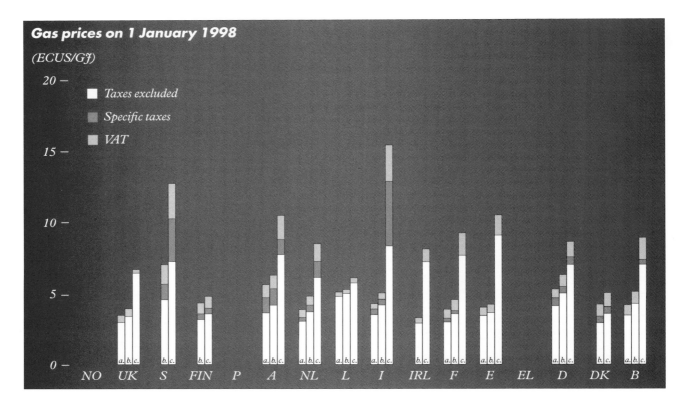

Electricity prices on 1 January 1998

(ECUS/100kwh)

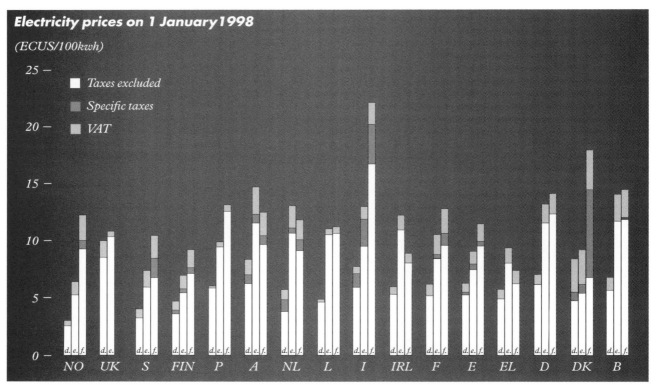

a. Gas: Household 83.7 GJ/year
b. Gas: Industrial consumer 41 860 GJ/year (200 days, 1600 hours)
c. Gas: Industrial consumer 418 600 GJ/year (250 days, 4000 hours)
d. Electricity: Household 3 500 kWh/year (of which 1300 night)
e. Electricity: Industrial consumer 0.160 GWh/year (100 kW, 1600 hours)
f. Electricity: Industrial consumer 24 GWh/year (4000 kW, 6000 hours)

levelling off. It is noticeable that the higher the level of gas consumption, the lower the price differences between the Member States. Domestic users saw prices rise up until 1985–1986, before dropping between 1986 and 1987. They rose again between 1988 and 1991 and then stabilised.

GLOSSARY

W:Watt:
> *is the power of a system in which the energy of 1 joule is transformed at constant rate during 1 second.*

toe: tonne of oil equivalent:
> *a standardised conventional unit defined on the basis of a tonne of oil with a net calorific value of 41 868 kJ/kg.*

FURTHER READING

Eurostat publications

Energy Balance sheets
Energy Yearly statistics
Energy, monthly
Operation of nuclear power stations, annual
Energy and industry, Statistics in Focus
Renewable energy sources Statistics 1989–1996
Gas prices
Electricity prices

Electronic products

Eurostat Yearbook CD-ROM
Comext CD-ROM
Eurostat's New Cronos database

Other publications

Energy in Europe
Annual energy review

13 Industry

13.1 The world's leading industrial producer

With industrial production of ECU 3,380 billion in 1996, the EU was the world's leading industrial producer. US output was ECU 2,910 billion and that of Japan ECU 2,330 billion. The four largest EU industrial countries accounted for 73.2% of the Union's total industrial production. Germany led easily with 28.8%; France was next (16.8%) followed by Italy (14.7%) and the UK (12.9%). The five largest EU industries in 1996 (based on share of total industrial value-added) were: electronics and electrical engineering; food, drink and tobacco; transport equipment; basic metals and metal products; and chemicals. These accounted for nearly 60% of total industrial value-added.

Employment in manufacturing fell from 27 million in 1980 to 22.6 million in 1996. This compares with 17 million in USA and under 10 million in Japan.

EU industrial production grew steadily from the mid-1980s to 1991. Then followed two years of decline, followed by modest recovery in 1994 and 1995 and stabilisation in 1996. The average annual growth rates of production in Member States in the 10 years to 1996 ranged from zero to 5.5%. In Germany it was 2.2%, France 2.9%, Italy 4.0% and UK 1.9%.

The increased output from newly-industrialised countries (NICs), such as those in south-east Asia, in the 1990s – not to mention economic globalisation – is putting the EU economy under growing pressure in traditional markets. To maintain their position EU manufacturers must continue to be at the forefront of innovation in design, marketing and cost-saving.

The European Commission's White Paper on Growth, Competitiveness and Employment has the goal of

creating a new economic climate in Europe. It identifies the need for growth while respecting the diversity of human and natural resources. It confronts the challenge of creating employment and equal opportunities within a 'Social Europe' while, at the same time, increasing competitiveness and facing economic realities.

Wages are a key issue. From 1986–1994, in real terms, average hourly wages in manufacturing rose by an average annual rate of 2.1% in Germany and 1.7% in the UK. In the USA they fell by 1.2% a year. However, productivity is also an important element of competitiveness. From 1991 onwards, EU labour productivity grew faster than that of its competitors combined. This corresponded with a drop in EU employment, which shows that labour saving played a key part in this productivity growth.

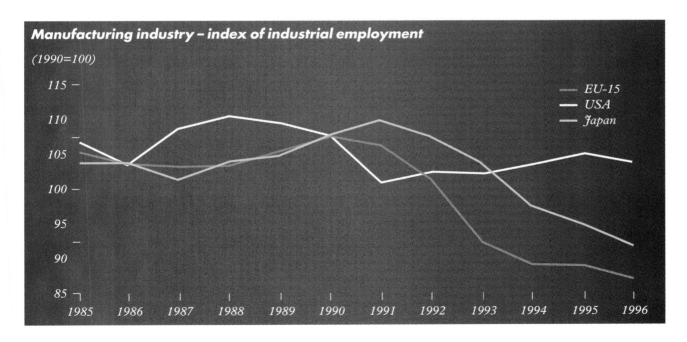

Manufacturing industry – index of industrial employment

Manufacturing industry – index of industrial production

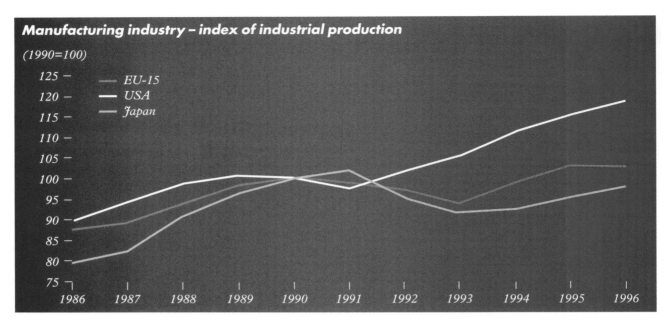

(1990=100)

Legend:
— EU-15
— USA
— Japan

Y-axis: 125, 120, 115, 110, 105, 100, 95, 90, 85, 80, 75

X-axis: 1986, 1987, 1988, 1989, 1990, 1991, 1992, 1993, 1994, 1995, 1996

Manufacturing industry – main indicators

(M ECU except where specified

	1988	1989	1990	1991	1992	1993	1994	1995	1996
Apparent consumption	2,486,900	2,773,894	2,911,758	3,015,002	3,023,496	2,839,720	3,046,990	3,226,648	3,287,077
Production	2,502,602	2,785,283	2,919,266	3,004,598	3,021,977	2,880,367	3,098,183	3,288,160	3,378,046
Exports	264,967	298,847	300,755	307,547	316,844	368,286	412,617	446,452	492,276
Trade Balance	15,702	11,389	7,508	−10,404	−1,519	40,647	51,193	61,512	90,970
Employment ('000)	25,554	25,969	26,321	26,094	25,209	23,605	23,065	22,946	22,623

Manufacturing industry – Comparison of production at current prices

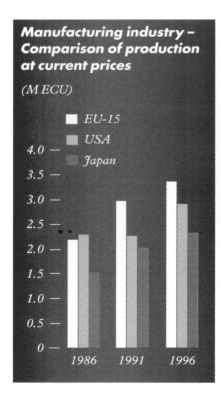

(M ECU)

Legend:
■ EU-15
■ USA
■ Japan

Y-axis: 4.0, 3.5, 3.0, 2.5, 2.0, 1.5, 1.0, 0.5, 0

X-axis: 1986, 1991, 1996

Sector shares of value added of total industry – 1996

Electrical and electronic engineering	12.9%
Food, drink and tobacco	11.9%
Transport equipment	11.6%
Metals and metal products	11.2%
Chemicals	11.2%
Mechanical engineering	10.9%
Paper, printing and publishing	8.2%
Other industries	8.0%
Textiles and leather	5.3%
Non metallic minerals	4.4%
Rubber and plastics	4.4%

13.2 Food, drink and tobacco – a picture of plenty

Food, drink and tobacco is one of the EU's main industries. It employs 2.6 million people and total production value was over ECU 545 billion in 1996. In almost all sectors, production exceeds consumption, giving the EU an overall trade balance of ECU 4.4 billion. The EU is the world's largest producer of food drink and tobacco products. It has increased its lead over the USA in the past decade.

Meat, dairy products and tobacco are the most important sectors. Employment has fallen from the 1991 peak of 2.8 million but remains over 2.6 million.

The EU is the largest global consumer and producer of processed food products, followed by the USA. The industry is very fragmented with a large number of small and medium sized enterprises. Nevertheless, mergers and takeovers have led to food items increasingly produced and marketed by a small number of multinational companies.

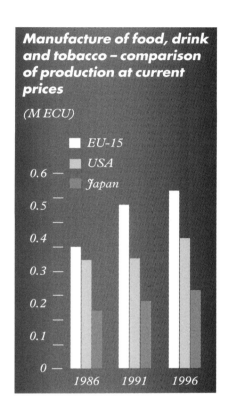

Manufacture of food, drink and tobacco – comparison of production at current prices

(M ECU)

- EU-15
- USA
- Japan

Manufacture of food, drink and tobacco – main indicators

(M ECU except where specified)

	1988	1989	1990	1991	1992	1993	1994	1995	1996
Apparent consumption	405,228	439,692	468,938	503,032	515,944	503,709	517,728	522,194	541,260
Production	402,922	439,488	468,897	502,113	516,267	506,746	520,184	527,163	545,676
Exports	19,229	22,780	22,642	23,136	24,876	27,439	29,740	31,209	32,949
Trade Balance	–2,306	–204	–41	–919	323	3,037	2,455	4,969	4,416
Employment ('000)	2,720	2,745	2,803	2,843	2,802	2,718	2,678	2,647	2,632

13.3 Textiles, clothing, leather and footwear – a shift east

Total production value in textiles, clothing, leather and footwear was ECU 179 billion in 1996 having peaked at ECU 184 billion in 1991. Long-term trends towards contraction and restructuring of the industry were reinforced by the 1990s recession. In 1983 there were 3.7 million workers in the industry. By 1996 this figure had dropped to 2.1 million.

Much production has been relocated to lower-cost regions of the world such as south and south-east Asia, while EU companies often contract-out part of their production to eastern European firms.

In this sector, the EU is self-sufficient only in the leather industry. It is a net importer of textiles, clothing and footwear, with an overall trade deficit of some ECU 14 billion in 1996. Small and medium sized enterprises are particularly strong in this industry, accounting for more than half of total employment. There is a big concentration in Italy, Spain and Portugal.

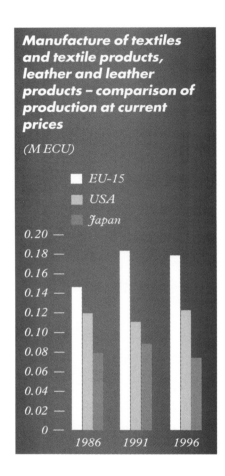

Manufacture of textiles and textile products, leather and leather products – comparison of production at current prices

(M ECU)

- EU-15
- USA
- Japan

Manufacture of textiles and textile products, leather and leather products – main indicators									
(M ECU except where specified)	1988	1989	1990	1991	1992	1993	1994	1995	1996
Apparent consumption	168,682	181,968	192,849	202,595	198,931	187,968	196,162	192,483	192,990
Production	159,664	173,358	181,411	184,461	181,390	169,832	178,835	178,388	178,971
Exports	19,841	23,423	23,791	23,152	24,086	25,833	30,133	31,955	34,995
Trade Balance	−9,018	−8,610	−11,438	−18,133	−17,540	−18,136	−17,327	−14,095	−14,019
Employment ('000)	2,850	2,810	2,828	2,747	2,579	2,409	2,334	2,240	2,138

13.4 Paper, printing and publishing - strong exports

The EU paper, printing and publishing industry ranks second behind the USA with 1996 production of ECU 240 billion against ECU 273 billion, although the gap is closing. It employs some 1.7 million people, although the recession led to employment falling by over 10% between 1991–1996.

The EU is the largest OECD exporter in both paper and printing, with over 60% of OECD exports in 1995. The trade balance has grown strongly over recent years to nearly ECU 7 billion. The UK, in particular, has benefited because of the wide use of the English language. The entry into the EU of Sweden and Finland led to the Community's pulp production trebling and paper and board output rising by 50%. Most of the EU's largest companies in this field are Scandinavian.

Printing and publishing is highly fragmented with tens of thousands of small companies, although the industry is polarised by the presence at the other end of some very large multimedia conglomerates.

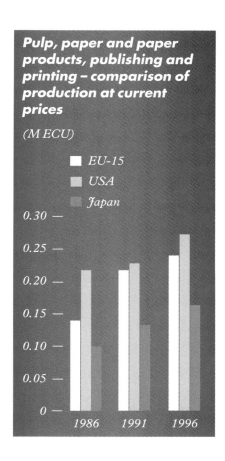

Pulp, paper and paper products, publishing and printing – comparison of production at current prices

(M ECU)

- EU-15
- USA
- Japan

Pulp, paper and paper products, publishing and printing – main indicators

(M ECU except where specified)

	1988	1989	1990	1991	1992	1993	1994	1995	1996
Apparent consumption	177,651	199,141	208,965	215,912	213,177	202,759	218,694	237,764	232,686
Production	181,062	201,662	211,341	217,915	215,665	207,184	223,380	242,757	239,507
Exports	10,849	11,891	11,422	11,208	11,543	12,980	14,861	17,890	18,405
Trade Balance	3,412	2,521	2,376	2,002	2,488	4,426	4,686	4,993	6,821
Employment ('000)	1,834	1,893	1,921	1,916	1,863	1,779	1,758	1,735	1,712

13.5 The chemical industry – the world's largest

The EU chemical industry is big both in the EU and internationally. It remains the world's largest, with production some 10% more than the USA and twice Japan's. It accounts for 11% of EU value-added. The recession in the early 1990s led to falling employment and static production. But in 1996 production stabilised at ECU 364 billion, 20% of which was exported. Employment, at 1.68 million, was some 230,000 below its 1989/1990 peak. Large enterprises account for over 70% of employment. Seven of the world's 10 largest chemical companies have their headquarters in Europe.

In recent years the trade balance has improved rapidly, topping ECU 25 billion in 1996. The EU is responsible for over 60% of OECD chemicals' exports.

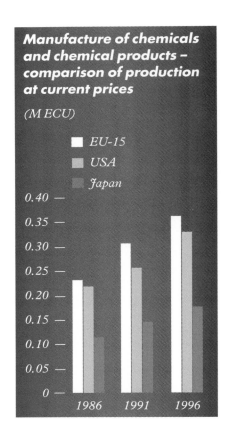

Manufacture of chemicals and chemical products – comparison of production at current prices

(M ECU)

■ EU-15
■ USA
■ Japan

Manufacture of chemicals and chemical products – main indicators

(M ECU except where specified)

	1988	1989	1990	1991	1992	1993	1994	1995	1996
Apparent consumption	261,791	289,226	291,708	297,582	299,773	285,263	306,799	344,476	338,137
Production	273,423	299,650	300,381	307,257	310,660	304,985	328,683	363,391	363,784
Exports	35,204	38,605	38,058	40,248	42,516	51,016	57,881	60,360	68,267
Trade Balance	11,633	10,424	8,673	9,675	10,887	19,722	21,884	18,915	25,647
Employment ('000)	1,885	1,907	1,906	1,902	1,865	1,777	1,716	1,703	1,675

13.6 Rubber and plastics – the EU leads

In 1996, over 1.1 million people were employed in rubber and plastics, little changed from 10 years previously. The industry had a production value of over ECU 125 billion. The EU has overtaken the USA in recent years with Japan in third place. Some 10% of EU output is exported. The industry's trade balance is positive and rose to over ECU 3 billion in 1996.

In value terms, the plastics processing industry is about three times the size of the rubber industry. Tyres are the rubber industry's largest product. The world tyre market is dominated by large multinationals with three European companies in the top 10. In contrast, only a dozen EU plastics companies employ over 1,000 people.

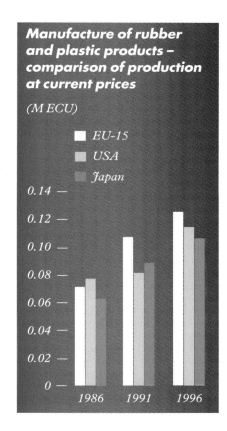

Manufacture of rubber and plastic products – comparison of production at current prices

(M ECU)

■ EU-15
■ USA
■ Japan

1986 · 1991 · 1996

Manufacture of rubber and plastic products – main indicators

(M ECU except where specified)	1988	1989	1990	1991	1992	1993	1994	1995	1996
Apparent consumption	83,389	94,154	100,626	106,362	109,209	105,380	114,667	122,913	122,191
Production	85,924	96,735	102,752	107,949	110,553	107,580	117,066	125,641	125,484
Exports	7,225	8,129	8,009	8,129	8,502	9,662	10,845	12,361	13,606
Trade Balance	2,535	2,581	2,126	1,587	1,344	2,201	2,399	2,728	3,292
Employment ('000)	1,097	1,148	1,190	1,194	1,169	1,120	1,120	1,136	1,113

13.7 Non-metallic minerals – the EU leads again

Non-metallic mineral products are used mainly in construction. In 1996, EU production was over ECU 120 billion and the industry employed just over a million people, about 200, 000 below its 1990 peak. Over the last decade the EU has significantly increased its lead both over Japan, which lies in second place, and over the USA.

Some 10% of output is exported. The industry's trade surplus rose to ECU 7.3 billion in 1996. Companies range from major international construction groups to small family-owned firms. The location of production sites is often governed by the presence of raw materials and by transport costs.

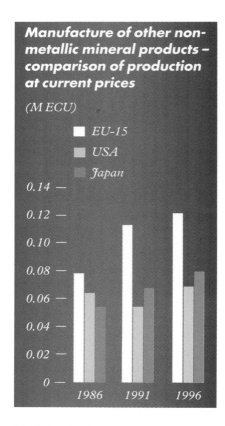

Manufacture of other non-metallic mineral products – comparison of production at current prices

(M ECU)

■ EU-15
■ USA
■ Japan

Manufacture of other non-metallic mineral products – main indicators

(M ECU except where specified)

	1988	1989	1990	1991	1992	1993	1994	1995	1996
Apparent consumption	89,229	98,994	103,440	107,455	109,839	103,409	108,613	113,885	113,247
Production	94,072	104,312	108,392	111,939	114,072	108,351	114,526	120,095	120,552
Exports	7,158	8,083	7,933	7,963	8,040	8,863	10,220	10,987	12,215
Trade Balance	4,844	5,318	4,952	4,483	4,233	4,942	5,914	6,210	7,305
Employment ('000)	1,215	1,238	1,245	1,235	1,195	1,106	1,077	1,075	1,034

13.8 Metals – the largest manufacturing employer

Basic metals and metal products is the largest industry in employment terms in EU manufacturing (although not in industry as a whole where it is second to construction). It includes three sectors – iron and steel, non-ferrous metals and metalworking. At 2.84 million in 1996, employment was over half-a-million below its 1990 peak.

After falling in the early 1990s recession, production stabilised at ECU 358 billion in 1996. The EU remains ahead of USA.

In 1996, 12% of production was exported. Over the last decade the trade balance has fluctuated from positive to negative.

Metalworking produces mainly for downstream industries such as mechanical engineering, construction and the motor industry, hard hit by the recession. But production recovered to ECU 190 billion in 1996 with employment at 1.9 million, 10% below the peak. In 1996, the EU was the world's largest producer of metal products with a trade surplus of over ECU 8 billion.

Non-ferrous metals extraction is very low in the EU with refining more significant. The industry employed just under 200,000 in 1996. Production was worth ECU 45 billion and there was a trade deficit of over ECU 14 billion.

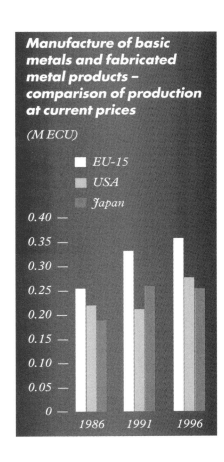

Manufacture of basic metals and fabricated metal products – comparison of production at current prices

(M ECU)

- EU-15
- USA
- Japan

Manufacture of basic metals and fabricated metal products – main indicators

(M ECU except where specified)	1988	1989	1990	1991	1992	1993	1994	1995	1996
Apparent consumption	299,855	344,266	338,381	333,371	327,808	293,270	324,965	367,187	356,165
Production	297,689	343,700	337,015	332,193	324,738	296,709	326,233	361,562	358,087
Exports	30,563	33,809	29,966	30,261	28,890	34,899	38,021	39,634	43,416
Trade Balance	−2,166	−566	−1,366	−1,178	−3,070	3,439	1,269	−5,625	1,923
Employment ('000)	3,290	3,357	3,378	3,341	3,236	2,931	2,882	2,885	2,836

13.9 Mechanical engineering industry – export success

Mechanical engineering plays a central role in manufacturing in supplying capital goods to other sectors. Production declined in the recession of the early 1990s but then recovered slightly to ECU 317 billion in 1996. Employment fell from nearly 3.1 million in 1990 to a low of just over 2.6 million in 1994, recovering slightly afterwards. In the 10 years to 1996 the EU industry remained the world's largest. The Japanese overtook the USA to gain second place.

In 1996 the EU exported over 30% of its output and the extra-EU trade balance reached an all-time high of over ECU 63 billion. This was over two-thirds the total industrial trade balance and over twice that of the next most successful industry, chemicals. This success helped to cushion the effects of recession. It is an industry with processes that lend themselves to small firms. It consists of some 140,000 companies but only about 800 have over 500 employees.

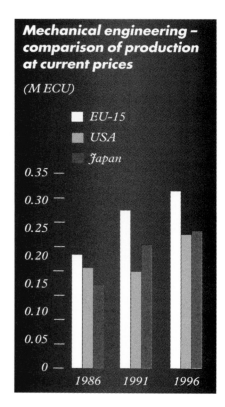

Mechanical engineering – comparison of production at current prices

(M ECU)

- EU-15
- USA
- Japan

Mechanical engineering – main indicators

(M ECU except where specified)

	1988	1989	1990	1991	1992	1993	1994	1995	1996
Apparent consumption	199,865	227,741	245,606	247,965	243,351	215,821	230,235	252,370	253,819
Production	228,860	260,097	280,377	282,398	279,060	261,850	280,729	307,153	317,316
Exports	49,271	56,251	59,837	60,526	61,520	71,219	78,546	86,467	98,280
Trade Balance	28,995	32,356	34,771	34,434	35,709	46,029	50,494	54,784	63,497
Employment ('000)	2,914	2,998	3,088	3,042	2,916	2,708	2,608	2,620	2,628

13.10 Electrical and electronic engineering – greatest value-added

The electrical and electronic engineering industry manufactures a wide range of products, including household appliances, computers and telecommunications equipment. It is the biggest contributor to total EU industrial value-added. In 1996 the industry's production value topped ECU 371 billion. This was 60% higher than ten years earlier. Over 2 million people were employed. While the numbers employed were half-a-million below those at the the 1989 peak, the industry was still the second most important employer in manufacturing.

Unlike most sectors of manufacturing industry, however, EU output is less than that of both Japan and the USA. Just over 20% of production is exported, but the trade balance is strongly negative at ECU –22.6 billion. Despite improved efficiency and productivity, the EU has lost ground, especially to Japanese competition.

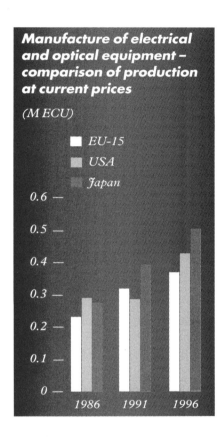

Manufacture of electrical and optical equipment – comparison of production at current prices

(M ECU)

- EU-15
- USA
- Japan

Manufacture of electrical and optical equipment – main indicators

(M ECU except where specified)

	1988	1989	1990	1991	1992	1993	1994	1995	1996
Apparent consumption	286,459	319,446	334,551	349,179	347,323	331,365	356,256	375,910	393,658
Production	264,982	294,176	310,194	319,611	319,748	307,984	330,746	352,305	371,028
Exports	34,730	38,467	40,403	42,283	44,265	52,477	61,522	69,288	76,762
Trade Balance	–21,476	–25,270	–24,357	–29,568	–27,575	–23,381	–25,510	–23,605	–22,630
Employment ('000)	3,279	3,343	3,335	3,310	3,162	2,943	2,846	2,842	2,806

13.11 Transport equipment – motor-vehicles dominate

Motor-vehicle construction dominates the transport equipment industry, accounting for over two-thirds of production. In 1996, EU production of ECU 424 billion was about 10% more than USA and a further 10% ahead of Japan. Following the recession of the early 1990s, employment in 1996, at 2.43 million, was 450,000 below the 1990 peak.

Transport equipment production is concentrated in Germany, France, the UK and Italy. Germany dominates motor vehicle construction, railway rolling stock is mainly in French hands, and France and UK share over 70% of aircraft construction. In the motor vehicles industry in 1992, 3% of firms employed 86% of the workforce.

Some 13% of production is exported. The EU had a positive trade balance of ECU 16 billion in 1996. It accounts for about a third of world production and sales of motor vehicles.

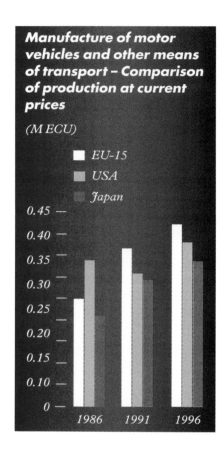

Manufacture of motor vehicles and other means of transport – Comparison of production at current prices

(M ECU)

- EU-15
- USA
- Japan

Manufacture of motor vehicles and other means of transport – main indicators									
(M ECU except where specified)									
	1988	1989	1990	1991	1992	1993	1994	1995	1996
Apparent consumption	293,771	337,163	356,886	367,576	380,875	331,999	364,102	381,747	407,828
Production	296,631	335,265	356,184	364,754	379,909	335,771	373,636	396,250	423,918
Exports	26,376	29,859	30,816	33,113	34,309	39,714	44,585	49,236	54,691
Trade Balance	2,860	−1,897	−702	−2,823	−966	3,772	9,534	14,503	16,090
Employment ('000)	2,779	2,814	2,882	2,828	2,737	2,529	2,430	2,426	2,433

13.12 Other manufacturing – substantial growth

Other manufacturing industries – woodworking, furniture, jewellery, toys, sporting goods etc. – experienced substantial growth in the 10 years to 1996 with relatively stable employment and improved productivity.

The sector had production of ECU 140 billion in 1996 and employed just under 1.5 million.
It exported 17% of production with a trade deficit of ECU –3.8 billion.

13.13 Construction – the largest workforce

Construction – building and civil engineering – is a key EU industry. It accounts for some 7% of total EU employment and nearly 6% of gross value-added. After being hit by the recession, it suffered a new decline in output volume in 1996. The employment index for 1996 also showed a new fall (–2.1%).

In 1994, small and medium-sized enterprises of under 250 employees represented over 99% of all construction businesses and provided about 86% of jobs. Some 9.5 million workers were employed in construction out of an estimated 41.6 million in industry overall. This makes it larger than any other EU industrial sector in terms of the numbers of workers. An estimated 21% of all in the sector are self-employed.

FURTHER READING

Eurostat publications

Monthly Panorama of European Industry
Enterprises in Europe
Iron and steel, Yearly statistics
Iron and steel, monthly
Energy and industry, Rapid Reports/Statistics in Focus

Electronic products

Eurostat Yearbook CD-ROM
Panorama of EU industry 1995–96
Competitiveness indicators CD-ROM
Comext CD-ROM
Eurostat's New Cronos database
European on the move
Increasing industrial competitiveness

Other publications

Panorama of EU Industry 1997
White Paper on growth, competitiveness and employment

Employment in the construction industry – annual growth rates(1)

	1991	1992	1993	1994	1995	1996
EU-15	0.3	–4.0	–4.3	–0.3	2.2	–2.1
B	4.7	0.5	–3.0	–1.4	2.1	-0.8
DK	–4.7	0.7	–1.9	7.5	3.2	0.2
D(2)	1.6	3.0	4.4	5.1	4.0	–6.3
EL	:	:	:	:	:	:
E	4.3	–6.1	–8.8	–2.9	7.2	3.6
F	–0.7	–3.6	–5.6	–1.6	–0.5	–4.2
IRL	–3.2	–2.1	–6.0	2.5	4.4	8.2
I	5.6	–5.7	–8.0	–3.6	–2.4	–1.1
L	3.7	0.6	–0.5	–4.8	–2.5	–2.8
NL	0.0	–0.6	–3.7	–0.9	1.2	:
A	0.8	4.8	0.8	1.3	–3.4	:
P	:	:	:	:	:	:
FIN	–13.0	–17.0	–17.0	–10.5	6.7	2.5
S	2.6	–15.8	–14.1	–7.0	4.4	0.5
UK	–7.3	–10.5	–7.2	–1.9	–0.7	–0.4

(1) Derived from short term indices
(2) Including the former East Germany. Data prior to 1991 have been estimated by Eurostat.

14 Services
14.1 The post-industrial society

For over two decades, European economies have been undergoing a major structural change due to the increased 'deindustrialisation' of economic activity. Europe has entered a stage of 'post-industrial' economy or 'information society', with the services sector as the cornerstone. Services now dominate the European economies both in terms of wealth created and of employment. Market services (those supplied on a commercial basis) alone give work to around 65 million Europeans, almost half the total number of persons employed. They create more than half of the total output or 'value added'.

The increasing importance of the services sector is normal for advanced economies. It was also encouraged by the restructuring of the industrial sector which occurred after the oil crisis of 1973/74. As a result of the re-organisation of the production process that followed this crisis, manufacturing industries have increasingly outsourced non-core activities to independent service providers. Consequently, the services sector now plays a considerable role in the overall competitiveness of manufacturing industries. Indeed, the ability of a product to compete depends on a variety of services. Even before the production process begins, services come into play in the form of feasibility studies, market research, product design, etc. Business services such as quality control, equipment leasing, maintenance and repair are an integral part of the production process itself. In the final stage, services play an essential role not only in the advertising, transport and distribution of a product but also in after-sales support (maintenance, repairs and client training, for example). Lastly, software, accountancy, management consultancy, training, telecommunications, insurance and financial intermediation services are all crucial to the smooth running of a business.

In addition to this economic mutation, European economies have had to face profound sociological changes, such as the increased weight of the elderly population and of working women, rising environmental awareness, or the reduction in working time. These changes created new or increased needs in such fields as local services, information services (Internet), audio-visual, leisure and cultural services, and health services, improving the quality of life and environmental protection.

14.2 Services dominate the EU economy

In 1995, market and non-market services accounted for ECU 3,978 billion – two-thirds of total EU GDP. This lies between the USA figure of 72% and the Japanese figure of 60%. Japan is the only one of the three where industry has grown more than services.

Small firms, much employment

Services employed over 94 million people in 1995 – 66% of the EU's total active population. Since 1982, the EU has created 17 million new jobs in this sector. Services are the largest contributor to employment in the USA and Japan as well as in Europe. Market services alone gave work to almost 65 million people in the EU in 1995, 45% of the total. That was more than twice the number of persons employed by manufacturing industries during the same year. A comparable ratio could be observed in Japan but in the USA market services employed three times more people than manufacturing industries at 62 million persons against 19 million. Together with non-market services, a total of 94 million Europeans, 90 million Americans and 39 million Japanese are active in the tertiary sector, compared to 40 million, 26 million and 23 million in industry.

This prevalence of service activities within the economy is clear. In Europe, employment in services represents two out of three jobs and in the USA three out of four. The

Breakdown of total employment, 1995

(%)

■ Services
■ Industry
■ Agriculture

EU-15   USA(1)   JPN

(1) 1994

Japanese economy witnesses the lowest weight of services in employment terms (59%) and the highest share of persons active in industry and agriculture, 34% and 7% respectively. This compares with 28% and 5% in Europe and only 22% and 3% in the USA.

The relative shares in employment of each of the main national accounts branches (agriculture, industry and services) show that the European Union stands between the USA and Japan. Services employ relatively more people in the USA and relatively less in Japan. Industry and agriculture employ relatively more people in Japan and less in the USA.

Over the long term, the share of services in total employment has witnessed a strong upward trend in all three markets. In 1970, around 45% of people in employment in Japan and Europe worked in

Employment by major industrial branch, 1995

(millions)

	EU-15	EUR-11	USA(1)	JPN
Agriculture	7.8	6.2	3.3	4.9
Energy	1.7	1.1	1.3	0.4
Construction	8.1	7.7	6.3	7.0
Manufacturing and mining	30.6	22.7	18.6	15.1
Market services	64.6	45.6	62.4	33.4
Non-market services	29.7	22.8	27.7	5.8
Total	142.5	106.1	119.6	66.7

(1) 1994.

services compared with 65% in the USA. Since then, Europe has been closing the gap with the USA at a faster rate than Japan.

Value added

It can be clearly seen that the service economy is the largest contributor to value added in the EU, just as it is in the USA and Japan. Market services' contribution to wealth creation is even larger than its contribution to employment, accounting for just over half the total value added generated by the whole EU economy (ECU 3,100 billion in 1995 out of ECU 5,883 billion). This was two and a half

times as much as the value added of manufacturing industries. The same pattern can be observed in the USA and Japan, although the gap between market services and industry is somewhat narrower in Japan and somewhat wider in the USA. In the latter case, market services represent no less than 60% of total value added (almost ECU 3,500 billion). It can be seen that market services is the only branch in which the EU generated less value added than the USA.

Total services – market and non-market – account for 66% of EU value added. The corresponding figure for the USA is 6 percentage

points higher, at 72% while for Japan it is six percentage points lower, at 60%. The structural analysis section of this chapter provides greater detail on the contribution of each branch of services to total value added. Over the long term, services value added has grown faster than other branches of the economy. In 1970, services represented about half of European total value added while the corresponding shares were 47% in Japan and 63% in the USA. Since then, the growth of services' share of the total in the EU has been faster than in either the USA or Japan.

Value added by major industrial branch, 1995

(bn ECU)

	EU-15	EUR-11	USA(1)	JPN
Agriculture	136.5	104.0	100.8	75.8
Energy	281.9	221.6	164.8	111.0
Construction	324.8	264.6	229.3	404.0
Manufacturing and mining	1,271.0	1,029.0	1,092.2	978.1
Market services	3,089.2	2,485.5	3,462.5	1,951.8
Non-market services	889.3	705.1	651.7	405.2
Total	5,992.7	4,809.7	5,701.2	3,925.9

(1) 1994.

14.3 Structural analysis

In the previous section we saw that services account for over 66% of employment and value added in the EU. This analysis will examine in more detail which branches within services have contributed to this dominant position.

Services are grouped into two main branches: market services and non-market services. Market services are further broken down into:

- distributive trades and repair services
- lodging and catering services (referred to as Horeca – hotels, restaurants and cafes – in this analysis)
- transport services,
- communication services
- credit, financial intermediation and insurance services (referred to as financial services in this analysis)
- other market services.

Services employed 94 million persons and generated ECU 4,000 billion of value added in Europe in 1995. Market services accounted for 69% of employment in services and for 78% of the wealth created.

Thus market services has a higher level of labour productivity. Indeed, the value added by each person occupied in market services exceeded ECU 47, 800 per capita, whilst it was only ECU 29,900 per capita in non-market services. By comparison, labour productivity was ECU 41,500 per capita in the manufacturing branch of the European economy and ECU 42,000 per capita for the European economy in total.

Distributive trades and repair activities account for over one third of market services employment but due to lower levels of labour productivity, the branch contributes only a quarter of total value added in market services. The " other market services" branch is the second most important for employment accounting for nearly 32% of the persons employed in market services. This branch groups miscellaneous service activities not fitting into the definition of other branches, such as business services to enterprises, computer and related activities, real estate, renting, and research and development. It has experienced spectacular growth during the past 25 years. With very high labour productivity, the total wealth created in the EU by other market services represents no less than 47% of the total value added of market services, some 15 percentage points more than its employment share.

Horeca and transport services (inland, maritime and air transport plus auxiliary transport services) both employ approximately 10% of the total market services workforce. In both cases, their share in total market services value added is lower than the corresponding employment figure. The difference

Structure of services in the EU, 1995(1)

	Employment(2) (millions)	Value added (billion ECU)
Market services	64.6	3,089.2
of which (% breakdown)		
distributive trades	36.5%	24.9%
horeca (3)	9.9%	5.5%
transport services	10.0%	8.5%
communication services	3.9%	4.5%
financial services	6.9%	10.6%
other market services	31.5%	46.5%
Non-market services	29.7	889.3

(1) Earlier years had to be used for the breakdown of market services branches.
(2) Excluding Greece, except for market services and non-marketservices totals.
(3) Excluding Greece for value added.

is wider for Horeca (4.4 percentage points) than for transport services (1.5 percentage points). This suggests that labour productivity in Horeca is lower than in transport services. Indeed, a look at the data from 1990 onwards shows that value added per capita is consistently higher in transport services in all Member States (except Spain).

Financial services display particularly high performance ratios. They employ about 7% of the persons active in market services in Europe, but they represent a much higher share of the creation of wealth (10.6%). Labour productivity is slightly higher even than other market services. Communication services (4% of employment and 4.5% of value added in market services) also have above-average labour productivity.

14.4 EU transport dominated by roads

Transport accounts for around 7.5% of EU GDP and around 4% of total employment. Total transport accounts for around 30% of energy consumption with a serious impact on the environment including approximately 25% of CO_2 and 60% of NO_x emissions.

The EU has one of the world's densest transport networks. Germany, the Netherlands, Luxembourg and Belgium have the densest motorway networks with 30–55 km of motorway per 1,000 km² of land area. Motorway density is lower in Italy, France, UK and Denmark – 10–20 km per 1,000 km² – and relatively sparse in other Member States.

The Rhine, navigable for 1,000 km, is the backbone of the inland waterway network. Most sea transport is concentrated in some 60 ports, each handling upwards of 10 million tonnes of cargo a year and six with more than 50 million tonnes. Rotterdam is the world's largest port – handling 291 million tonnes in 1995.

Air traffic is particularly dense in the London-Paris-Frankfurt triangle. Of the 18 airports with a total of more than 10 million passengers embarked and disembarked in 1995, 8 were in this area.

Transport infrastructure is crucial to the single market and EU social cohesion. The EU has launched a series of strategic projects covering the period up to the year 2010 to establish a genuine trans-European transport network covering major arteries. Eventually, 70,000 km of rail track, 23,000 km of it permitting speeds up to 200 km an hour, will link key centres of activity. The trans-European road network will total 58,000 km while the inland waterways network will comprise 12,000 km.

Most goods go by road

In 1995, 41% of EU external trade goods – exports and imports – went by road. Sea transport accounted for 30%, rail for 6% and inland waterways for 13%. Road transport dominates transport of traded manufactured products (65%), carrying 62% of food, 58% of chemicals, and 55% of agricultural produce.

When internal trade is included roads transport counted for 82% of total EU transport tonnage – 10.7 billion tonnes out of a total of 13.0 billion tonnes. Two-thirds of freight carried by domestic road haulage travels less than 50 km.

In total, when tonnage and distance are both considered, road freight transport accounts for some 58% of the EU's 1,920 billion tonne-kilometres (tkm), rail 11% and inland waterways 6%. Twenty-five years ago, with 890 billion tkm, the figures were 48%, 32% and 12% respectively. This means road haulage has more than doubled while rail and inland waterway have remained more or less stable. A top

Length of transport networks in 1995

(km)

	Motorways	Railway lines	Inland waterways
EU-15	47,376	155,836	30,551
B	1,666	3,368	1,513
DK	830	2,349	-
D	11,190	41,719	7,343
EL	420	2,474	–
E	6,485(1)	12,280	–
F	8,275	31,939	5,962
IRL	72	1,947	–
I	8,860	15,998	1,466
L	123	275	37
NL	2,208	2,739	5,046
A	1,596	5,672	351
P	687	2,850	–
FIN	394	5,880	6,120
S	1,262	9,782(2)	360(3)
UK	3,308	16,564	2,353

(1) 1994.
(2) Not including private lines (614km in 1994
(3) Used by seagoing vessels.

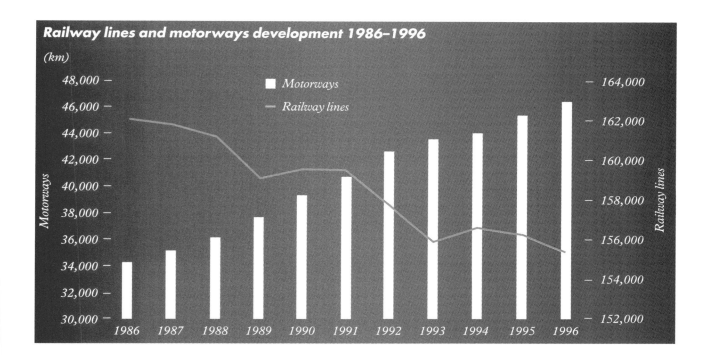

Railway lines and motorways development 1986–1996

Transport equipment in 1995

	Passenger cars ('000)	Buses and coaches (number)	Lorries and road tractors 1994 ('000)	Rail – Passenger transport vehicles (2) (number)	Rail – Goods transport wagons 1994 (number)	Inland water- ways – goods transport vessels (5) 1994 (number)	Number of aircraft over 9 tonnes (8) 1993 (number)	Total merchant fleet controlled 1996 (mio dwt)
EU-15	163,215	536,301	18,463	77,370	734,729	:	:	217.0
B	4,273	14,667	443	3,139	19,927	1,604(6)	96	3.9
DK	1,674	14,000	449	1,688	5,099	-	114	11.4
D	40,404	86,000	2,234	18,944	318,511	4,597	501	17.0
EL	2,209	24,600	850(1)	869	11,103	-	59	118.3
E	14,212	47,400	2,826(1)	4,273	31,484	-	253	3.3
F	27,762	48,274	3,774	15,799	146,150	2,368	637	6.9
IRL	952	6,082	130(1)	331	1,885	-	144	0.2
I	31,001	77,000	2,605	13,494	89,993(3)	3,136(4)	255	10.8
L	229	846	25	146	2,611	29(7)	:	0.1
NL	5,883	12,000	650(1)	2,611	4,290	5,792	145	5.0
A	3,593	9,752	689	3,792	34,770	151	:	0.5
P	3,751	15,020	621	1,380	4,819	-	50	1.2
FIN	1,901	8,083	249	957	15,110	153	58	3.6
S	3,631	14,577	308	1,633	21,343	:	148	13.4
UK	21,740	158,000	2,610	8,314	27,634(4)	:	656	21.3

(1) Not including road tractors
(2) Rail coaches, railcars and trailers
(3) Ente Ferrovie dello Stato only
(4) 1993
(5) Self propelled, dumb and pushed vessels
(6) 1992
(7) Self propelled vessels only
(8) Source: ICAO (International Civil Aviation Organization)

EU priority is developing combined rail/road transport.

In 1979, almost 30% of world merchant fleet tonnage belonged to the EU, then 9 countries. By 1992 this was down to 15%.

Air transport skyrockets

In 1995, slightly more than 270,000 million passenger kilometres were done by rail. The number has increased by almost 25% since 1970 whereas air transport has incresead by more than 500%, from 43,000 million passenger-kilometres to 274,000 million passenger-kilometres overtaking rail transport in 1995. The most important airports are London (Heathrow and Gatwick), Paris (Charles de Gaulle and Orly) and Frankfurt, with 67 million, 34 million and 30 million international passengers embarked or disembarked in 1995. Nevertheless transport by car accounts for around 80% of all passenger kilometres.

Inland goods transport 1995

		Road		Rail		Inland waterways	
	Total(1)	bn tkm	%	bn tkm	%	bn tkm	%
EU-15	1,439.0	1,102.0	77	220.0	15	116.0	8
B	55.5	42.6	77	7.3	13	5.6	10
DK	11.2	9.3	83	1.9	17	–	–
D	404.9	271.1	67	69.8	17	64.0	16
EL	15.8	15.5	98	0.3	2	–	–
E	190.0	180.0	95	10.0	5	–	–
F	185.8	132.0	71	47.9	26	5.9	3
IRL	6.0	5.4	90	0.6	10	–	–
I	216.0	193.7	90	22.2	10	0.1	0
L	1.3	0.5	38	0.5	38	0.3	23
NL	64.7	27.1	42	3.1	5	34.5	53
A	31.7	15.7	50	13.9	44	2.1	7
P	13.1	11.1	85	2.0	15	–	–
FIN	35.3	22.4	63	9.6	27	3.3	9
S	47.8	29.3	61	18.5	39	–	–
UK	159.4	146.7	92	12.5	8	0.2	0

(1) excluding pipelines – 6% of EU total

14.5 The world's favourite tourism destination

The EU remains the world's most popular tourist destination and the main source of tourists to the rest of the world. In 1996 it had 40% of international arrivals, 38% of international tourism receipts and 42% of total spending.

Despite the difficulty of fully assessing the contribution of tourism to the general economy, it is estimated that EU tourism-related activities – hotels and other accommodation, restaurants and catering, travel services and recreation parks – contribute 6% of total employment, 5.5% of GDP and a third of international trade in services. Links with other key economic sectors probably makes its economic contribution even higher. At a global level, France remained second to the USA in 1996 in tourism earnings with receipts amounting to ECU 22.3

billion followed by Spain (21.8 billion) and Italy (21.5 billion).

In 1996 there were nearly 190,000 EU hotels and similar establishments compared to 180,000 in 1990. The number of beds has risen to 8.9 million from 7.8 million, reflecting also the fact that the average size of accommodation establishments was increasing. EU tourism demand amounted to ECU 1.69 billion in terms of nights spent by tourists in accommodation establishments in 1995 compared with 1.64 billion in 1994. Over 60% of tourist nights is attributable to domestic tourism. The annual rise was particularly strong in the Netherlands (10.2%), UK (10.2%) and Sweden (6.9%).

In 1996 the Germans confirmed their position as the EU's main world travellers, second only to the

Hotels and similar establishments

	Number of establishments				Number of beds		
	1994	*1995*	*1996*		*1994*	*1995*	*1996*
EU-15	188,413	189,443	189,568	EU-15	8,684,558	8,661,497	8,941227
B	1,946	2,038	2,062	B	108,811	114,887	117,299
DK	565	564	478	DK	99,275	98,991	60,080
D	37,307	38,226	38,565	D	1,380,713	1,494,024	1,490,769
EL	7,604	7,754	7,916	EL	508,408	557,188	571,656
E	10,063	10,422	9,482	E	1,053,355	1,031,684	1,025,208
F	19,645	20,147	20,849	F	1,379,955	1,193,340	1,472,424
IRL	5,034	5,039	5,274	IRL	100,000	96,900	96,905
I	34,549	34,296	34,080	I	1,724,333	1,738,031	176,4651
L	372	369	368	L	14,705	14,748	14,750
NL	1,726	1,749	1,739	NL	138,060	142,516	142,800
A	18,402	18,120	17,990	A	650,020	646,125	640,199
P	1,728	1,733	1,744	P	202,442	204,051	208,205
FIN	951	936	958	FIN	106,374	105,030	108,438
S	1,855	1,829	1,842	S	173,521	173,759	177,620
UK	46,666	46,221	4,6221	UK	1,044,586	1,050,223	1,050,223

(1) Only establishments with 40 beds or more
(2) Figures for beds are estimated on the basis of 1.8 beds per room
(3) 1996 figures not comparable with previous years due to a break in the series

Main originating countries in 1994

(figures based on overnight stays in all tourist accommodation establishments)

	First market		Second market		Third market		Fourth market		Share of top four markets
B	The Netherlands	34%	Germany	21%	United Kingdom	11%	France	11%	77%
DK	Germany	43%	Sweden	18%	Norway	11%	The Netherlands	7%	79%
D	The Netherlands	20%	CEEC	10%	United Kingdom	10%	USA	9%	49%
EL	Germany	37%	United Kingdom	16%	Italy	6%	France	5%	64%
E	Germany	33%	United Kingdom	28%	France	7%	Italy	6%	74%
F	The Netherlands	19%	Germany	19%	United Kingdom	19%	Italy	10%	67%
IRL(1)	United Kingdom	37%	USA	22%	Germany	8%	France	8%	75%
I	Germany	40%	United Kingdom	7%	France	6%	USA	6%	59%
L	The Netherlands	45%	Belgium	22%	Germany	10%	France	5%	82%
NL	Germany	53%	United Kingdom	10%	Belgium	7%	USA	5%	75%
A	Germany	63%	The Netherlands	8%	United Kingdom	4%	Switzerland	4%	79%
P	United Kingdom	27%	Germany	23%	Spain	10%	The Netherlands	9%	69%
FIN	Germany	20%	Sweden	20%	United Kingdom	5%	USA	5%	51%
S	Germany	28%	Norway	20%	Denmark	11%	The Netherlands	6%	64%
UK(2)	USA	17%	France	16%	Germany	15%	Ireland	8%	56%
EU-15	Germany	26%	United Kingdom	12%	Netherlands	9%	USA	4%	51%

(1) Nights spent by non-residents in hotels and similar establishments only
(2) Arrivals in all accommodation types including non commercial

Nights spent in all types of tourist accommodation

(’000)

	1995			1996		
	Nights spent by residents	Nights spent by non-residents	Nights spent total	Nights spent by residents	Nights spent by non-residents	Nights spent total
B	14,133	13,878	28,010	14,288	14,441	28,729
DK	14,835	10,791	25,626	17,059	10,778	27,837
D	288,283	35,481	323,764	285,930	35,460	321,390
EL	13,061	39,565	52,626	12,932	36,243	49,175
E	72,536	107,787	180,323	71,762	106,658	178,420
F	155,126	87,548	242,674	150,694	83,622	234,316
IRL	12,722	14,011	26,733	10,011	16,974	26,985
I	173,494	113,001	286,495	173,347	118,024	291,371
L	228	2,327	2,555	217	2,153	2,370
NL	42,179	19,736	61,915	42,334	19,043	61,377
A	24,452	63,840	88,292	23,413	62,411	85,824
P	13,965	22,240	36,205	14,528	21,708	36,236
FIN	10,631	3,292	13,923	10,729	3,288	14,017
S	29,428	7,861	37,289	28,848	7,701	36,549
UK	172,600	131,740	304,340	181,500	137,160	318,660
EU-15	1,037,673	673,098	1,710,770	1,037,592	675,664	1,713,256

USA. Their spending in this field was ECU 39.2 billion – followed by UK (20.5 billion), France (13.8 billion) and Italy (10.2 billion). Europe is expected to remain the biggest single international tourism market – by origin and by destination – thanks to its richness and diversity.

FURTHER READING

Eurostat publications

Tourism in Europe – Key Figures 1995–1996, 1996–1997

Tourism in the Mediterranean countries – Key Figures 1994–1995, 1996–1997

Tourism in Europe 1995

Tourism Annual Statistics 1994

Services – Annual Statistics 1996

Statistics on selected service sectors in the EU

Insurance in Europe

Electronic products

Services – Annual Statistics CD-ROM 1996

Eurostat Yearbook CD-ROM

Panorama of EU Industry CD-ROM

Eurostat's New Cronos database (Regio)

European documentation

Commission proposal for a Council Decision on a First multi-annual programme to assist European tourism "Philoxenia" (1997–2000) [COM(96)635 Final of 04.12.96]

Report from the Commission on Community measures affecting tourism (COM(97)332 final of 02.07.1997)

Other publications

Putting services to work – Communication from the Commission, November 1996

15 Economic and Monetary Union (EMU)

15.1 Growing financial integration

European financial integration continues day by day with funds reinvested ever more freely by financial intermediaries regardless of national borders. The euro – the European single currency – replaced the ECU at the start of the third stage of Economic and Monetary Union (EMU) on 1 January 1999. For eleven of the fifteen Member States exchange rates are now irrevocably locked and a common monetary policy is in place.

Why EMU?

Economic and Monetary Union (EMU) began as an historic European project – a crucial step in European economic and political integration. It is the logical conclusion of the single market and a symbol of the progress of political integration in Europe since World War Two.

Why is Europe introducing the euro, the new single currency? The positive effects fall into three broad categories: significant enhancement of the single market; stabilising effects on the economic environment; and increased stability of the global monetary system. The single market has already transformed Europe's trading environment. The evidence suggests that it has created many new jobs and added significantly to EU growth since its creation.

The euro will take the single market further still. Just two examples:

- *Costs associated with converting one Community currency to another will be eliminated. These currently account for 0.5 % of EU GDP.*
- *It will increase price transparency. Consumers will be able to compare prices more directly. Firms will be able to compare costs more easily. This will boost competition which, in turn, should bring down prices.*

The institutional arrangements supporting EMU are designed to deliver a stable economic environment, with low inflation, sound public finances and low interest rates. The independent European Central Bank (ECB) will pursue price stability as its key objective. Inflation expectations will remain low and national economies converge, leading to lower interest rates and thus stronger economic growth.

The euro-zone will be a pole of stability in the international monetary system and the euro will progressively become an international currency. Although the euro is not leading to an overnight shift on currency markets, the European Commission expects to see a continued move away from the dollar – a process already underway.

EMU = a better EU

EMU, of course, is not exclusively an economic objective in itself but also a political one: the aim is to improve, at all levels, the lives of EU citizens – as much in civil liberties and culture as in economic achievement. It is seen as a key step forward in the process of European integration that began way back in 1952.

15.2 The road to EMU

Early developments

Although it was not explicitly mentioned in the Treaty of Rome, monetary union – the use of a single currency – became an early goal of the European Community. However initial attempts in the early 1970s foundered due to world-wide financial turmoil in the wake of the collapse of the global fixed-exchange rate system and the first oil crisis.

A subsequent attempt was made later in the 1970s and the European Monetary System (EMS) was set up by the European Council on 12 March 1979. Its three main components were the ECU, the exchange rate mechanism (ERM) and the credit mechanism. They were administered initially by the European Monetary Cooperation Fund (EMCF) and then, from 1994, by the European Monetary Institute (EMI).

ECU – the first currency for Europe

The European Currency Unit or ECU was a notional currency valued in terms of a basket of fixed amounts of Member State currencies. At its inception on 13 March 1979, the ECU was made up of a basket of the then nine EU currencies weighted according to countries' GDP and share of internal EC trade. The ECU was redefined twice: in September 1984, when the Greek drachma became part of the basket, and in September 1989, when the Spanish peseta and the Portuguese escudo were introduced. Neither occasion affected its external value.

The ECU did not become a formal currency in the sense that notes and coins were issued (apart from small commemorative issues). However,

in addition to official use it became an instrument for commercial transactions used by many private companies. The ECU Banking Association and the Bank for International Settlements were jointly responsible for clearing ECU transactions. An average of ECU 46.9 billion was cleared daily in 1997.

ECU-denominated bonds were also actively traded on financial markets. At end-1997 the total amount outstanding of national and international ECU-denominated bonds was ECU 116 billion although this was an ECU 20 billion decline from end-1994.

Exchange rate mechanism

The goal of the exchange rate mechanism (ERM) was to minimise currency fluctuations between participating currencies. It was based on a grid of central parities between each pair of individual currencies and between each currency and the ECU. Each currency was allowed to fluctuate around the central parity up to an agreed margin, initially set at 2.25% for most currencies with a broader 6% band for some. Currencies were traded freely on financial markets within these margins but when the limits were approached central banks were obliged to intervene on foreign exchange markets to attempt to maintain the currency within its permitted band. Most EU currencies were in the ERM but some countries remained temporarily or permanently outside it. The ERM survived successfully until the advent of the euro but suffered severe turmoil in 1992, when currency speculation forced the pound sterling, which had only joined the ERM in 1990, and the

Italian lira (which subsequently rejoined) out. A further bout of severe currency speculation in 1993 resulted in the agreed currency bands being widened to 15%.

The initial ERM disappeared with the advent of the euro in 1999 but ERM 2 was set up by the Dublin meeting of the European Council in December 1996. This is intended as a stepping-stone for EU currencies remaining outside the euro. In principle all countries acceding to the EU will be required to join it, although not necessarily immediately, and successful membership of it for at least two years will be a criterion for any Member State wishing to join the euro zone. Currency bands in ERM 2 remain at 15%.

Giving credit

To assist EMS central banks' obligation to intervene on the foreign exchange markets should currency fluctuations approach their limit, a credit mechanism was put in place. This consisted of a very short-term financing facility (VSTF), a short-term monetary support mechanism (STMS), a medium-term financial assistance (MTFA) and a mobilisation mechanism for official ECU holdings. The credit system was initially overseen by the European Monetary Cooperation Fund (EMCF) and all EU member states deposited 20% of their gold and foreign exchange holdings with it in return for ECU.

The path to EMU

In 1988, under the presidency of Jacques Delors, work began on preparing a way towards closer Economic and Monetary Union (EMU). The Delors report, as it became known, set out a three-stage plan to achieve monetary union by 1999 at the latest. The provisions governing EMU were included in the 1992 Treaty on European Union (Maastricht Treaty).

Stage 1 of the process started, prior to Maastricht, in July 1990 and consisted of the final removal of exchange controls in eight of the then twelve participating members of the ERM, with the others to follow, and measures to encourage economic convergence.

Stage 2 started in January 1994. The EMCF was replaced by the European Monetary Institute (EMI) which took over the EMCF's functions and in addition had the task of taking a coordinating role and preparing for monetary union. Most Member States took steps to give their central banks the power to set interest rates independently. During this stage economic conditions in Member States were intended to converge sufficiently for Economic and Monetary Union to become feasible.

Stage 3 consisted of the irrevocable locking of currencies and the start of the euro and began in January 1999. The euro was set so that one euro = one ECU. The EMI was replaced by the European Central Bank (ECB) which was set up in June 1998 and Member States' deposits of gold and foreign exchange with the EMI were returned to them at the end of 1998.

15.3 Economic convergence

A high degree of economic convergence is necessary for EMU to work. In particular, the Maastricht Treaty stipulated that Member States who wished to join the single currency had to demonstrate that they met five key criteria in respect of the year 1997. These were:

- a rate of inflation no more than 1.5 percentage points above the three Member States with the lowest inflation rates
- long-term interest rates not exceeding the average rates of these low inflation states by more than 2 percentage points for the previous twelve months
- exchange rates which have fluctuated within the normal margins of the ERM for at least two years
- a general government deficit not exceeding 3% of GDP although a small and temporary excess would be permissible
- a general government outstanding debt level not more than 60% of GDP although a higher figure would be permissible if 'sufficiently diminishing'.

Inflation and interest rates moved downwards

Inflation in the EU has been on a downward trend for most of the 1990s and by 1997 only Greece had a rate in excess of the Maastricht criterion.

Day-to-day money rates are market-led but closely reflect changes in official interest rates, and monetary policy. After relatively high short-term interest rates in most countries at beginning of the 1990s, rates fell significantly EU-wide from 1992. At first this reflected an easing of monetary policy in response to an economic downturn. Subsequently it was more an indication of weakening inflation and growing stability within the Exchange Rate Mechanism (ERM). The yield on government bonds is a good indicator of long-term interest rates as government bond markets generally form a large and liquid part of capital markets. Many factors may influence yields, including evaluation by the market of national budgetary positions, economic growth and inflation prospects, and current and expected short-term interest rates. Prospects for EMU were also a key influence

EMU convergence criteria				
	Inflation: Harmonised indices of consumer prices: 09/97–09/98	Interest Rates: Long-term interest rates: 09/97–09/98	General government budgetary position: Deficit /GDP ratio 1997	General government budgetary position: Debt/GDP ratio 1997
	(1)	(2)	(3) (4)	(3)
B	1.0	5.1	2.0	121.9
DK	1.4	5.3	−0.5	64.1
D	1.0	4.9	2.7	61.2
EL	4.7	9.1	4.0	109.5
E	1.9	5.2	2.6	68.9
F	0.9	5.0	3.0	58.1
IRL	1.8	5.2	−0.9	63.4
I	2.0	5.3	2.7	121.6
L	1.2	5.1	−3.0	6.7
NL	2.0	5.0	0.9	71.4
A	0.9	5.0	1.9	64.3
P	2.0	5.3	2.5	61.5
FIN	1.5	5.1	1.1	55.1
S	1.7	5.4	0.8	76.6
UK	1.7	6.0	2.1	53.5
EU-15	1.5	5.3	2.3	71.9
EUR-11	1.3	5.1	2.5	74.5

(1) *Inflation : arithmetic average of twelve monthly Harmonised Indices of Consumer Prices (HICP) relative to the arithmetic average of the twelve monthly HICP of the previous period.*
(2) *Yield on government bonds of around 10 years to maturity: average of the last 12 monthly averages.*
(3) *as notified by Member States in September 1998*
(4) *a negative sign indicates a surplus.*

on the degree of convergence of EU interest rates. In the case of government bond yields, the differential between the highest and lowest (excluding Greece) narrowed to 1.1 percentage points at end-1997 while among the countries which eventually participated in EMU the gap narrowed to 0.5 percentage points. In the first half of 1998 EU government bond yields generally fell to historical lows.

Improving government finances

Luxembourg was the only EU country where general government finances were in surplus in 1996 but it was joined by Denmark and Ireland in 1997. Most countries had budgetary deficits in 1990–97. These deficits generally rose in the early years of the decade as a result of the 1992–93 recession (which reduced government revenue from taxation of income and spending but increased government social security spending). Deficits subsequently fell as economic conditions improved and as governments took active steps to improve their finances in order to meet the Maastricht criteria.

The recession in the early 1990s also contributed to a rise in outstanding general government debt, which continued to rise afterwards in some countries although it fell in others. The most notable decline in debt from 1990–97 was in Ireland. Finland's debt rose very steeply up to 1994 but then fell. Reunification contributed to the rise in Germany's debt from 1990–97.

15.4 The birth of the euro

Eleven countries qualify

At the start of May 1998, EU Heads of State and Government decided on which countries would mover to the third stage of EMU and adopt the euro from 1 January 1999. Eleven Member States – Belgium, Germany, Spain, France, Ireland, Italy, Luxembourg, Netherlands, Austria, Portugal and Finland – were deemed to have met the Maastricht conditions and be ready to move to stage 3. The other four Member States – Denmark, Greece, Sweden and the UK – either did not qualify or had decided not to adopt the euro initially.

On 1 January 1999, the exchange rates between the currencies of participating Member States and the euro were irrevocably fixed. This was the start of monetary union. The euro, with one euro equal to one ECU on December 31 1998, became the currency of participating Member States, with national currencies existing as sub-divisions of the euro. Foreign exchange markets between participating currencies ceased to exist. During transition, to end-2001, economic agents are free, and not forced, to use the euro. This

Irrevocable euro conversion rates	one euro = the following units of national currency
B	40.34
D	1.96
E	166.39
F	6.56
IRL	0.79
I	1,936.27
L	40.34
NL	2.20
A	13.76
P	200.48
FIN	5.95

Note: 1 euro = 1 ECU on 31 December 1998

Exchange rates against the ecu/euro

(year averages, national currency per ecu/euro)

	1980	1985	1990	1991	1992	1993
Belgium/Luxembourg (franc)	40.6	44.91	42.43	42.22	41.59	40.4:
Denmark (krone)	7.83	8.02	7.86	7.91	7.81	7.5:
Germany (Deutsche Mark)	2.52	2.23	2.05	2.05	2.02	1.9:
Greece (drachma)	59.42	105.74	201.41	225.22	247.03	268.5:
Spain (peseta)	99.70	129.14	129.41	128.47	132.53	149.1:
France (franc)	5.87	6.8	6.91	6.97	6.85	6.6:
Ireland (punt)	0.68	0.72	0.77	0.77	0.76	0.8
Italy (lira)	1189.21	1447.99	1521.98	1533.24	1595.52	1841.2:
Netherlands (guilder)	2.76	2.51	2.31	2.31	2.27	2.1:
Austria (schilling)	17.97	15.64	14.44	14.43	14.22	13.6:
Portugal (escudo)	69.55	130.25	181.11	178.61	174.71	188.3:
Finland (markka)	5.17	4.69	4.85	5.0	5.81	6.7
Sweden (krona)	5.88	6.52	7.52		7.53	9.1:
UK (pound)	0.6	0.59	0.71	0.70	0.74	0.7:
Japan (yen)	315.04	180.56	183.66	166.49	164.22	130.1:
USA (dollar)	1.39	0.76	1.27	1.24	1.3	1.1:

means the changeover will be largely market-driven. Companies will have to decide for themselves when it is best to change over. National public administrations can be expected to make the changeover sometime during this second phase.

Finally, from 1 January 2002, all economic transactions or contracts have to be defined and implemented in euro. Public and private operators will have completed the changeover and will operate exclusively in euro. The new euro notes and coins will come into circulation as legal tender by this date at the latest. National notes and coins will be withdrawn from circulation by 1 June 2002 at the latest, but the Commission expects that the final changeover to euro notes and coins will, in fact, happen much more rapidly and last perhaps only a month or two.

Notes and coins

Production of euro notes and coins began by the end of 1998. This is no easy task – a total of more than 70 billion coins weighing nearly 300,000 tonnes are used by the EU's 370 million inhabitants. The EMI first made designs of the new euro notes public in December 1996, outlining the main features – size, number, colours etc. Final versions were then announced in July 1997 after a number of detailed changes had been made.

Euro policy matters

The single monetary policy of the euro area is conducted by the European System of Central Banks (ESCB). This is composed of the ECB, which has superseded the EMI and is based in Frankfurt, and national central banks (NCBs). The Statutes of the ESCB and the ECB are contained in a Protocol of the Maastricht Treaty, and thus have constitutional value. They can be changed only by a modification of the Treaty, unanimously agreed and ratified by all Member States. The capital of the ECB was set at 5 billion euros to be subscribed by the NCBs, according to a share of population and GNP of respective Member States. In practice only 4 billion euros (15% in gold, the remainder in foreign exchange) has so far been transferred since the four countries who are not eurozone members have only contributed 5% of their respective shares and their central banks will not take part in policy decisions affecting the eurozone area.

The ECB and members of its decision-making body are independent from any Community or national institution or body. The primary objective of the ESCB is to maintain price stability in the euro area and it does this by periodically making appropriate changes in official interest rates.

Eurozone NCBs have kept their gold and foreign exchange reserves with the exception of those transferred to form the initial capital of the ECB. However the management of all the foreign reserves of the Eurozone is determined according to guidelines issued by the ECB.

At its meeting in Amsterdam in June 1997, the European Council adopted the stability and growth pact. This sought to ensure that the efforts made by countries to achieve economic convergence continued in order to foster stability and

1994	1995	1996	1997	1998	
39.66	38.55	39.3	40.53	40.62	*Belgium/Luxembourg (franc)*
7.54	7.33	7.36	7.48	7.45	*Denmark (krone)*
1.92	1.88	1.91	1.96	1.97	*Germany (Deutsche Mark*
288.03	302.99	305.55	309.36	330.74	*Greece (drachma)*
158.92	163.0	160.75	165.89	167.18	*Spain (peseta)*
6.58	6.53	6.49	6.61	6.6	*France (franc)*
0.79	0.82	0.79	0.75	0.79	*Ireland (punt)*
1915.06	2130.14	1958.96	1929.30	1943.65	*Italy (lira)*
2.16	2.1	2.14	2.21	2.22	*Netherlands (guilder)*
13.54	13.18	13.44	13.82	13.85	*Austria (schilling)*
196.9	196.11	195.76	198.59	201.7	*Portugal (escudo)*
6.19	5.71	5.83	5.88	5.98	*Finland (markka)*
9.16	9.33	8.51	8.65	8.92	*Sweden (krona)*
0.78	0.83	0.81	0.69	0.68	*UK (pound)*
121.32	123.01	138.08	137.08	146.42	*Japan (yen)*
1.19	1.31	1.27	1.13	1.12	*USA (dollar)*

economic growth. In particular, the pact emphasises the need to maintain sound government finances.

Changes to financial markets

Complementing the single internal market, the advent of the euro is creating a large single capital market in Europe. This will have important effects on the existing markets, both in terms of their functioning as well as in terms of their structure. Eurozone stock exchanges – in a 'big bang' at the start of January 1999 – switched to quoting all listed securities in euro. This aligned the stock markets with the money markets and wholesale banking operations, all of whom are now operating in euro. EMU will also bring enormous changes in the bond markets. The current nationally based securities' markets – each with its own set of conventions and market practices – will be transformed into a single market with common conventions.

16 Accounting for the economy
16.1 Measuring GDP

Gross domestic product (GDP), one of the main national accounts aggregates, summarises the outcome of activities of economic operators within a country or other defined territory. It corresponds to the cash value of all goods and services produced by economic units within a given period, less the value of intermediate goods used in the production process, but plus value added tax (VAT) and net taxes (taxes minus subsidies) on imports.

Three different approaches may be used to calculate GDP, based on output (as in the previous paragraph), income and expenditure. In theory these should give the same result. In the expenditure approach, GDP is the sum of: spending by private households and non-profit institutions serving households on goods and services (private consumption); the current spending (public consumption) of general government; gross fixed investment (gross fixed capital formation); changes in stocks; and the balance of exports less imports.

GDP is calculated in accordance with a system of national accounts. EU Member States use the European System of Integrated Economic Accounts (ESA79 in this publication changing to ESA95 from 1999). This system comprises a coherent set of detailed tables and accounts which reveal various aggregates, one of the most important of which is GDP. These aggregates are essential indicators for macroeconomic analysis and economic policy.

Data from national accounts are frequently used in implementing European Union policies. The indicators, especially GDP and GNP (gross national product), are used in fixing the budget contributions of the Member States and in the application

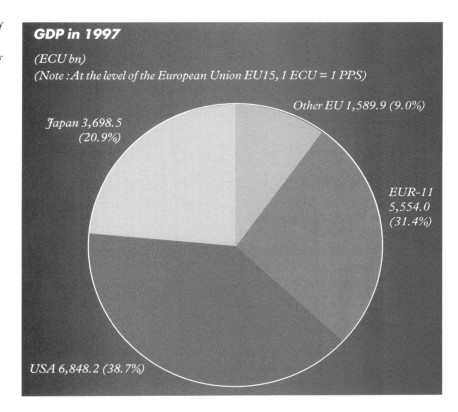

GDP in 1997

(ECU bn)
(Note: At the level of the European Union EU15, 1 ECU = 1 PPS)

Other EU 1,589.9 (9.0%)
Japan 3,698.5 (20.9%)
EUR-11 5,554.0 (31.4%)
USA 6,848.2 (38.7%)

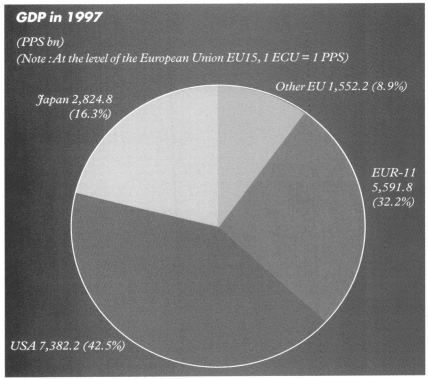

GDP in 1997

(PPS bn)
(Note: At the level of the European Union EU15, 1 ECU = 1 PPS)

Other EU 1,552.2 (8.9%)
Japan 2,824.8 (16.3%)
EUR-11 5,591.8 (32.2%)
USA 7,382.2 (42.5%)

of structural measures undertaken for the purpose of economic and social cohesion. The arrangements for Economic and Monetary Union provided for under the Treaty of Maastricht draw on criteria which are defined on the basis of national accounts data.

16.2 GDP per person continues to rise

In 1997 EU-15 GDP amounted to ECU 7,143.9bn while the figures for the United States and Japan were ECU 6,848.2bn and ECU 3,698.5bn respectively. When expressed in ECU, the GDP of the European Union is equivalent to a little less than a quarter of the GDP of the entire world economy It is around 40% of the total GDP of the three major economic powers: the EU, the USA amd Japan. However, the three powers' shares of their total GDP are significantly changed if the figures are expressed in terms of purchasing power instead of ecus. The purchasing power standard (PPS) is an artificial currency which is calculated to adjust for differences in the cost of living between countries. Whilst the Community's share remains fairly constant in both cases (40% and 41% respectively), the United States figure goes up from 39% to 43% and that for Japan decreases from 21% to 16%.

Almost 80% of the EU's GDP is generated by five Member States – Germany, France, Italy, Spain and the United Kingdom. Four other Member States (Ireland, Luxembourg, Portugal and Greece) together account for less than 5% of the Union's GDP. Member States' shares of Union GDP can vary considerably depending on whether the figures are expressed in ecus or PPS. This is particularly noticeable for Scandinavian countries (where the cost of living tends to be more expensive) and Mediterranean countries (where it tends to be cheaper).

Per capita GDP

Per capita GDP is often taken as a measure of a country's standard of living, but here differences between PPS and ecu data are quite striking.

Because of the high price levels in Denmark, for example, the country's per capita GDP in 1997 in terms of PPS is 4,872 lower than the figure in ecus (27,281 ecus but only 22,409 PPS). Another example is the fact that Luxembourg's GDP is 3.8 times higher than Portugal's in ecus but only 2.4 times higher when expressed in PPS. It is also interesting to see that whilst Japan's per capita GDP expressed in ecus is about 54% higher than the EU average for 1997, it is only 18% higher in real terms. In the United States, GDP is about 34% higher than the EU average for 1997 in ecu terms but is almost 45% higher when expressed in PPS. Indices based on PPS data show significantly reduced differences in standard of living between countries of the Union. The richer countries are in fact not as rich as the data based on current exchange rates would suggest, while the less favoured countries are not as badly off as it seems from the calculations in ecus based on these exchange rates.

Comparisons in such terms are particularly useful when exchange rates are shifting quickly. Thus, between 1990 and 1997, per capita GDP in Japan expressed in ecus increased by about 55% as a result of the sharp rise of the yen against the ecu, whilst in real terms the increase over the same period was only about 36%.

GDP, and especially per capita GDP, is often used as an indicator of a country's standard of living and

social progress, but there are some disadvantages in this. GDP can be influenced by factors such as the effects of a harsh winter, new fees or an increase in road accidents which do nothing to improve people's well-being. Furthermore, it is an average and says nothing about the distribution of GDP.

GDP by region

Comparing the regions of the European Union reveals even greater differences in per capita GDP than those found between the Member States (regional per capita GDP is in fact used as a criterion for the allocation of funds from the European Regional Development Fund). The less favoured regions – i.e. those where GDP is below the Community average – are situated on the edges of the Community, in mountain areas, in areas with a low level of industrialisation and in areas where old industries are in crisis. The richest regions are along the London-Milan axis and around separate centres such as Hamburg and the capital cities. These are highly populated regions with a concentration of growth industries and intense business activity.

Trend in GDP

Comparison over time is meaningful only if it is expressed in volume, or real, terms, i.e. the results of several successive years must be related to base year prices which are kept constant.

A volume comparison (i.e. at 1990 constant prices) of per capita GDP for 1980 and 1997 shows that the EU average rose over this period from ECU 12,154 to 15,807, an increase of about 30%. Over the same period, the figures rose from ECU 14,809 to 19,109 (+29%) in

GDP in 1997

	ECU bn	%	PPS bn	%
EU15	7,143.9	100.0	7,143.9	100.0
EUR-11	5,554.0	77.7	5,591.8	78.3
B	214.0	3.0	220.7	3.1
DK	144.2	2.0	118.4	1.7
D	1,844.9	25.8	1,664.1	23.3
EL	105.9	1.5	138.6	1.9
E	482.3	6.8	598.6	8.4
F	1,222.3	17.1	1,157.4	16.2
IRL	68.1	1.0	71.1	1.0
I	1,011.1	14.2	1,140.4	16.0
L	14.5	0.2	13.7	0.2
NL	319.2	4.5	320.3	4.5
A	181.9	2.5	173.4	2.4
P	90.0	1.3	135.8	1.9
FIN	105.8	1.5	96.3	1.3
S	201.0	2.8	167.9	2.3
UK	1,138.9	15.9	1,128.5	15.8
USA	6,848.2	95.9	7,382.2	103.3
JPN	3,698.5	51.8	2,824.8	39.5

GDP per head at current prices

	1990		1997	
	ECU	PPS	ECU	PPS
EU15	14,885.0	14,885.0	19,040.0	19,040.0
EUR-11	15,262.7	14,895.3	19,047.8	19,177.4
B	15,509.6	15,500.7	21,022.9	21,681.0
DK	19,761.9	15,281.5	27,280.8	22,408.5
D	18,690.2	17,046.2	22,483.7	20,281.0
EL	6,422.3	8,539.3	10,096.0	13,214.0
E	10,250.6	11,270.5	12,265.0	15,222.0
F	16,568.1	16,089.0	20,855.9	19,748.8
IRL	10,226.1	10,566.9	18,552.3	19,369.6
I	14,934.8	14,885.7	17,263.7	19,470.9
L	22,158.4	22,010.9	34,401.0	32,654.8
NL	14,888.9	14,774.7	20,456.1	20,526.8
A	16,249.0	15,487.3	22,532.7	21,479.7
P	5,487.8	8,905.8	9,051.4	13,652.2
FIN	21,292.8	15,003.7	20,581.5	18,738.1
S	21,126.6	15,762.2	22,721.8	18,977.1
UK	13,257.2	14,404.4	19,300.7	19,123.5
USA	17,449.2	20,574.4	25,567.4	27,561.3
JPN	18,969.2	16,511.3	29,330.1	22,401.8

the United States and from ECU 13,541 to 20,905 (+54%) in Japan. It was thus in Japan, where GDP per head increased by almost half, that growth was most spectacular.

Growth was rather varied within the EU. From 1980 to 1997, per capita GDP in Germany expressed in constant ecus increased by much less (15%) than the EU average (30%), but it should be remembered that this was mainly due to the effects of German unification.

The increases in per capita GDP in Greece (22%), France (24%) and Belgium (30%) are also below, or equal to, the EU average. However, it should be borne in mind that in 1980 the per capita GDP of these countries expressed in ecus was, with the exception of Greece, already above the average.

Over the period 1980–1997, the increase in per capita GDP was above the Community average in

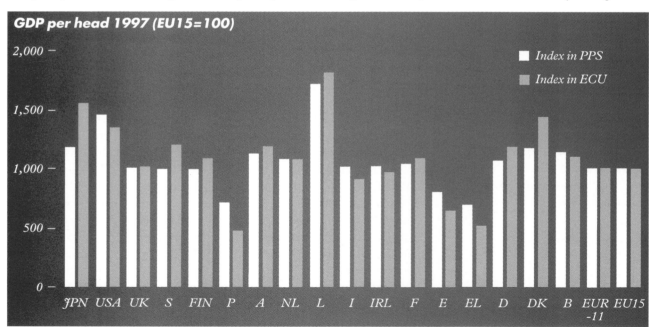

GDP per head 1997 (EU15=100)

Italy (30%), the Netherlands (33%), the United Kingdom (39%), Denmark (47%) and Spain (48%), Portugal (57%), Luxembourg (59%) and Ireland (122%). Of these countries, Greece, Spain, Portugal and Ireland had a particularly low per capita GDP in ecus in 1980. It is interesting to note that Denmark, where per capita GDP was already one of the highest in the EU of 1980, nonetheless enjoyed above-average growth between 1980 and 1997. In 1997 the figures for the new Member States (Austria, Finland and Sweden) are all above the Community average in ecus, but only Austria and Sweden are above it also in PPS.

Gross national product (GNP)

Alongside GDP, which relates to the activity of economic operators, regardless of their nationality, in the economic territory of a country, there is also the concept of gross national product (GNP), which is based on the nationality of the operators. GNP is calculated by adding together GDP and the balance of compensation of employees and entrepreneurial and property income with the rest of the world. GNP thus comprises employment, entrepreneurial and property income related to nationals within a given period, irrespective of where such income has been generated. GNP is also the basis for calculating the EU's fourth own resources (part of the Community's budget) and, as such, is covered by a Council Directive which aims to encourage comparability and comprehensiveness. For most Member States of the EU, the difference between GNP and GDP is very small.

Comparison of GDP in terms of purchasing power standards (PPS)

GDP, and especially GDP per head, is one of the main indicators for economic analysis and for comparisons both in time (assessment of growth) and space (international comparison of a country's production capacity).

For the international comparison of GDP and its components, the values expressed in national currencies must first be converted into a common currency (usually the ecu for the Member States of the EU and the US dollar for worldwide comparisons). This conversion is based on official exchange rates, but for various reasons these rates do not necessarily reflect the real purchasing power of a currency in the economic territory of a country and using them does not always provide a true indication of the volume of goods and services produced and consumed in the various countries during a given year. In order to get round this difficulty, calculations are based on a special artificial conversion rate which is the purchasing power parity (PPP). This rate uses the prices of a selection of comparable products and thus takes account of the real purchasing power of a currency. The amounts obtained using this rate are expressed in an artificial currency called purchasing power standard (PPS). For internal comparisons the constant prices or the constant PPS are used.

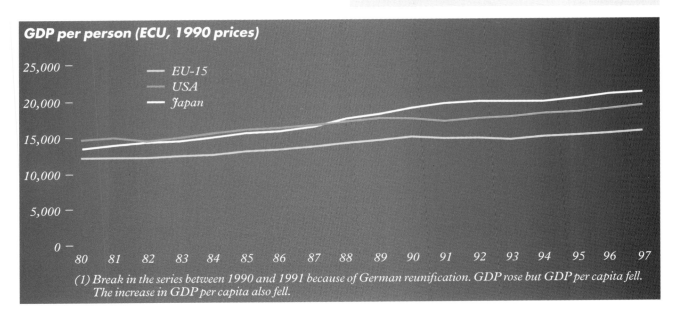

GDP per person (ECU, 1990 prices)

- EU-15
- USA
- Japan

(1) Break in the series between 1990 and 1991 because of German reunification. GDP rose but GDP per capita fell. The increase in GDP per capita also fell.

16.3 Household spending is the largest component

The most common approach in analysing GDP involves final uses ('expenditure approach'). This analysis, which involves breaking down the final uses of GDP into various sub-aggregates, reveals to what extent the goods and services produced by the economy of a country or imported are used for private consumption, public consumption, gross fixed-capital formation, changes in stocks or (re)exports.

For the EU-15 as a whole, the private consumption of households including the NPISH (non profit institutions serving households) accounted for approximately 64% of final expenditure in 1997, with the government sector accounting for 17% and fixed-capital formation 19%. In the United States in 1996, 67% of final expenditure was accounted for by private consumption, while the corresponding figure for Japan in 1997 was only 62%. The government sector accounts for 16% of final expenditure in the United States (1996) and 10% in Japan (1997). The United States uses approximately 18% (1996) of final expenditure for fixed-capital formation; Japan, however, remarkably invests 29% (1997) of it, which is also linked to this country's strong saving.

Uses of GDP

Per capita figures for private consumption in current prices are around the EU average for the majority of EU Member States, with the exception of Portugal (57% in ecus, 73% in PPS), Greece (36% in ecus, 80% in PPS), Spain (65% in ecus, 79% in PPS), Ireland (70% in ecus, 81% in PPS), Germany (137% in ecus, 115% in PPS) and Luxembourg (155% in ecus, 140% in PPS) . These differences depend to a certain extent on how some spending, such as expenditure on health, is classified. There are institutional differences in the

Final domestic expenditure per head

(ECU, 1990 prices)

	Private consumption			Compared with EU-15		Public consump[t]		
	1980	1997	Change %	1980 %	1997 %	1980	1997	Change %
EU-15	7,299.2	9,659.3	32.3	100.0	100.0	2,136.6	2,606.1	22.0
EUR-11	7,577.0	9,823.4	29.6	103.8	101.7	1,997.7	2,441.3	22.2
B	8,394.0	10,657.5	27.0	115.0	110.3	2,148.4	2,308.2	7.4
DK	9,098.9	12,144.0	33.5	124.7	125.7	4,526.9	5,916.2	30.7
D	9,615.8	11,534.9	20.0	131.7	119.4	2,116.4	2,049.2	−3.2
EL	3,830.7	5,217.1	36.2	52.5	54.0	768.6	978.8	27.4
E	5,090.2	7,008.7	37.7	69.7	72.6	949.1	1,782.2	87.8
F	8,292.2	10,361.9	25.0	113.6	107.3	2,518.4	3,329.4	32.2
IRL	4,758.2	7,741.1	62.7	65.2	80.1	1,545.1	1,749.9	13.3
I	7,105.5	9,602.0	35.1	97.3	99.4	2,125.3	2,609.3	22.8
L	10,662.9	13,258.3	24.3	146.1	137.3	2,375.7	3,064.3	29.0
NL	7,835.4	9,731.6	24.2	107.3	100.7	1,947.3	2,359.1	21.1
A	7,284.4	9,973.2	36.9	99.8	103.2	2,683.6	3,078.5	14.7
P	2,659.6	4,163.1	56.5	36.4	43.1	557.3	1,040.7	86.7
FIN	8,270.6	10,968.0	32.6	113.3	113.5	3,341.8	4,367.8	30.7
S	9,586.8	10,646.0	11.0	131.3	110.2	5,082.5	5,538.4	9.0
UK	6,114.8	9,267.7	51.6	83.8	95.9	2,358.9	2,973.7	26.1
USA	9,462.4	12,882.1	36.1	129.6	133.4	2,606.2	2,863.8	9.9
JPN	8,062.8	12,329.1	52.9	110.5	127.6	1,412.5	1,912.4	35.4

provision of health, education and leisure. These services, especially health, may be provided exclusively by the government sector and thus serve to inflate public consumption, as happens in Denmark. Alternatively, they can be regarded as market services and come under the final consumption of households. In order to obtain more meaningful international comparisons, these types of services are often transferred from government to household consumption in statistical analyses.

Gross fixed-capital formation constitutes a relatively high proportion of GDP in Austria (24%) and in Portugal (25%), and a relatively low one in Sweden (18%), as well as in Denmark (21%), in Finland (19%) and in the United Kingdom (18%).

In 1995, government consumption per head in Denmark was 2.4 times higher than the EU average (ECU 2,868), whilst in Sweden it was almost 1.8 times the EU average (and, respectively, 1.9 and 1.6 in PPS terms). In Greece, on the other hand, government consumption per head is only 46% of the EU average (62% in PPS) and is equivalent to only 19% of the Danish figure in ecus and 33% in PPS terms.

In 1997, gross fixed capital formation (GFCF) per head in the Union averaged ECU 3,087; the figure for Luxembourg was 2.3 times as high and that for Greece just 48% of the average.

Very detailed study of final uses reveals differences in how the Member States use GDP, as well as changes over time (see Section 9.3).

Trend in final uses of GDP

Comparison over the period 1980–1997 shows that per capita household consumption in the EU increased in volume by 32%, per capita public consumption by 22% and per capita fixed-capital formation by 21%. Per capita private consumption in Japan went up by 53%, but rose less than investment, which jumped by 63%.

The greatest volume increase in per capita household consumption within the EU was recorded in Ireland (63%) and Portugal (+57%), whereas in Sweden this increase was only 11%.

As for per capita consumption in the government sector, the volume increases were greatest in Spain (88%) and Portugal (+87%). In Germany, per capita consumption in volume in the government sector

Gross fixed capital formation

Compared with EU-15					Compared with EU-15		Total	
1980 %	1997 %	1980	1997	Change %	1980	1997	1997	
100.0	100.0	2,552.0	3,087.5	21.0	100.0	100.0	15,353.0	EU-15
93.5	93.7	2,719.8	3,201.4	17.7	106.6	103.7	15,466.1	EUR-11
100.6	88.6	2,520.3	3,155.8	25.2	98.8	102.2	16,121.4	B
211.9	227.0	2,962.4	5,267.7	77.8	116.1	170.6	23,327.9	DK
99.1	78.6	3,436.6	3,718.8	8.2	134.7	120.4	17,302.9	D
36.0	37.6	1,526.7	1,697.1	11.2	59.8	55.0	7,893.1	EL
44.4	68.4	1,530.8	2,593.0	69.4	60.0	84.0	11,384.0	E
117.9	127.8	2,986.7	3,199.4	7.1	117.0	103.6	16,890.8	F
72.3	67.1	1,788.1	2,545.1	42.3	70.1	82.4	12,036.1	IRL
99.5	100.1	2,652.8	2,799.4	5.5	103.9	90.7	15,010.8	I
111.2	117.6	3,814.6	6,125.9	60.6	149.5	198.4	22,448.4	L
91.1	90.5	2,741.8	3,536.5	29.0	107.4	114.5	15,627.2	NL
125.6	118.1	3,032.8	4,363.5	43.9	118.8	141.3	17,415.2	A
26.1	39.9	1,137.8	1,986.8	74.6	44.6	64.4	7,190.7	P
156.4	167.6	4,294.3	4,025.4	-6.3	168.3	130.4	19,361.1	FIN
237.9	212.5	3,379.1	3,346.9	-1.0	132.4	108.4	19,531.3	S
110.4	114.1	1,796.4	2,537.8	41.3	70.4	82.2	14,779.2	UK
122.0	109.89	2,677.4	3,744.6	39.9	104.9	121.28	19,490.5	USA
66.1	73.379	3,845.2	6,270.6	63.1	150.7	203.1	20,512.1	JPN

decreased by 3% between 1980 and 1997.

Per capita gross fixed-capital formation in volume fell in Finland (−6%) and Sweden (−1%) but there was a dramatic rise in Denmark (78%), Portugal (75%) and Spain (69%).

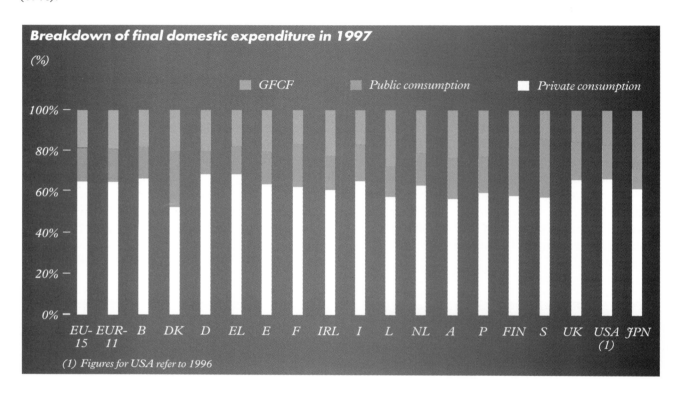

Breakdown of final domestic expenditure in 1997

(%)

■ GFCF   ■ Public comsumption   ■ Private consumption

(1) Figures for USA refer to 1996

Components of final uses of GDP ('Expenditure approach of GDP')

The components of the final uses shown in the national accounts are:

- *final consumption of households, which represents the value of goods and market services used for the direct satisfaction of individual needs. The main categories are food and beverages, clothing and footwear, housing services, furniture, health services, transport, recreation and cultural services. Households includes NPISH (non profit institutions serving households).*

- *collective consumption (public consumption) of general government and private non-profit institutions, which comprises non-market services, i.e. community services which are provided without any direct payment. These services benefit all economic operators, whether they are businesses or households. The main services are those provided by general government, national defence, health, education, research, recreation and cultural services, welfare services, etc.*

- *gross fixed capital formation, which represents the value of durable goods with a value of more than ECU 100 (originally defined as 100 Units of Account of 1970) acquired by producer units and used for a period of more than a year in the production process This covers mainly machinery and other equipment, transport equipment, housing (even if produced and occupied by households), non-residential buildings and other civil construction and works. Military equipment and construction are included in collective consumption.*

- *changes in stocks held by producer units (stocks held by households are automatically included in the final consumption of households).*

- *the balance of exports and imports.*

16.4 Agriculture and manufacturing fall, services boom

Gross domestic product broadly constitutes the sum of the figures for value added (total production less intermediate consumption) of the various branches of production, with the VAT on products and the net taxes on imports (i.e. taxes minus subsides). Taking value added as a basis, it is possible to find out which branches contribute to GDP formation.

Updated figures on value added are available for six major branches of production in the EU, in the United States and Japan for 1997. If value added in these three major economic powers is compared, considerable differences also emerge for the most recent year for which figures are available.

Looking at the period from 1980 to 1997, it can be seen that trends are very similar in the three major economies. The following structural changes are clearly discernable :

- The shares of GDP accounted for by agriculture are declining everywhere.
- The shares of GDP accounted for by manufacturing are declining, except in Ireland and in the Netherlands.
- The share of construction is declining everywhere, except in Austria and Japan.
- The share represented by market services, on the other hand, is increasing everywhere.
- Differing trends can be seen only in the 'fuel and power products' sector (a 9 out of 15 majority decreasing in the EU and in the USA, with Japan increasing) and in the 'non-market services' sector (a 9 out of 15 majority decreasing in the EU as a whole and in Japan, the USA and the eurozone increasing).

The 'fuel and power products'

branch in 1997 has the largest share of GDP in Italy (5.7%) The share of value added accounted for by manufacturing in 1996 is almost six points lower in the USA (17.3%) than in Japan (23.1%) with the EU at 20.7%. In every country the largest sectors in 1997 are market services the share of which ranges from 41% (Ireland) to 66% (Luxembourg), followed by manufacturing ranging from 13% (Greece) to 33% (Ireland).

In 1997, the differences between EU Member States as regards the shares of value added accounted for by fuel and power products (Luxembourg 1.4% up to the United Kingdom 5.9%) and construction (Germany and France 4.5% up to Austria 7.8%) are limited.

Agriculture's share, on the other hand, is more than eight times larger in Greece (8.1%) than in Germany (1.0%) and ten times larger than in Luxembourg (0.8%).

Manufacturing makes the most significant contribution in Ireland (33%), the least in Greece (13%). Market services make the largest contribution to GDP in Luxembourg (66%) and in the Netherlands (49%), the smallest in Finland and Ireland (both 41%). As regards non-market services, Sweden has the highest share with 26%, more than twice the figure in Greece (12%).

Contribution of different industries to gross value added in 1997

(%)
Percentage of total

	Agricultural, forestry and fishery products [Nace Clio 01]	Ful and power products [Nace Clio 06]	Manufactured products [Nace Clio 30]	Building and construction [Nace Clio 53]	Market services [Nace Clio 68]	Non-market services [Nace Clio 86]	Total
EU-15	2.1	4.6	20.7	5.1	52.4	15.1	100.0
EUR-11	2.1	4.4	20.9	5.1	52.3	15.1	100.0
B	1.2	4.4	19.2	5.2	56.5	13.5	100.0
DK	3.2	2.8	19.2	5.2	47.1	22.5	100.0
D	1.0	3.9	23.4	4.5	53.9	13.3	100.0
EL	8.1	2.6	13.0	7.4	56.9	12.0	100.0
E	3.3	5.2	18.2	7.7	51.8	13.7	100.0
F	2.4	4.0	19.0	4.5	51.9	18.2	100.0
IRL	4.5	2.8	33.2	5.0	41.0	13.5	100.0
I	2.7	5.7	20.4	5.0	52.8	13.4	100.0
L	0.8	1.4	14.2	5.5	65.9	12.2	100.0
NL	3.0	4.6	18.6	5.3	48.8	19.7	100.0
A	1.4	4.1	20.4	7.8	52.3	14.0	100.0
P	4.1	4.1	23.5	6.0	45.7	16.6	100.0
FIN	3.9	2.5	26.1	6.2	41.4	19.9	100.0
S	1.8	3.3	20.9	4.7	43.3	26.0	100.0
UK	1.5	5.9	20.6	5.1	54.5	12.5	100.0
USA	2.0	3.5	17.3	4.1	54.8	18.5	100.0
JPN	1.7	3.5	22.9	9.6	54.5	7.9	100.0

Contribution of different industries to gross value added in 1997

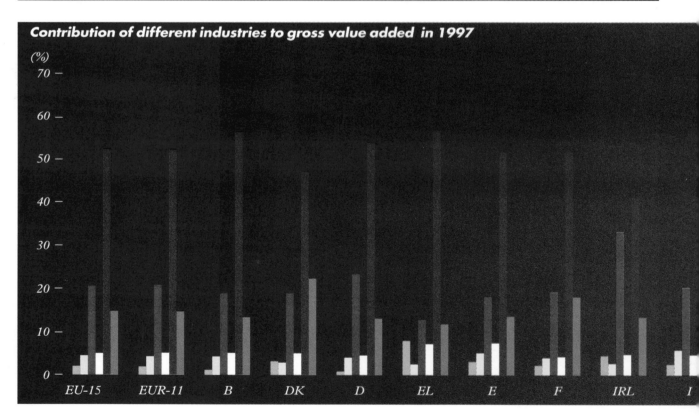

FURTHER READING

Eurostat publications

Quarterly national accounts ESA
National accounts ESA,
aggregates 1970–1997
National accounts ESA, detailed
tables by branch, 1970–1997
Economy and Finance, Rapid
Reports

Electronic products

Eurostat CD
New Cronos database (Regio)

Other publications

The economies of 1995–1996
The economic and social situation
in the Community, Economic and
Social Committee
Annual Economic Report

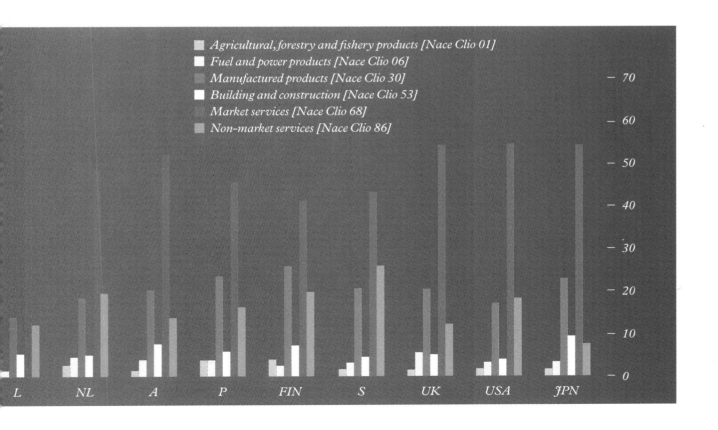

17 Trade and foreign investment
17.1 The world's largest trader

A fundamental EU principle since its earliest days has been the promotion of free trade among its members. It is also an area very open to trade with the outside world. The EU is the world's biggest exporter and importer of goods and services – and a leading contributor to international flows of direct investment. The European Commission is a very active member of the World Trade Organisation (WTO), whose birth on 1 January 1995 marked a new era in the regulation – and de-regulation – of world trade. The EU is also the most active promoter of the change to market economies in former Soviet-bloc countries. It has contributed to a large extent to the transformation of societies in Central and Eastern Europe, preparing them for possible EU membership. In addition, trade with the USA, Canada and Japan has increased in intensity. The development and liberalisation of world trade – including that in services – remain cornerstones of EU policies.

A world-beater in export of goods

In 1997, the EU was the world's leading exporter of goods (also known as merchandise or visible trade) accounting for 20% of global exports. It ranked second in imports (17%) after the USA (20%). This chapter focuses primarily on 'extra-EU' trade – ie trade between EU Members and other countries excluding trade between Member States ('intra-trade'). Before looking in detail at 'extra' trade in goods it is worth noting that trade among EU Member States has always represented over half the EU's total trade; since Austria, Sweden and Finland joined the Union in 1995, almost two-thirds of goods trade is 'intra' trade since these three Member States were geared strongly to the EU market. All data for trade in goods refer to EU-15, including those for years before all fifteen countries were Members.

Extra-EU trade rose from 1960–97, although inflation sometimes makes it difficult to measure the 'real' increase. Since 1960, extra-EU trade generally has shown a structural deficit with imports normally exceeding exports. Only since 1993 has there been a shift to a surplus.

Key export partners . . .

From 1960–1997, USA, Japan and EFTA were the key EU markets. But there has been a big change in the last few years. The export share of USA, Japan and EFTA taken together fell from 42.8% in 1990 to 35.5% in 1997. The USA and EFTA became less important – although the USA is still the EU's main trading partner with a 19.6% share in 1997 – but Japan's share

rose from 3.1% in 1985 to 5.0% in 1997. EU exports to six Developing Asian Economies (DAE – Singapore, Taiwan, Hong Kong, South Korea, Thailand and Malaysia) rose remarkably from 4.8% in 1985 to 10.8% in 1997. However the EU has a relatively low share of exports to China. Central and Eastern European countries (CECs) and the Commonwealth of Independent States (NIS) together received 16.7% of extra-EU exports in 1997. CEC figures rose sharply from 5.1% in 1985 to 12.1% in 1997, underlining the reorientation of former communist countries towards the EU. African markets dramatically reduced their share by over 13 percentage points between 1960–1997 – partly the loosening of old colonial ties. Latin America's share of EU exports fell from 10% in 1960 to 6.3% in 1997.

. . . and main suppliers

USA, Japan and EFTA are by far the most important EU suppliers. Their imports share was up from 31.1% in 1960 to 41.4% in 1997. But since 1990 (45.8%) it has been going down – due to Japan's share falling from 12.1% in 1991 to 8.9% in 1997. That their share is still over 40% of total extra-EU imports – together with rising EU imports from newly-industrialised countries (especially DAE) – can be explained partly by the growing importance of intra-industry trade in the last 20 years. Falling raw materials' prices in the 1980s was the main cause of the big drop in the share of EU imports from other areas, such as the Middle East, Africa and Latin America. For example, the Middle East and other Asia group accounted for only 4.5% of EU imports in 1997 compared with 18.7% in 1985 and 29.4% in 1975. CEC and NIS partners, which contributed 7.6% in 1960 and 9.9% in 1990, were the source of 13.7% of total extra-EU imports in 1997 although the growth was primarily in the CEC's share. The DAE and China have become key EU suppliers. Their shares of total EU imports rose from 5.2% and 1.0% respectively in 1985 to 10.1% and 5.6% in 1997.

Striking a balance

The EU's biggest goods trade deficit in 1997 was in trade with Japan – ECU 23.2 billion. However, if the deficit is considered as a percentage of exports and imports, then that in trade with China was the largest (38.9%) in 1997 with Japan second (24.4%). The EU has witnessed remarkable improvements in trade with CECs and the NIS. Its deficit with these countries of –ECU 9.1 billion in 1985 shifted to an ECU 28.6 billion surplus in 1997, due mainly to an improved position with CECs. The EU had a surplus of ECU 10.1 billion with the DAE group in 1997 while its surplus with Oceania rose from ECU 2.2 billion in 1991 to ECU 7.2 billion in 1997. This was the biggest surplus in relative terms, at 28.5% of exports plus imports.

Producing the goods

The EU is a traditional and growing exporter of manufactured products – 71% of total extra-EU exports in 1980, reaching 87% in 1997. Among such products, the biggest share of extra-EU exports was held by machinery and transport equipment – 45.8% of the total in 1997 with continuous growth since 1985. The trend in extra-EU imports also shows clearly the growing role of manufactured products. Raw materials, with a 53.1% share of total extra-EU imports in 1980, accounted for only 26.2% in 1997. Over the same period manufactured imports' share rose from 32.1% to 70.7%. In the early 1980s, fuel products were the key category with a 34.3% share of total extra-EU imports. But, from 1985, when raw material prices fell, the machinery and transport equipment share started rising. It reached 33.8% in 1997 compared with 12.7% for fuel products. Other manufactured products also rose substantially – from 16.7% of the total in 1980 to 29.2% in 1997. These figures demonstrate the growing importance of intra-industry flows in EU external trade.

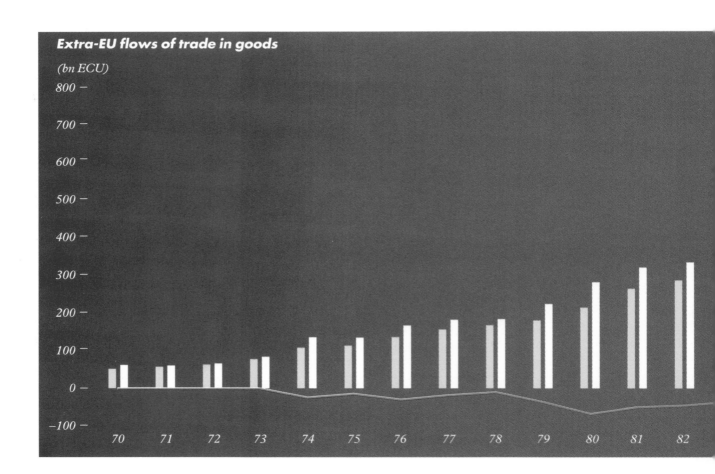

Extra-EU flows of trade in goods

(bn ECU)

Extra-EU trade in goods, by partner

	Extra-EU export shares by partner Share (%)				Extra-EU import shares by partner Share (%)				Extra-EU trade balance by partner (Bn ECU)			
	1970	*1980*	*1990*	*1997*	*1970*	*1980*	*1990*	*1997*	*1970*	*1980*	*1990*	*1997*
USA	20.2	14.0	21.2	19.6	23.9	18.1	20.8	20.5	−3.9	−21.2	−8.7	4.2
Japan	2.9	2.5	6.3	5.0	3.9	5.5	11.7	8.9	−0.8	−10.2	−26.9	−23.2
EFTA(1)	15.0	15.5	15.3	10.9	8.8	9.8	13.3	12.0	2.5	5.3	1.1	−1.9
CEC(2)	8.6	7.1	6.2	12.1	5.7	4.3	5.4	9.0	1.0	3.0	0.5	26.8
NIS	3.7	4.9	3.8	4.6	3.5	5.4	4.5	4.7	−0.2	−4.8	−4.8	1.8
Africa	16.1	19.1	11.9	7.2	18.3	15.8	11.6	8.4	−2.7	−4.0	−4.5	−4.6
Latin America	8.2	7.0	4.3	6.3	9.1	6.5	6.2	5.1	−1.2	−3.4	−10.1	10.6
DAE(3)	3.3	3.9	7.9	10.8	2.8	4.9	8.2	10.1	0.1	−5.6	−5.2	10.1
China	1.0	0.9	1.5	2.3	0.6	0.7	2.6	5.6	0.1	−0.1	−5.6	−20.9
Middle East and other Asia	8.8	16.3	11.5	7.1	12.2	23.0	8.9	4.5	−2.8	−30.0	5.8	21.1
Oceania	4.2	2.2	2.6	2.3	3.5	1.6	1.6	1.4	0.0	0.0	2.9	7.2
Total, bn ECU	51.6	211.1	390.6	717.9	59.8	280.6	439.4	667.4	−8.3	−69.5	−48.9	50.5

(1) Switzerland, Norway, Iceland, Liechtenstein
(2) Poland, Czech Republic, Slovakia, Hungary, Romania, Bulgaria, Albania, Latvia, Lithuania, Estonia, Slovenia, Croazia, Bosnia-Herzegovina., Serbia, FYROM
(3) Singapore, Taiwan, Hong Kong, South Korea, Thailand, Malaysia
(4) Lebanon, Syria, Iraq, Iran, Israel, Gaza, Jordan, Saudi-Arabia, Kuwait, Bahrain, Qatar, United Arab Emirates, Oman, Yemen, Afghanistan, Pakistan, India, Bangladesh, Maldives, Sri Lanka, Nepal, Bhutan, Burma, Laos, Vietnam, Cambodia, Indonesia, Brunei, Philippines, Mongolia, North Korea, Macao

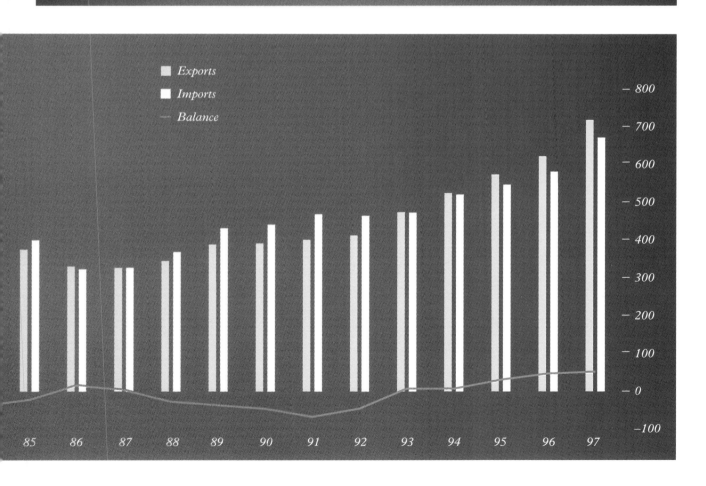

Extra-EU export and import shares by products

(%)

	Extra-EU export shares by products					Extra-EU import shares by products				
	1980	1985	1990	1995	1997	1980	1985	1990	1995	1997
Raw materials (0-4)	14.6	14.0	12.3	11.5	10.8	53.1	48.0	33.4	27.2	26.2
Food, etc. (0+1)	7.9	7.3	7.5	6.8	6.3	9.3	9.3	8.5	7.9	7.2
Crude materials (2+4)	1.8	1.9	2.3	2.4	2.2	9.6	9.1	7.7	7.4	6.4
Fuel products (3)	4.9	4.8	2.5	2.3	2.3	34.3	29.6	17.2	11.9	12.7
Manufactured goods (5-8)	71.0	70.9	83.3	86.8	87	32.1	38.4	61.7	70.0	70.7
Chemicals (5)	9.3	10.0	11.5	12.8	12.9	3.8	4.9	6.5	7.9	7.6
Machinery, Transport (7)	33.5	32.9	40.7	44.7	45.8	11.6	16.7	28.6	31.8	33.8
Other Manufactures (6+8)	28.1	28.0	31.1	29.2	28.3	16.7	16.8	26.6	30.2	29.2
Not classified elsewhere (9)	14.4	15.1	4.4	1.7	2.2	14.8	13.6	4.9	2.8	3.1
Total (bn ECU)	211.1	372.6	390.6	572.8	717.9	280.6	397.9	439.4	545.1	667.4

Source: Eurostat-Comext, International Monetary Fund – Direction of Trade Statistics (IMF-DOTS) for total products and UN-Comtrade for products breakdown

Note: The classification refers to Product list SITC Rev 3

(0-4): 0: Food and live animals + 1: Beverages and tobacco + 2: Crude materials, except fuels + 3: Energy + 4: Oils, fats and waxes

(0+1): 0: Food and live animals + 1: Beverages and tobacco

(2+4): 2: Crude materials, except fuels + 4: Oils, fats and waxes

(3): 3: Energy

(5-8): 5: Chemical products + 6: Manufactured goods classified by material + 7: Machinery and transport equipment + 8: Miscellaneous manufactured articles

(5): 5: Chemical products

(7): 7: Machinery and transport equipment

(6+8): 6: Manufactured goods classified by material + 8: Miscellaneous manufactured articles

17.2 Providing a service

The contribution of services to EU external trade is about a third that of goods. Total EU service transactions, including those within the EU, have followed an upward trend. They more than doubled to reach ECU 867.7 billion in 1996. Since 1992 most EU international services transactions have been 'intra-EU' – 56% in 1996 compared with 46% in 1986.

The EU's balance of extra-trade in services is gradually being eroded. An excellent surplus of ECU 30 billion in 1986 fell to just over ECU 8 billion by 1996. Over the same period, the USA saw a striking rise in its services balance – from ECU 7 billion to 62 billion. Japan is different. It is a major net purchaser of external services with a big deficit. This rose from –ECU 15 billion in 1986 to –ECU 49 billion in 1996. In addition to the EU's apparent loss of competitiveness vis-à-vis the US, it is possible that certain services, particularly financial, have migrated to 'off-shore' centres. This makes it difficult to analyse the international economic health of European services on the basis of trade in services alone.

From transport to tourism . . .

In sea transport, closely connected with trade in goods, the EU has consistently been in deficit for many years. It has a consistent surplus in

EU(1) external trade in services

(M ECU)

	1986 Exports	1986 Imports	1990 Exports	1990 Imports	1994 Exports	1994 Imports	1995 Exports	1995 Imports	1996 Exports	1996 Imports
Transportation	31,834	31,439	44,858	43,478	46,841	44,580	46,735	46,054	48,902	50,551
of which:										
Sea transport	8,778	10,820	11,416	12,987	20,810	21,546	20,897	21,941	20,645	24,269
Air transport	8,736	7,907	12,979	10,973	19,989	17,808	19,903	18,130	22,404	19,629
Travel	29,342	21,671	37,733	34,086	40,831	41,653	43,813	43,733	49,508	49,407
Other services	47,557	32,021	52,194	44,633	82,685	74,472	85,063	74,873	96,421	80,022
of which:										
Communications services	2,356	2,236	2,604	2,305	2,603	2,996	2,883	3,440	3,011	3,469
Construction services	6,497	2,642	4,800	2,513	9,659	5,218	11,419	7,077	11,521	6,823
Insurance services	5,696	1,855	2,032	2,084	6,316	3,940	4,579	1,825	6,077	2,753
Financial services	3,917	1,719	8,717	5,131	9,817	7,173	8,039	4,442	8,498	4,649
Computer and information services	:	:	:	:	2,609	2,906	3,249	3,472	4,070	3,837
Royalties and licence fees	2,626	4,847	4,220	8,179	6,520	10,304	6,597	10,795	6,930	12,046
Other business services	14,379	13,922	15,301	16,685	33,599	32,421	38,769	33,895	46,848	36,497
Personal, cultural and recreational services	749	1,039	2,457	2,756	3,182	4,230	2,627	4,500	2,997	4,808
Government services, n i e	11,343	3,753	12,063	4,980	8,381	5,283	6,900	5,426	6,472	5,142
Services not allocated	13,720	9,415	25,215	18,529	3,340	1,695	2,014	886	1,040	2,973
Services	122,454	94,546	160,000	140,725	173,696	162,398	177,628	165,546	195,871	182,953

(1) EU-12 for 1986 and 1990; EU-15 for 1994–1996

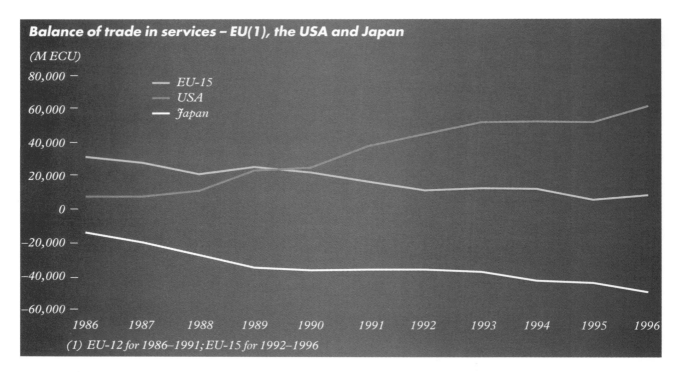

Balance of trade in services – EU(1), the USA and Japan

(M ECU)

Legend: EU-15, USA, Japan

(1) EU-12 for 1986–1991; EU-15 for 1992–1996

air transport. The tourism balance has also slipped from a record ECU 13 billion surplus in 1985 primarily because EU tourist spending in the rest of the world has been growing quicker (annual average growth of 8%) than that of visitors to the EU (4.4%). There is no real reduction in Europe's appeal. The closely linked sectors of communications and computer and information services registered small deficits but are expanding rapidly. The EU has been in surplus on insurance since 1993 and still records surpluses on services in the financial and construction sectors.

Key partners in services

The USA is the main partner with 33% of EU external trade in services. Asia comes second with 22%, one quarter of which is trade with Japan. EFTA accounts for 16%, other European countries 11%. Africa represents 7%.

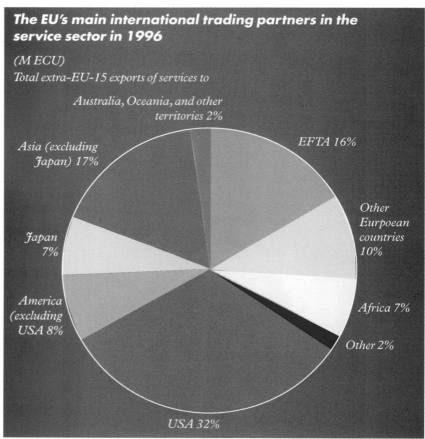

The EU's main international trading partners in the service sector in 1996

(M ECU)
Total extra-EU-15 exports of services to

- Australia, Oceania, and other territories 2%
- EFTA 16%
- Asia (excluding Japan) 17%
- Other Eurpoean countries 10%
- Japan 7%
- Africa 7%
- America (excluding USA 8%
- Other 2%
- USA 32%

The EU's main international trading partners in the service sector in 1996

(M ECU)
Total extra-EU-15 imports of services from

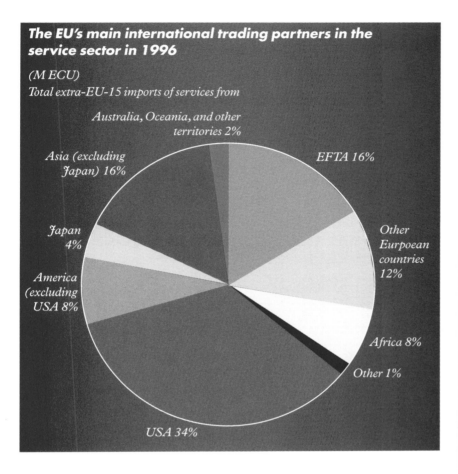

Australia, Oceania, and other territories 2%

Asia (excluding Japan) 16%

EFTA 16%

Japan 4%

America (excluding USA 8%

Other Eurpoean countries 12%

Africa 8%

Other 1%

USA 34%

The EU's main international trading partners in the service sector in 1996

(M ECU)

Total 1996 extra-EU-15 exports of services to:	
USA	63,308
Asia (excluding Japan)	32,348
EFTA	32,073
Other European countries	18,876
America (excluding USA)	14,811
Japan	13,347
Africa	13,286
Australia, Oceania and other territories	4,803
Other	3,019
Total 1996 extra-EU-15 imports of services from:	
USA	62,182
Asia (excluding Japan)	28,613
EFTA	29,487
Other European countries	21,313
America (excluding USA)	15,022
Japan	7,265
Africa	13,926
Australia, Oceania and other territories	3,227
Other	1,918

17.3 Current transactions

The EU's balance of trade (goods and services) has seen a decade of surpluses. The only exception was in 1991 due to a big deficit in the balance of goods. The overall current account balance surplus (which includes some other items such as investment income and non-commercial transfers), reached ECU 43 billion in 1986. It returned to surplus in 1993 after being in the red since 1990 and plummeting to –ECU 64.6 billion in 1992. There now seems to be an upward trend, due mainly to a substantial improvement in the goods surplus since 1993, and the current account surplus reached ECU 88 billion in 1996.

The USA managed to reduce a huge current account deficit of –ECU 166 billion in 1986 to almost zero by 1991. Since then, it has sunk again, reaching –ECU 122 billion in 1996. Japan has maintained a surplus, although it has declined slightly since 1993.

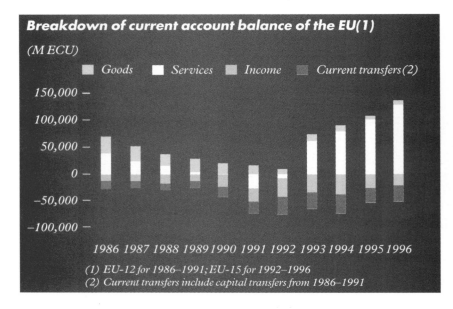

Breakdown of current account balance of the EU(1)

(M ECU)

■ Goods ■ Services ■ Income ■ Current transfers (2)

(1) EU-12 for 1986–1991; EU-15 for 1992–1996
(2) Current transfers include capital transfers from 1986–1991

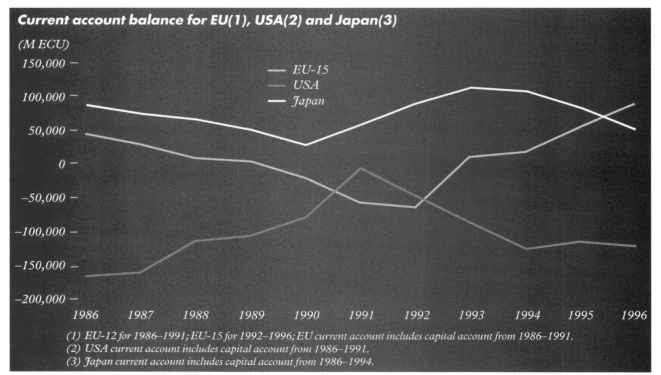

Current account balance for EU(1), USA(2) and Japan(3)

(M ECU)

— EU-15
— USA
— Japan

(1) EU-12 for 1986–1991; EU-15 for 1992–1996; EU current account includes capital account from 1986–1991.
(2) USA current account includes capital account from 1986–1991.
(3) Japan current account includes capital account from 1986–1994.

17.4 Investing abroad

Foreign direct investment (FDI) is international investment with the intention of a lasting interest in an enterprise operating in another economy. It is a driving force of 'globalisation'. Outward flows from the EU to the rest of the world surged in 1997 to ECU 96.4 billion. Corresponding inward flows grew slightly to ECU 44 billion. FDI among EU Member States showed an upturn to ECU 85.3 billion, by far the highest value of the 1990s.

The increasing trend of EU net exports of FDI capital continued in 1997, doubling the 1996 figure to ECU 52.4 billion. At the end of 1996 the EU held direct investment assets of ECU 543 billion abroad. These exceeded liabilities by ECU 121 billion. Over half the assets were held in the USA (43%), Switzerland (9%) and Australia (5%). The Union had net asset positions with nearly all countries and markets.

Outward and inward FDI – EU, the US and Japan

(M ECU)

	1988	1989	1990	1991	1992	1993	1994	1995	1996	1997
EU with the rest of the world										
Outward flows	31,680	33,282	20,527	26,732	17,828	24,157	24,129	60,805	62,421	96,431
Inward flows	18,141	27,943	32,753	20,933	22,760	21,504	21,814	42,133	36,281	43,976
USA										
Outward flows	3,850	22,608	6,873	12,851	20,301	35,106	32,891	65,072	67,383	:
Inward flows	47,872	69,347	49,149	35,424	23,872	43,061	36,264	53,068	62,082	:
Japan										
Outward flows	28,931	40,056	37,718	24,796	13,267	11,711	15,080	17,304	18,456	22,943
Inward flows	−410	−957	1,377	1,104	2,102	73	747	32	180	2,846
Intra EU flows	20,219	35,736	44,998	37,477	49,279	40,204	50,320	62,668	65,582	85,315

The figures are the sum of equity + other capital flows, and from 1995 onwards they represent total capital flows (incl. reinvested earnings).
All 1987 to 1991 EU figures cover the EU with 12 Member States only.
All 1992 to 1997 figures cover the EU with 15 Member States.
Intra EU flows are the sum of all Member States' outward flows to other Member States.

MK	PL	RO	SI	SK	CEC-12	EU-15	
							I. Basic and demographic indicators
25	313	238	20	49	1132	3231	*Total area ('000 km²)*
)5.3	38,660	22,526.1	1,984.9	5,387.6	110,180.4	374,565.7	*Total population, end of period ('000)*
6.4	0.8	-2.3	-0.3	1.3	-0.8	0.9	*Rate of natural increase (per '000 inhabitants)*
59.6(3)	68.5	65.2	71	68.9	67.5	74.1(2)	*Life expectancy: men (years)*
73.5(3)	77.0	73.0	78.6	76.7	75.7	80.5(2)	*Life expectancy: women (years)*
8.3	9.8	12.4	9.5	9.7	11.2	9.9	*Mortality rate (per '000 inhabitants)*
'4.8	10.7	10.1	9.1	11	10.3	10.8	*Birth rate (per '000 inhabitants)*
					150,070		***II. Labour market indicators***
54.9(2)	57.7	64.8	57.6(2)	59.5	:	55.4	*Economic Activity rate (ILO methodology)*
1.9(2)	11.2	6	7.3(2)	11.6	:	10.8	*Unemployment rate (ILO methodology)*
:	20.5	39	10.1(2)	8.6	:	5.0	*Employment in agriculture (% of total employment)*
:	25.4	26.2	36.8(2)	30.4	:	21.6	*Employment in industry (% of total employment)*
:	6.6	4.2	5.4(2)	8.9	:	7.8	*Employment in construction (% of total employment)*
:	47.5	30.6	52.3(2)	52.1	:	65.3	*Employment in services (% of total employment)*
							III. Non-financial national accounts
2.9(2)	119.7	30.6	16.1	17.2	300.6	6,770.6(2)	*Gross Domestic Product at current prices (billion ECU)*
:	6.9	-6.6	3.8	6.5	3.6	1.7(2)	*Gross Domestic Product Growth (in %)*
0	3,100	1,400	8,100	3,200	2,750	18,100(2)	*Gross Domestic Product per capita (ECU)*
:	7,500	5,800	13,000	8,900	7,500	18,100(2)	*Gross Domestic Product per capita (PPS)*
							Gross Value Added by branches (%):
1.3(2)	6.9(2)	20.1	4.4(2)	6.0(3)	8.7(3)	2.4(2)	*agriculture*
9.5(2)	31.5(2)	38.0	32.0(2)	28.0(3)	31.2(3)	25.9(2)	*industry*
5.0(2)	6.2(2)	5.7	5.6(2)	4.7(3)	6.2(3)	5.3(2)	*construction*
6.0(2)	55.3(2)	36.2	58.0(2)	61.3(3)	53.8(3)	66.5(2)	*services*
							IV. Main economic and financial indicators
2.3(2)	14.9	54.8	8.3	6.1		1.7	*Inflation rate (% change of year av. over prev. year)*
9.3(2)	26.1(2)	72.5	21.3	18.7	:	:	*Average short-term lending interest rate (%)*
9.0(2)	20.0(2)	55.8	13.2	13.4	:	:	*Average short-term deposit interest rate (%)*
3.0(2)	24.4(2)	19.1(2)	16.0(2)	21.6(2)	:	:	*Gross foreign debt (as % of GDP)*
0.0	3.9	8111.5	181.0	38.1	:	:	*ECU exchange rates (period average): 1ECU = x NCs*
'5.4	3.9	8859.1	186.8	38.4	:	:	*ECU exchange rates (end of period): 1ECU = x NCs*
4.6	121.6	103.4	102.0	105.3	:	99.87	*Industrial production volume indices (1995=100)*
							V. External trade
:	37,307	9,947	8,252	9,051	121,968	1,760,700	*Imports (M ECU)*
:	22,707	7,436	7,383	7,754	92,851	1,871,800	*Exports (MECU)*
:	-14,600	-2,511	-869	-1,298	-29,053	111,100	*Balance of trade (M ECU)*
:	63.8	52.5	67.4	39.5	:	:	*EU Share in total imports*
:	64.2	56.6	63.6	45.0	:	:	*EU Share in total exports*

play the leading role. Enacting, implementing and enforcing the necessary laws can be undertaken only by themselves, although support will be provided by the EU and its Member States.

In coming years, the EU faces enlargement from 15 Member States to as many as 26. Applications are now on the table from Hungary, Poland, Romania, Slovakia, Latvia, Estonia, Lithuania, Bulgaria, the Czech Republic and Slovenia – plus Cyprus. It is an historic development. Never before has Europe had the opportunity to unite in democracy. If properly managed, an enlarged EU could bring increased security, stability and prosperity but it could add over 100 million to its present 370 million population with a host of different economic and social situations.

At the end of 1997 the first decisive steps were taken along the path towards enlargement to the east. Applicant countries should start to join the Union at the beginning of the new century. To do so they must have stable institutions that guarantee democracy, the rule of law, human rights and respect and protection for minorities. There must be a viable market economy capable of withstanding EU competition – and they must be able to sign up to EU objectives. Enlargement is a crucial step towards a reconciled, peaceful and democratic Europe. Achieving it first became a realistic goal in 1989 when the collapse of Communism in Central and Eastern Europe and the fall of the Berlin Wall lifted the Iron Curtain, opening the way both to German unification and to free, democratic elections in Central and Eastern Europe.

The Obnova Programme is an EU initiative for the rehabilitation and reconstruction of Bosnia and Herzegovina, Croatia, the Federal Republic of Yugoslavia and the Former Yugoslav Republic of Macedonia (FYROM). Created in July 1996, it aims to reinforce the Dayton Accord and the peace agreements signed in Paris on 14 December 1995.

CECs: 110 million people

In 1996 12 Central European countries (CECs) – Bosnia and Croatia are excluded from this analysis due to lack of some data – had a combined population of 110.3 million . This was 30% of the EU population in an area about 35% its size. The transition process to a market economy differs substantially between the countries. The total GDP (in current prices) of all CECs in 1996 was equivalent to only 4% of the EU total – and about 10% on the basis of purchasing power standards (PPS). This means that average CEC living standards are about 32% of those in the EU. However they vary widely between countries – from about 18% in Latvia to 59% in Slovenia. Most CECs have overcome the immediate deep economic slump that followed their initial exposure to market economies and the consequent decline in inefficient and over-manned state industries – but much remains to be done to develop modern basic infrastructure and adjust to market-oriented production. Double digit inflation, huge public and external deficits and high unemployment are persistent features. After great effort and sacrifice, most CECs now have real growth. But a continuation of this trend will be necessary for many years to come – even for the best-performing CECs – to close the gap with average EU living standards.

East-West trade-off

Trade between the EU and CECs has developed dynamically. From 1991–1996, EU exports to CECs rose annually by 29.8%; EU imports from CECs soared by 24.2%. CECs boosted their share in total EU trade from 3.7% in 1991 to 9.4% in 1996. The EU's share in total CEC trade rocketed from 26.1% to 57.4%. Germany (44%), Italy (15%) and Austria (9%) accounted for more than two-thirds of EU trade with CECs. On the CEC side, the leading countries were Poland (27%), the Czech Republic (20%) and Hungary (16%).

Trade with CECs

| | Exports | | | | Imports | | | | Trade Balance M ECU | |
| | 1996 | | 1997 | | 1996 | | 1997 | | | |
	M ECU	%	M ECU	%	M ECU	%	M ECU	%	1996	1997
Reporting countries										
BLEU	2,663.0	3.8	3,370.6	3.9	1,627.3	3.3	1,947.8	3.3	1,035.7	1,422.8
Denmark	1,424.3	2.0	1,663.4	1.9	1,033.2	2.1	1,229.0	2.1	391.1	434.4
Germany	28,671.8	41.2	34,841.0	40.8	23,129.5	46.7	27,483.0	46.3	5,542.3	7,358.0
Greece	1,010.9	1.5	1,260.4	1.5	767.3	1.5	936.8	1.6	243.6	323.6
Spain	1,439.1	2.1	1,854.0	2.2	949.7	1.9	1,112.6	1.9	489.4	741.5
France	5,163.0	7.4	6,395.3	7.5	3,365.9	6.8	3,685.3	6.2	1,797.1	2,710.0
Ireland	407.4	0.6	486.0	0.6	153.2	0.3	189.9	0.3	254.2	296.1
Italy	11,184.0	16.1	12,755.7	14.9	6,502.8	13.1	7,933.1	13.4	4,681.3	4,822.6
Netherlands	3,152.3	4.5	4,104.0	4.8	2,602.4	5.3	3,101.4	5.2	549.9	1,002.6
Austria	6,112.1	8.8	8,000.2	9.4	4,419.1	8.9	5,327.7	9.0	1,692.9	2,672.5
Portugal	134.3	0.2	160.1	0.2	133.0	0.3	142.5	0.2	1.3	17.5
Finland	2,171.1	3.1	2,786.7	3.3	777.1	1.6	965.0	1.6	1,393.9	1,821.7
Sweden	2,181.4	3.1	2,918.1	3.4	1,342.6	2.7	1,705.1	2.9	838.8	1,213.0
United Kingdom	3,872.7	5.6	4,903.0	5.7	2,764.4	5.6	3,613.2	6.1	1,108.3	1,289.8
EU-15	69,587.3	100.0	85,498.6	100.0	49,567.5	100.0	59,372.3	100.0	20,019.8	26,126.2
Partner countries										
Albania	743.7	1.1	596.3	0.7	197.6	0.4	190.4	0.3	546.1	406.0
Bosnia–Herzegovina	527.1	0.8	759.8	0.9	68.2	0.1	161.5	0.3	458.9	598.4
Bulgaria	1,699.2	2.4	1,814.4	2.2	1,709.7	3.4	2,082.3	3.5	−10.5	−240.8
Croatia	3,889.5	5.6	4,775.0	5.6	1,741.7	3.5	1,774.6	3.0	2,147.8	3,000.4
Czech Republic	13,975.4	20.1	15,846.2	18.5	9,755.0	19.7	11,742.5	19.8	4,220.5	4,103.7
Estonia	1,696.7	2.4	2,387.1	2.8	1,088.8	2.2	1,497.4	2.5	608.0	889.7
FYROM	807.1	1.2	845.7	1.0	426.0	0.9	487.7	0.8	381.1	358.0
Hungary	10,000.8	14.4	13,580.7	15.9	8,826.6	17.8	11,597.2	19.5	1,174.1	1,983.6
Latvia	1,109.8	1.6	1,531.7	1.8	1,125.3	2.3	1,276.7	2.2	−15.5	255.0
Lithuania	1,460.3	2.1	2,149.9	2.5	1,087.4	2.2	1,308.7	2.2	372.9	841.2
Poland	19,857.5	28.5	25,058.5	29.3	12,252.4	24.7	14,194.5	23.9	7,605.1	10,863.9
Romania	4,445.1	6.4	5,011.4	5.9	3,597.4	7.3	4,419.3	7.4	847.8	592.1
Slovakia	3,997.9	5.7	4,805.4	5.6	3,421.0	6.9	3,978.2	6.7	576.9	827.2
Slovenia	5,377.1	7.7	6,309.2	7.4	4,270.4	8.6	4,661.3	7.9	1,106.6	1,647.9
CEC	69,587.3	100.0	85,471.3	100.0	49,567.5	100.0	59,372.3	100.0	20,019.8	26,126.2

Source COMEXT2 16/9/98

18.3 Forging links even farther east

Together with Mongolia, the newly independent states that emerged from collapse of the Soviet Union are ten times the size of the EU – 9,600 km from east to west with 11 time zones. The EU has set up aid and assistance programmes with them and signed Partnership and Cooperation Agreements (PCAs) covering political, economic, commercial and cultural issues. PCAs are a 'halfway house' between standard framework agreements, which the Commission has negotiated with a number of countries round the world, and the European Agreements negotiated with CECs. They foresee institutionalised political dialogue and contain detailed trade and investment related provisions. The PCA with Russia signed in 1994 establishes political dialogue at all levels.

The Tacis Programme (Technical Assistance to the Commonwealth of Independent States) fosters the development of harmonious and prosperous economic and political links between the EU and these partner countries. It provides money to support the

Key NIS indicators in 1996

	Armenia	Azerbaijan	Belarus	Georgia	Kazakhstan	Kyrgystan	Moldo
Total population ('000)	3,780.7	7,574.5	10,284	5,423.6	15,992.9	4,606.8	4,320
Total area ('000 km²)	29.8	86.6	207.6	69.7	2,724.9	199.9	33.
Population density (inhabitants per km²)	126.9	87.5	49.5	77.8	5.9	23	127.
Life expectancy: men (years)	67(1)	65(2)	63	69(1)	64(1)	62	63
Life expectancy: women (years)	73(1)	74(2)	74	76(1)	73(1)	71	70
Proportion of total jobs in agriculture (%)	40.5	28.8	17.8	–	23	45.9	42.
Proportion of total jobs in industry (%) (5)	22.5	18	34.8	–	21	14.6	15.
Proportion of total jobs in services	37	53.2	47.4	–	56	39.5	42.
Unemployment rate (%) (6)	10	1.1	4	1.7	4.2	4.5	1.
Gross domestic product (M ECU)	1,258	2,517	10,431	2,835	16,569	1,381	1,253
Per capita GDP (ECU)	332.6	332.3	1,014.3	522.7	1,036	299.8	290
Proportion of GDP from agriculture (%) (7)	38.8	26.7	17	32.6	13	43.1	32.
Proportion of GDP from industry (%) (7)	24.4	29.3	30.7	15.9	24.6	12.9	26.
Proportion of GDP from construction (%) (7)	8.6	3.9	5.9	5.1	6.7	6.5	3.
Proportion of GDP from services (%) (7)	28.2	40.1	46.4	46.4	55.7	37.5	36.
Total exports (M ECU)	290.3	631.2	5,462.7	199.4	6,230.4	505.4	801.
Total imports (M ECU)	855.8	960.6	6,939.3	718.4	4,261.3	837.7	1,079.
Trade balance (M ECU)	−565.5	−329.4	−1,476.6	−519	1,969.1	−332.3	−277.
Exchange rate 8 (1 ECU = … national currency)	525.1	5454.7	17238	1.6	85.5	16.3	5.

(1) 1990
(2) 1993
(3) 1994
(4) 1991
(5) Including construction
(6) Registered.
(7) Gross value added; 1994 – Tadjikistan; 1995 – Armenia, Azerbaidjan, Belarus, Kazakhstan, Kyrgystan, Moldova, Ukraine, Uzbekistan.
(8) Annual average.
(9) Estimated.
(10) Extra EU15 trade.
Source: National statistics (for the NIS data), Eurostat (for the EU data).

transformation to market economies and democratic societies. In its first six years, 1991–1996, Tacis committed ECU 2,807 million to over 2,250 projects. Tacis works closely with the partner countries to determine how funds should be spent thus ensuring that funding is relevant to each country's own reform policies and priorities. It provides know-how from a wide range of public and private organisations. This allows experience of market economies and democracies to be combined with local knowledge and skills. Tacis is also a catalyst – unlocking funds from major lenders by providing pre-investment and feasibility studies. Key targets are:

public administration reform; restructuring of state enterprises and private sector development; transport and telecommunications infrastructure; energy, nuclear safety and the environment; an effective food production, processing and distribution system; and social services and education.

In the NIS, Russia alone accounts for 52% of the population and 80% of GDP. The NIS has a population density of only 13 people per km compared with the EU's 117. NIS economic backwardness is reflected in life expectancy – on average some 10 years lower than in the EU. In 1996 total NIS GDP and GDP per person were only 6.4% and 8.3%

respectively of EU figures. Unemployment is low, although there are doubts about the reliability of the figures. Services account for the biggest share of GDP – 51.2% in 1996 – but are still below the EU's 63.7%. griculture and industry accounted for 40.2% compared with 27.1% in the EU. Foreign trade, which represented 2.6% of world trade in 1996, enabled the NIS to generate a 43 billion ECU surplus.

Over 40% of trade with EU

In 1996, over 40% of NIS trade was with the EU although the NIS accounted for only 4.3% of the EU's total trade. However, in the three

Russia	Tadjikistan	Turkmenistan	Uzbekistan	Ukraine	NIS 12(9)	EU(10)	
7,502.4	5,969.7	4,627.9	23,443.7	50,893.5	284,419.7	373,111	Total population ('000)
7,075.4	143.1	488.1	447.4	603.7	22,110	3,191	Total area ('000 km²)
8.6	41.7	9.5	52.4	84.3	12.8	116.9	Population density (inhabitants per km²)
60	64(3)	62(4)	66(1)	63(3)	61.2	74	Life expectancy: men (years)
73	69(3)	69(4)	72(1)	73(3)	72.9	80.5	Life expectancy: women (years)
14.4	59.5	45.6	40.1	21.5	21.3	5.5	Proportion of total jobs in agriculture (%)
34.3	12.7	18.5	19.2	29.5	29.7	28.4	Proportion of total jobs in industry (%) (5)
51.3	27.8	35.9	40.7	49	49	66.2	Proportion of total jobs in services
3.4	2.4	–	0.3	1.5	2.9	10.9	Unemployment rate (%) (6)
6719	817	1,483	10,985	34,698	430,946	6,764,864	Gross domestic product (M ECU)
2350.6	136.9	320.4	468.6	681.8	1,515	18,154	Per capita GDP (ECU)
7.5	19.6	17.1	31.3	15	9.8	2.3	Proportion of GDP from agriculture (%) (7)
30.8	25.5	43.9	19.3	34.1	30.4	24.8	Proportion of GDP from industry (%) (7)
9	11.9	10.4	7.9	7.5	8.6	5.3	Proportion of GDP from construction (%) (7)
52.7	43	28.6	41.5	43.4	51.2	63.7	Proportion of GDP from services (%) (7)
7629	770.1	1,692.6	4,210.8	14,331	122,754.5	623,396	Total exports (M ECU)
6238	668.1	1,313.5	4,711.7	17,623.9	86,207.5	579,990	Total imports (M ECU)
1391	102	379.1	–500.9	–3,292.9	36,547	43,406	Trade balance (M ECU)
6507.5	372	4456.9	50.99	2.32	–	–	Exchange rate (8) (1 ECU = … national currency)

years to 1996, the growth rate of EU trade with the NIS was significantly higher than with other third countries growing by 53% against 31%. EU imports from the NIS rose by 36% compared to 23% for other countries. In 1996, Russia alone accounted for 82.4% of EU trade with the NIS, and Ukraine accounted for 7.9%. In that year, the EU ran a trade deficit of ECU 1.7 billion with the NIS.

Total EU trade with NIS in 1996

	M ECU	%
EU imports from:		
Russia	19,093.8	76.8
Ukraine	2,624.6	10.6
Uzbekistan	699.3	2.8
Kasakhstan	562.0	2.3
Belarus	916.9	3.7
Other NIS	970.8	3.9
Total NIS	24,867.4	100.0
EU exports to:		
Russia	23,299.2	87.6
Ukraine	1,462.0	5.5
Uzbekistan	518.8	2.0
Kasakhstan	514.6	1.9
Belarus	416.9	1.6
Other NIS	386.1	1.5
Total NIS	26,597.5	100.0

18.4 EU links with the Mediterranean

Mediterranean countries, as a group, are a priority area of political and economic strategic importance for the EU. Apart from being key trading partners, they have close historical and cultural ties with certain EU Member States. Today, the EU is connected with almost all Mediterranean countries by a network of cooperation or association agreements. The Barcelona conference in November 1995 provided the foundation of a process based on respect for the essential principles of international law and the construction of a shared prosperity area.

EU-15 (excepting Greece) bilateral aid to (12) Mediterranean countries 1990–1996

(Annual average, M ECU)

Algeria	408.9
Cyprus	7.8
Egypt	1,252.1
Israel	284.1
Jordan	174.9
Lebanon	70.6
Malta	29.6
Morocco	618.3
Syria	71.3
Tunisia	306.8
Turkey	471.5
West Bank and Gaza Strip	:

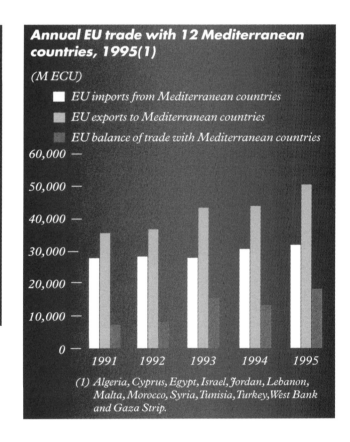

Annual EU trade with 12 Mediterranean countries, 1995(1)

(M ECU)

■ *EU imports from Mediterranean countries*
■ *EU exports to Mediterranean countries*
■ *EU balance of trade with Mediterranean countries*

(1) Algeria, Cyprus, Egypt, Israel, Jordan, Lebanon, Malta, Morocco, Syria, Tunisia, Turkey, West Bank and Gaza Strip.

Mediterranean countries – key data in 1995

		Population			Education	Health	Economy
	Area (km²)	Estimate ('000)	Fertility rate (births per woman)	Projection, 2025 ('000)	Primary school: enrolment ratio (%) (2)	Infant mortality rate per 1,000 live births	Per capita GNP (ECU)
Algeria	2,381,741	27,939	3.4	45,475	97	44	1,223
Cyprus	9,251	742	2.4	927	102(1)	7	7,844
Egypt	997,738	62,931	3.4	97,301	104	54	604
Israel	20,700	5,629	2.7	7,808	94(1)	8	12,171
Jordan	88,946	5,439	5.1	12,039	105	30	1,154
Lebanon	10,230	3,009	2.8	4,424	129	29	2,034
Malta	316	366	2.1	422	110	8	6,047
Morocco	458,730	27,028	3.1	40,650	70	56	849
Syria	185,180	14,661	5.4	33,505	110	33	856
Tunisia	164,150	8,896	2.8	13,290	118	37	1,391
Turkey	779,452	61,945	3.0	90,937	110	52	2,125
West Bank and Gaza Strip	7,433	2,462	6.2	1,405	99	28	:

(1) 1992

(2 The rates of enrolment in education are taken from the 'Enrolment estimates and projections', produced by the United Nations Educational, Scientific and Cultural Organisation (UNESCO).

The gross rate of enrolment used is defined as a ratio between the number of young people enrolled for a given level of education (regardless of whether or not they are of the usual age to attend) and the number of young people who belong, according to the national system, to the age group for which the level is designed. This rate is expressed in percentages and may be over 100% because of late admissions, pupils repeating a year or inconsistencies in the data.

18.5 A key north-south agreement

The Lomé Convention, initially signed in 1975 and subsequently renewed on several occasions, connects 71 states of Africa, the Caribbean and the Pacific (ACP) to the 15 EU Member States. It is the most important collective cooperation agreement in the history of relations between developed and developing countries. The latest agreement – apart from traditional priorities of food security, industrial development and human resources – attaches greater importance to the promotion of human rights and democracy, the strengthening of women's position, environmental protection, decentralised cooperation and the private sector.

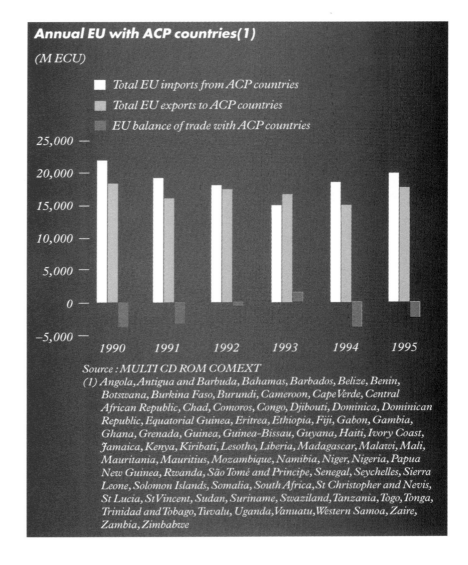

Annual EU with ACP countries(1)

(M ECU)

- ☐ *Total EU imports from ACP countries*
- ☐ *Total EU exports to ACP countries*
- ☐ *EU balance of trade with ACP countries*

Source : *MULTI CD ROM COMEXT*
(1) Angola, Antigua and Barbuda, Bahamas, Barbados, Belize, Benin, Botswana, Burkina Faso, Burundi, Cameroon, Cape Verde, Central African Republic, Chad, Comoros, Congo, Djibouti, Dominica, Dominican Republic, Equatorial Guinea, Eritrea, Ethiopia, Fiji, Gabon, Gambia, Ghana, Grenada, Guinea, Guinea-Bissau, Guyana, Haiti, Ivory Coast, Jamaica, Kenya, Kiribati, Lesotho, Liberia, Madagascar, Malawi, Mali, Mauritania, Mauritius, Mozambique, Namibia, Niger, Nigeria, Papua New Guinea, Rwanda, São Tomé and Principe, Senegal, Seychelles, Sierra Leone, Solomon Islands, Somalia, South Africa, St Christopher and Nevis, St Lucia, St Vincent, Sudan, Suriname, Swaziland, Tanzania, Togo, Tonga, Trinidad and Tobago, Tuvalu, Uganda, Vanuatu, Western Samoa, Zaire, Zambia, Zimbabwe

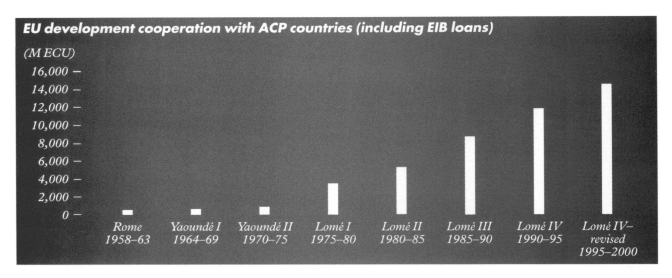

EU development cooperation with ACP countries (including EIB loans)

(M ECU)

16,000							
14,000							
12,000							
10,000							
8,000							
6,000							
4,000							
2,000							
0	Rome 1958–63	Yaoundé I 1964–69	Yaoundé II 1970–75	Lomé I 1975–80	Lomé II 1980–85	Lomé III 1985–90	Lomé IV 1990–95	Lomé IV– revised 1995–2000

Pacific ACP countries – key data in 1995

		Population			Education	Health	Economy
	Area (km²)	1995 estimate ('000)	Fertility rate (births per woman)	Projection, 2025 ('000)	Primary school: enrolment ratio (%)	Infant mortality rate per 1,000 live births	Per capita GNP (ECU)
Fiji	18,376	784	2.8	1,161	124	20	1,865
Kiribati	811	79	4.2(1)	144	:	57(1)	703
Papua New Guinea	462,840	4,302	4.6	7,532	74	61	887
Solomon islands	28,370	378	5.0	844	90(2)	23	696
Tonga	750	98	4.0(1)	134	133(1)	22(1)	1,246
Tuvalu	24	10	3.1(1)	15	:	33(1)	249
Vanuatu	12,190	169	4.4	334	94 1	38	917
Western Samoa	2,831	171	4.0	307	136	58	856

(1) 1990
(2) 1992

Caribbean ACP countries – key data in 1995

		Population			Education	Health	Economy
	Area (km²)	Estimate ('000)	Fertility rate (births per woman)	Projection, 2025 ('000)	Primary school: enrolment ratio (%)	Infant mortality rate per 1,000 live births	Per capita GNP (ECU)
Antigua and Barbuda	442	66	1.9(1)	84	:	19(1)	5,336
Bahamas	13,939	276	2	378	99	19	9,128
Barbados	430	262	1.83	309	115	9	5,015
Belize	22,965	215	3.66	386	109(2)	30	2,011
Dominica	750	71	2.8(1)	82	:	16(1)	2,286
Dominican Republic	48,422	7,823	2.8	11,164	94	34	1,116
Grenada	345	92	3.1(1)	113	:	31(1)	2,278
Guyana	215,083	835	2.32	1,141	112	42	451
Haiti	27,750	7,180	4.6	13,128	57	77	191
Jamaica	10,991	2,447	2.1	3,301	106	12	1,154
St Christopher and Nevis	269	41	2.6	47	:	36	3,953
St Lucia	616	142	4.4	199	:	19	2,576
St Vincent	389	112	2.6	147	:	22	1,743
Surinam	163,820	423	2.39	599	127	24	673
Trinidad and Tobago	5,128	1,306	2.25	1,808	97	16	2,882

(1) 1990
(2) 1992

African ACP countries – key data in 1995

		Population			Education	Health
	Area (km²)	1995 Estimate ('000)	Fertility rate (births per woman)	Projection, 2025 ('000)	Primary school: enrolment ratio (%)	Infant mortality rate per 1,000 live births
Angola	1,246,700	11,072	6.7	26,619	99	112
Benin	112,622	5,409	6.6	12,252	61	79
Botswana	582,000	1,487	4.5	2,980	114	37
Burkina Faso	274,000	10,319	6.1	21,654	37	123
Burundi	27,834	6,393	6.3	13,490	69	96
Cameroon	475,442	13,233	5.3	29,173	101	55
Cape Verde	4,033	392	4.0	735	112	41
Central African Republic	622,436	3,315	5.3	6,360	68	96
Chad	1,284,000	6,361	5.5	12,907	57	112
Comoros	1,862	653	6.5	1,646	75	79
Congo	342,000	2,590	5.9	5,677	:	83
Côte d'Ivoire	322,462	14,253	6.9	36,817	69	88
Democratic Republic of Congo	2,344,858	43,901	6.2	104,639	76	86
Djibouti	23,200	577	5.4	1,055	44	106
Equatorial Guinea	28,051	400	5.5	798	:	107
Eritrea	121,144	3,531	5.3	7,043	47(1)	94
Ethiopia	1,133,380	55,053	6.5	126,886	26	107
Gabon	267,667	1,320	5.7	2,697	134	85
Gambia	10,689	1,118	5.2	2,102	68	122
Ghana	238,537	17,453	5.5	37,988	77	73
Guinea	245,857	6,700	6.5	15,088	37	124
Guinea – Bissau	36,125	1,073	5.4	1,978	59	129
Kenya	582,656	28,261	5.8	63,360	95	66
Lesotho	30,355	2,050	4.9	4,172	108	69
Liberia	99,067	3,039	6.3	7,240	:	113
Madagascar	587,041	14,763	5.7	34,419	92	93
Malawi	118,484	11,129	6.7	22,348	66	136
Mali	1,240,192	10,795	6.6	24,575	24	149
Mauritania	1,030,700	2,274	5.0	4,443	55	92
Mauritius	2,040	1,117	2.3	1,481	107	15
Mozambique	812,379	16,004	6.1	35,139	66	136
Namibia	825,118	1,540	4.9	3,049	119	53
Niger	1,186,408	9,151	7.1	22,385	29	114
Nigeria	923,768	111,721	6.0	238,397	71	77
Rwanda	26,338	7,952	6.0	15,797	71	105
São Tomé and Principe	1,001	133	5.1(2)	215	:	25(3)
Senegal	196,722	8,312	5.6	16,896	56	62
Seychelles	454	73	2.8(2)	95	96	17(3)
Sierra Leone	71,740	4,509	6.1	8,690	48	154
Somalia	637,657	9,250	6.5	21,276	:	112
South Africa	1,219,080	:	:	:	:	:
Sudan	2,503,890	28,098	5.4	58,388	104	71
Swaziland	17,363	855	4.5	1,647	109	65
Tanzania	942,799	29,685	5.5	62,894	69	81
Togo	56,785	4,138	6.1	9,377	111	77
Uganda	241,040	21,297	6.7	48,056	81	111
Zambia	752,614	9,456	5.5	19,130	92	99
Zimbabwe	390,759	11,261	4.5	19,631	123	65

(1) 1993
(2) 1990
(3) 1991

18.6 EU and Latin America

From the first cooperation project – in 1961 on the peaceful use of nuclear energy – EU relations with Latin America have expanded considerably. Initially, simple agreements were aimed at promoting cooperation in fields such as energy, science and the environment. Today they tend to have a complementary political dimension based on joint statements on democracy, human rights, peace and international order. The accession of Spain and Portugal to the Community in 1986 added an important new dimension to the EU's relationship with Latin America. The budget allocated by the EU for aid to and cooperation with Latin America from 1990–1994 was ECU 935 million. It stands at ECU 1,343 million for 1995–1999.

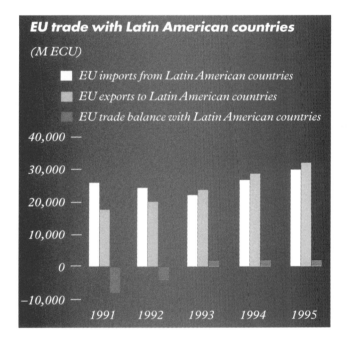

EU trade with Latin American countries

(M ECU)

- ☐ EU imports from Latin American countries
- ☐ EU exports to Latin American countries
- ☐ EU trade balance with Latin American countries

40,000 —
30,000 —
20,000 —
10,000 —
0 —
−10,000 —

1991   1992   1993   1994   1995

EU-15 (except Greece) bilateral aid to Latin American countries 1990–1996

(Annual average, M ECU)

Argentina	230.6
Bolivia	318.7
Brazil	208.6
Chile	144.6
Colombia	148.5
Costa Rica	74.7
Cuba	26.5
Ecuador	153.4
El Salvador	76.8
Guatemala	77.0
Honduras	92.8
Mexico	222.7
Nicaragua	107.3
Panama	12.5
Paraguay	39.4
Peru	235.4
Uruguay	58.0
Venezuela	41.1

Latin American countries – key data in 1995

	Area (km²)	Population 1995 estimate ('000)	Fertility rate (births per woman)	Projection, 2025 ('000)	Education Primary school: enrolment ratio (%)	Health Infant mortality rate per 1,000 live births	Economy Per capita GNP (ECU)
Argentina	2,766,889	34,587	2.6	46,133	111	22	6,139
Bolivia	1,098,581	7,414	4.4	13,131	87	66	612
Brazil	8,511,996	161,790	2.7	230,250	106	53	2,783
Chile	756,626	14,262	2.4	19,775	99	14	3,180
Colombia	1,141,748	35,101	2.5	49,359	115	34	1,460
Costa Rica	51,100	3,424	3.0	5,608	105	12	1,995
Cuba	110,860	11,041	1.8	12,658	102	11	:
Ecuador	272,045	11,460	3.1	17,792	120	46	1,063
El Salvador	21,041	5,768	3.6	9,735	80	39	1,231
Guatemala	108,889	10,621	4.9	21,668	79	40	1,024
Honduras	112,088	5,654	4.3	10,656	107	35	459
Mexico	1,958,201	93,674	2.8	136,594	114	33	2,538
Nicaragua	131,670	4,433	4.5	9,079	97	45	291
Panama	75,517	2,631	2.6	3,767	108	21	2,102
Paraguay	406,752	4,960	3.9	9,017	107	35	1,292
Peru	1,285,216	23,780	3.1	36,692	125	59	1,766
Uruguay	176,215	3,186	2.3	3,691	107	17	3,953
Venezuela	912,050	21,844	3.0	34,775	94	21	2,309

18.7 EU and Asia

EU relations with Asian developing countries are less structured than those of ACP and Mediterranean countries. Bilateral relations take the form of cooperation agreements with individual countries or emerging blocs. Financial and technical cooperation between the EU and Asia goes back to 1976. For a long time priority was given to rural development and, in particular, to improvement of the food supply. The current priority is human development – health, education etc. – and, in south-east Asia and China, economic development.

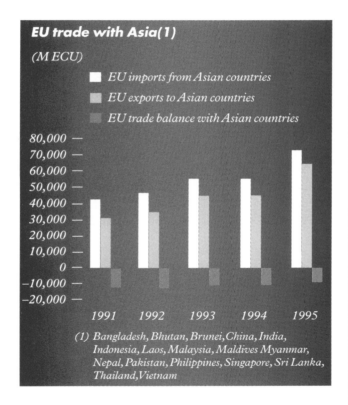

EU trade with Asia(1)

(M ECU)

- ☐ *EU imports from Asian countries*
- ▨ *EU exports to Asian countries*
- ▨ *EU trade balance with Asian countries*

80,000
70,000
60,000
50,000
40,000
30,000
20,000
10,000
0
−10,000
−20,000

1991   1992   1993   1994   1995

(1) Bangladesh, Bhutan, Brunei, China, India, Indonesia, Laos, Malaysia, Maldives Myanmar, Nepal, Pakistan, Philippines, Singapore, Sri Lanka, Thailand, Vietnam

EU-15 (excepti Greece) bilateral aid to Asian countries, 1990–1996

(Annual average, M ECU)	
Bangladesh	445.7
Bhutan	20.4
Brunei 0.2(1)	
China	1,041.8
India	995.6
Indonesia	842.0
Laos	56.0
Malaysia	59.5
Maldives	5.0
Myanmar	12.0
Nepal	131.5
Pakistan	378.5
Philippines	232.2
Singapore 9.8(1)	
Sri Lanka	124.8
Thailand	212.5

Asian countries – key data in 1995

		Population			Education	Health	Economy
	Area (km²)	1995 estimate ('000)	Fertility rate (births per woman)	Projection, 2025 ('000)	Primary school: enrolment ratio (%)	Infant mortality rate per 1,000 live births	Per capita GNP (ECU)
Argentina	2,766,889	34,587	2.6	46,133	111	22	6,139
Bangladesh	147,750	120,433	3.9	196,128	81	96	183
Bhutan	46,500	1,638	5.4	3,136	33	107	321
Brunei	5,765	285	2.8	425	110	8	19,235
China	9,571,300	1,221,462	2.0	1,526,106	123	38	474
India	3,166,414	935,744	3.4	1,392,086	104	72	260
Indonesia	1,919,317	197,588	2.6	275,598	116	48	749
Laos	236,800	4,882	6.0	9,688	112	86	268
Malaysia	330,442	20,140	3.2	31,577	95	11	2,974
Maldives	298	254	6.1	559	148	49	757
Myanmar	676,552	46,527	3.8	75,564	124	72	:
Nepal	147,181	21,918	5.0	40,693	89	86	153
Pakistan	796,095	140,497	5.6	284,827	44	74	352
Philippines	300,076	67,581	3.6	104,522	109	35	803
Singapore	641	2,848	1.7	3,355	107	5	20,436
Sri Lanka	65,610	18,354	2.3	25,031	112	15	535
Thailand	513,115	58,791	2.1	73,584	90	34	2,095
Vietnam	331,041	74,545	3.5	118,151	108	37	183